Analyzing Music in Advertising

The study of music in commercials is well suited for exploring the persuasive impact that music has beyond the ability to entertain, edify, and purify its audience. This book focuses on music in commercials from an interpretive text analytical perspective, answering hitherto neglected questions: What characterizes music in commercials compared to other commercial music and other music on TV? How does music in commercials relate to music "outside" the universe of commercials? How and what can music in commercials signify? Author Nicolai Graakjær sets a new benchmark for the international scholarly study of music on television and its pervading influence on consumer choice.

Nicolai Jørgensgaard Graakjær was born in 1972 in Denmark. He is Professor (WRS) of Mediated Communication in the Department of Communication and Psychology at the University of Aalborg, Denmark. He has published his research in, for example, *Popular Music & Society*, *Critical Discourse Studies*, and *Visual Communication*.

Routledge Interpretive Marketing Research

Edited by Stephen Brown, *University of Ulster, Northern Ireland*

Recent years have witnessed an "interpretive turn" in marketing and consumer research. Methodologies from the humanities are taking their place alongside those drawn from the traditional social sciences.

Qualitative and literary modes of marketing discourse are growing in popularity. Art and aesthetics are increasingly firing the marketing imagination.

This series brings together the most innovative work in the burgeoning interpretive marketing research tradition. It ranges across the methodological spectrum from grounded theory to personal introspection, covers all aspects of the postmodern marketing "mix," from advertising to product development, and embraces marketing's principal subdisciplines.

Also available in Routledge Interpretive Marketing Research series:

Analyzing Music in Advertising
Television Commercials and Consumer
Choice

Nicolai Jørgensgaard Graakjær

Routledge
Taylor & Francis Group

LONDON AND NEW YORK

First published 2015
by Routledge

2 Park Square, Milton Park, Abingdon, Oxfordshire OX14 4RN
711 Third Avenue, New York, NY 10017

*Routledge is an imprint of the Taylor & Francis Group,
an informa business*

First issued in paperback 2018

Library of Congress Cataloging-in-Publication Data
Graakjaer, Nicolai, author.
  Analyzing music in TV commercials : television commercials and
consumer choice / Nicolai Graakjaer.
    pages cm. — (Routledge interpretive marketing research ; 20)
    Includes bibliographical references and index.
  1. Music in advertising.   2. Television advertising.   3. Television and
music.   I. Title.
  ML3790.G676 2014
  781.5'4—dc23
  2014030440

ISBN: 978-1-138-78108-5 (hbk)
ISBN: 978-1-138-61681-3 (pbk)

Typeset in Sabon
by Apex CoVantage, LLC

Contents

Acknowledgments

I am grateful to Christian Jantzen and Alf Björnberg for having sparked and encouraged my interest in the subject of this book. I thank Christian Jantzen also for his comments on an earlier version of the manuscript.

Thanks to Stephen Brown, Manjula Raman, Steve Oakes, and the rest of the review and editorial team at Routledge for their enthusiasm and guidance.

Portions of the included case analysis of the use of The Blue Van's "There Goes My Love" in Parts I and II have appeared in *Popular Music & Society*. Also, portions of Chapter 3 and 7 have appeared in a book on Aalborg University Press; I thank the publishers for allowing me to include the revised versions here.

Nicolai Jørgensgaard Graakjær
Aalborg, Denmark
July 12, 2014

1 Introduction

This book is based on two premises. First, insufficient scholarly attention has been devoted to the interpretive text analysis of music in advertising. In this book, interpretive text analysis refers to the qualitative examination of textual structure, that is, text elements and the relations between elements. This examination does not include a systematic focus on the reception and uses of music in advertising, for example, in the form of an interpretive phenomenological analysis of actual listeners. Second, interpretive text analysis offers relevant and necessary insights into processes of musical signification in advertising, that is, the issue of how music can be interpreted as contributing to the construction of meaning. Thus, this book focuses on music in advertising from a text analytical perspective and aims to improve understanding of the significance, structures, and functions of music in advertising. "Music in advertising" includes all uses of music in market communication, including various media settings, such as radio commercials, television commercials, web banners, websites, telephone waiting lines, computer-based presentations, stores, and brandscapes. This book focuses primarily on music in commercials (i.e., audiovisual films promoting a product or service aired on television and paid for by an advertiser), although it will also include analytical perspectives on music in television, web ads, and stores.

With this purpose and perspective, I intend to address a lacuna in the research. As I illustrate in greater detail in the following, there appears to exist a discrepancy between the existing knowledge of music in advertising and commercials and prevalence and significance of this type of music. This discrepancy has been observed from various perspectives by many scholars. For example, "[music in advertising] is . . . an area in dire need of development" (Kassabian, 2013b, p. 100), and from the perspective of music in television, "substantial work remains to be undertaken for scholarship to obtain an understanding of how the musical realm beyond normal programming functions in television" (Deaville, 2011, p. 22). Thus far, searching for information on how to understand music in advertising from an interpretive text analytical perspective returns a relatively scarce, uneven and fragmented body of research; see Graakjær & Jantzen (2009a) for a review. With this book, I hope to remedy this situation.

From an interpretive text analytical perspective, the following questions are examined: How does music in commercials relate to music distributed prior to and outside the specific setting of the commercial? How does music in commercials compare to other forms of music in television and in advertising? How does music in commercials relate to visual and (other) auditory elements of commercials? How does music in commercials contribute to processes of signification? What are the typical structures and functions of music in commercials? In answering these questions, this book is primarily intended for university students, researchers, and lecturers in marketing, advertising, consumer behavior, and media and communication studies departments. In those contexts, this book can illustrate that music is a significant element of marketing and a specific type of communication that can be fruitfully examined from an interpretive text analytical perspective. This book may also be of value to students, researchers, and lecturers in musicology departments. In this context, the book can illustrate that music in commercials is well suited for exploring the persuasive effects of music beyond the well-known qualities of classical and popular music, such as the ability to entertain, edify, and emotionally cleanse an audience. Moreover, although this book does not systematically offer insights into the processes of production or reception of music in commercials, it is hoped that it can also be of interest to producers of (music in) commercials and to scholars in the tradition of experimental research (see the following discussion). Producers are invited to apply the presented analytical perspectives to evaluate their own—and their colleagues'—practice and to reframe analytical perspectives as design options for productions.[1] Experimental researchers testing the effects of music in commercials on the responses of actual viewers may be inspired by the analytical approach presented for refining the ways in which music is treated as an independent variable. Given that "music can be hugely beneficial for advertising, but only when its role has been carefully thought through" (Millward Brown, 2008, p. 3), this book aims to illustrate how the role of music in commercials can be carefully examined. Considering the target groups mentioned, this book does not presuppose that the reader is familiar with music theory or has the ability to read music.

1.1   MUSIC IN COMMERCIALS—PREVALENCE AND IMPORTANCE

A number of indicators should be considered when assessing the prevalence and significance of music in commercials. To assess the prevalence of music, a delineation of music is necessary. For this purpose, I briefly present a typology of sounds. Because this typology is inspired by the subject of this book—that is, music in advertising with a special interest in commercials—it does not pretend to be universally applicable to the sounds used in other genres or soundscapes (Schafer, 1977). There is no universal definition of music (see, e.g., Nattiez, 1990), and the following must be regarded as a practical starting point for the present study, inspired by the recommendation that analyzing sound(scapes) entails that "some system or systems of generic classification will have to be devised" (Schafer, 1977, p. 9). With reference to such classification, such an analysis can "discover the significant features of the soundscape, those sounds which are important because of their individuality, their numerousness or their domination" (Schafer, 1977, p. 9). Theoretically, this perspective is inspired by researchers such as Leeuwen (1999) and Traux (2001), and it consists of a tripartite classification that includes speech, music, and object sounds. Thus, the typology differs from other available typologies that do not, for example, highlight the importance of music as a particular type of sound, for example, the typology of "natural, animal, technical, and human" sounds in Augoyard and Torgue (2006, p. 5).

In this context, music is defined as the sounds that conform to current norms of "music" by presenting, for example, a "clearly identifiable rhythmic and harmonic structure,"[2] as suggested by Bjurström and Lilliestam (1993, p. 36). Musical sounds are normally produced by humans via designated musical instruments or via human voicing (e.g., singing or rapping); however, nonmusical sounds (see the following discussion) may be "musicalized," that is, ordered according to a identifiable rhythmic structure that may be uncommon for that particular sound type but is common from the perspective of current musical norms. Conversely, sounds produced by humans via designated instruments are not necessarily musical (e.g., when the sounds of musical instruments are "de-musicalized" and do not conform to norms for musical structuring). The implication is that the rhythmic "musicalized" barking of a dog in a commercial should be considered music—for example, a dog barks two notes over a descending interval of a major third in a commercial for the Danish supermarket chain Netto (a sample from my April 2008 volume of commercials)—whereas the sounds produced by the destruction of a violin should be labeled a (nonmusical) object sound. "Speech" is the sound of a human's vocal and verbal intonation, and in commercials, speech typically originates from a voice-over, testimonial, presenter, or characters in a mini-drama.

In this book, the term *object sounds* refers to residual sounds that are neither speech nor music. Often, the term *sound effect* has been applied to identify similar types of sound (see, e.g., Flueckiger, 2009; Rodman, 2010). However, I have chosen the term *object sounds* to indicate this book's focus on the text rather than the production of the text. From the perspective of production, most if not all sounds in commercials are sound effects in the sense that audio technology has been used to fine-tune and produce specific effects not only from the sound of objects but also from the sounds of speech and music. Specifically, I define object sounds as those nonmusical(ized) and nonspeech sounds that are presented in the text as deriving from (the motion of) physical objects. For example, a "swoosh" sound represents the sound of wind resistance following the sudden motion of an object of considerable size and weight—in commercials, for example, such an object sound can accompany the visual introduction of animated price tags. To provide another example, the barking of a dog is an object sound if it is not musicalized (i.e., not presented as a harmonic, melodic, and/or rhythmic expression that conforms to current norms of musical expressions).

Apart from delineating music, collecting samples of commercials is necessary to precisely determine how frequently music is utilized in commercials. The ways in which music is delineated and samples are collected vary widely, and because the frequency of commercials with music cannot be expected to remain unchanged across time and across places, there is no universal ratio of this frequency. However, if we examine some of the systematically collected samples available (i.e., samples that provide precise information on the number of commercials examined and most of the criteria used for sampling), it is reasonable to suggest that most commercials include music. For example, a survey presented by Graakjær (2009a) indicated that 80% to 90% of all commercials include music.

Although the percentage of commercials that include music does not clarify the significance of this music, it strongly indicates that music serves a purpose in advertising through its significant influence on commercial messages and consumer responses. Moreover, because music in commercials arguably constitutes a fair proportion of the music that people listen to in most countries around the world, music in commercials represents an important setting for the production, reproduction, and modification of processes of musical signification. For example, on the most general level, music may help fulfill the essential purpose of commercials to *attract the attention of* potential consumers. Music and other types of sound are particularly advantageous in this respect. Viewers cannot easily close or redirect their ears in the same way that they can effortlessly close their eyes or redirect their visual attention. Music can thus be considered a type of "umbilical cord" between the commercial and potentially visually distracted television viewers. For example, "the viewer who 'glances' is a much more diversified subject with a more diverse set of relations to the screen than is the cinema spectator who 'looks' or 'gazes'" (Fiske, 1987, p. 59, inspired by Ellis, 1982; see also, e.g., Anderson & Kirkorian, 2006; Gauntlett & Hill, 1999, p. 21). The advent and spread of mobile technology further illustrate that "multitasking while watching TV is on the rise" (eMarketer, 2014; see also Zigmond & Stipp, 2010) and that a television set that is "switched on" (approximately 4 hours a day is the current expected average; see, e.g., Tagg, 2013, p. 35) does not necessarily imply that it is literally being "watched." In addition to attracting the attention of viewers, music can serve another essential purpose of commercials: to *make contact with* potential consumers. In establishing contact, music can prompt an interest in the advertised product and perhaps even in the music itself. Occasionally, it is precisely because of the music that a commercial engages us and causes us to remember specific messages and to prefer certain brands over others.

1.2 FOUNDATION AND PERSPECTIVE

As previously indicated, this book adopts a textual analysis perspective. I am generally inspired by Glifford Geertz in considering a text to be a "sample of culture" (Geertz, 1973, p. 11) and hence "culture as an assemblage of texts" (Geertz, 1973, p. 448). Geertz (1973) furthermore maintains "The concept of culture I expouse . . . is essentially a semiotic one" (p. 5), and motivated from this, I consider a "sample" as a sign characterized by a given number of meaningful elements that are systematically related to one another (see also Tagg, 2013). Music is one such element that is related to other textual elements, such as pictures, written words, and other types of sound in commercials. From this perspective, the analysis focuses on the structure of the text: "Analysis, then, is sorting out the structures of signification" (Geertz, 1973, p. 9), and in the words of a researcher who is particularly interested in the study of music, "textual analysis is concerned with identifying and analyzing the formal qualities of texts" (Shuker, 2005, p. 272).

Furthermore, the analytical perspective is interpretive and hence qualitative. Again, I am inspired by Geertz (1973): "Man is an animal suspended in webs of significance he himself has spun, I take culture to be those webs, and the analysis of it to be therefore not an experimental science in search of law but an interpretive one in search of meaning" (p. 5). This book's presentation of how to examine music in commercials is empirically informed by "specialized listening" to a number of cases. Therefore, on numerous occasions, I viewed a sample of stored texts with a systematic focus on their music and its structural relationships with other sign elements. This procedure is rather unusual compared with ordinary viewers' reception of commercials, but it presents a necessary basis for text analysis, particularly when considering the "ephemeral" nature of (music in) commercials, for example.

As indicated, I have selected a number of cases to demonstrate throughout this book how to understand and analyze music in commercials. I have selected cases based on two different strategies. First, I have employed an information-oriented selection strategy (Flyvbjerg, 2006). This strategy includes the selection of cases that I found particularly suitable for illustrating specific aspects of, for example, music placement and musical signification in commercials. Additionally, some cases have been chosen because they are potentially well known to at least some readers (i.e., most commercials have been broadcast internationally, and most can be accessed on YouTube).

Special attention will be devoted to one particular case: a commercial for Apple's iPad, which was broadcast for the first time in 2010 and includes extracts from the song "There Goes My Love" by the band The Blue Van (the inclusion of this case in this book presents a further development of Graakjær, 2014). This case first captured my interest in 2010 when the band's appearance in the Apple commercial was widely announced and applauded by independent commentators in the Danish media (see the following examples). Additionally, the band is from Broenderslev—a town located only 15 miles from where I lived in Northern Jutland, Denmark—and I was especially interested in how this relatively unknown band (on an international scale) could possibly benefit from this seemingly sensational placement of its music. Today, several years after the first broadcast, this question can be examined. Accordingly, that case will serve as a distinctive basis for exemplifying specific aspects of music in commercials. One of these aspects is *music placement*, which refers to the placement (typically based on a legal contract) of excerpts from a piece of preexisting music in a commercial for a nonmusical product, brand or company. Arguably, recent developments have encouraged a specific mode of music placement, including placing the music of a band unknown to viewers (e.g., Christian, 2011; Eckhardt & Bradshaw, 2014; Klein, 2009; Meier, 2011; Sanburn, 2012; Schug, 2010; Taylor, 2012). Certainly, music placement as a particular type of co-branding or cross-promotion is not new, and research on the use of music in television commercials and motion pictures has indeed shown some interest in the use of well-known—both recognizable and "symbolically rich"—preexisting music; however, studies performing a textual analysis of this type of unfamiliar preexisting music are rare.

Klein (2009) offers one of the most significant scholarly examinations of the context and varieties of this type of music placement to date. Focusing primarily on "secondary texts" (as coined by Moore, 2001, p. 1), Klein thoroughly examines the processes, ideologies and discourse from the perspective of production.[3] However, the "primary audiovisual text"—referring to a specific excerpt of the music and its precise placement in a commercial—is largely undisclosed and unexamined with respect to, for example, its relevance to processes of signification (Moore, 2010). In other words, Klein refrains from systematic textual analysis, as is common in many subsequent contributions on related issues (e.g., Carah, 2010; Christian, 2011; Eckhardt & Bradshaw, 2014; Magis, 2013; Meier, 2011; Powers, 2010; Stevens, 2011; Taylor, 2012). Additionally, there is little knowledge about the actual prevalence of and possible increase in the use of preexisting music in commercials. Consequently, given that the information-oriented selection procedure may result in a sample of extreme or deviant cases (Flyvbjerg, 2006), I supplement the information-oriented strategy in this work.

Second, I have performed a random selection of a larger number of cases (Flyvbjerg, 2006). The selected sample consists of 1,678 unique commercials broadcast on the Danish television channel TV 2[4] for the first time during the month of April[5] in six volumes: 1992 (210 commercials), 1996 (197 commercials), 2000 (269 commercials), 2004 (301 commercials), 2008 (258 commercials), and 2012 (443 commercials). Music is present in 1,490 (i.e., 88.8 %) of these commercials (see the following chapters for further details regarding this music). In addition, to exemplify the process of musical branding in commercials, I have included all newly broadcast commercials for the McDonald's campaign *i'm lovin' it* on TV 2 for the period from September 2003 to November 2011. This sample includes 267 unique commercials. Generally, the sample for this book includes both nationally and internationally produced commercials, and it is arguably representative of the commercials broadcast on TV 2.

The main purpose of including the random sample is the objective of including a wide variety of musical structures and functions. I include commercials from this sample throughout the book to illustrate particular aspects, and compared with the Apple/The Blue Van case, the music in these commercials are described in a much more cursory manner. I maintain that an illustration of the variety of musical expressions in the sample can inspire and allow for the presentation of wide-ranging analytical perspectives on music in commercials (i.e., perspectives applicable to commercials outside of the sample used in this book). Given the relatively small number of commercials included in the sample and given that my perspective is primarily interpretive text analytical (and not oriented toward, e.g., quantitative content analysis), a proper statistical analysis will not be effectuated. Furthermore, the following examinations are based on categories, which are rather subjective (e.g., the categorizations are not confirmed by intercoder reliability). This subjectivity is evident throughout the book, for example, from its delineation of different types of sound to the delimitation of musical origins and structures. Reliability is substantiated by the intention to analyze all commercials in a similar manner and by clarification of the method of analysis. I have previously examined some of the commercials from this sample—that is, the April 1992, 1996, 2000, and 2004 volumes—and I have indicated some tendencies regarding the appearance of music in this book (see Graakjær, 2009a). The inclusion of the 2008 and 2012 volumes allow for a follow-up on some of these issues.

Whereas the information-oriented selection primarily includes cases that have been broadcast internationally and that are available on YouTube, the random selection primarily includes cases that have been broadcast only in Denmark. This selection procedure presents a possible bias. Previous studies have identified qualities particular to Danish commercials; for example,

> If you are not funny, good humored or some kind of regional type (which is often funny or fascinating in itself), and if you do not by other means create a symbolic space, which invites and activates the audience's imagination in a playful way, then stay out. That seems to be the general message of the tendencies in Danish TV ads.
>
> (Stigel, 2001, p. 349)

However, I suggest that the present sample is appropriate for my purposes, and it is beyond the present scope to examine and compare possible cross-cultural differences among larger samples of commercials. Moreover, it is important to emphasize that the sample does not allow for deeper historical examination. Consequently, this book does not aim to present a history of music in commercials (see Rodman, 2010, and Taylor, 2012, for recent examples of historical accounts of music in [American] commercials).

In addition to the analysis of the appearance of music in the preceding sample of commercials, the insights of this book originate from the evaluation and integration of previous research on music in commercials and in advertising more generally, particularly music in web ads and in stores. When relevant to the examination of music in commercials and the processes of musical signification, I supplement this research with insights from the examination of other audiovisual media, such as music from music videos, motion pictures, and television series (however, it is well beyond the scope of this book to provide a comprehensive presentation of the use of music in these other audiovisual media).

Within the field of music in advertising, two major traditions have emerged: the tradition of musicology and the tradition of advertising research and market communication. The first tradition is concerned with the aesthetic, historical, and sociological aspects of music. This tradition adopts a predominantly interpretive approach to its subject, although quantitative methods are not entirely avoided. The second tradition is dominated by quantitative and experimental approaches focusing on the effects of music on viewers. Only a handful of qualitative or interpretive studies of advertising and marketing have contributed to this field, which is interested in the signification (rather than the effect) of music and commercials for consumers (L. Andersen, 2001; Bode, 2004; Holbrook, 2004; Jacke, Jünger, & Zurstiege, 2000; Scott, 1990). The point of reference of such studies has typically been interpretive research in other fields of market communication, advertising studies and consumer behavior rather than contributions from musicology. Musicology and the "experimentalists" have largely ignored one another.

In this book, I focus on interpretive approaches based on the following arguments: (a) This approach has been used less frequently in advertising research and market communication; (b) although a significant body of interpretive contributions exists (as will be shown), the field is marked by a lack of cross-citation, and knowledge has not been integrated into a comprehensive analytical framework; and (c) a number of reviews already exist within the advertising research and market communication tradition (e.g., Allan, 2007a; Bode, 2004; Bullerjahn, 2006; Oakes, 2007; Shevy & Hung, 2013; Vihn, 1994; Yoon, 1993). Because mutual inspiration between the traditions described is highly necessary, I supplement the interpretive focus by including contributions from the tradition of advertising research and market communication when it seems relevant. Moreover, as a service to readers who demand a brief account of major experimental contributions, Table 1.1 provides a chronological overview specifying the scope (the variables) and design (the quality of the stimuli and the number of respondents) of the research.[6]

With respect to the results of this research, I agree with the following evaluations. Generally, it is "not possible to directly measure the impact of

Table 1.1 A survey of experimental research on music in television commercials presented in chronological order (adapted from Graakjær & Janzten 2009)

Contribution	Independent variable	Dependent variable	Stimuli	Respondents
Wintle, 1978	Supporting and contradicting music	Emotion, meaning	Constructed	120 undergraduate students
Aaker & Bruzzone, 1985	Music, no music	Irritation (attitude toward ad)	Real	780 households
Park & Young, 1986	Involvement	Attitude toward brand	Constructed	120 women (21–60 years old)
Stout & Rust, 1986	Music, no music	Recall, attitude, emotion	Real (?)	60 women
Paltschik & Lindqvist, 1987	Feelings aroused, sex, television exposure, former experience	Recall	Real	76 students
Macklin, 1988	Jingle, background music, no music	Attitude toward ad and brand, product choice, behavioral intent, recall	Constructed	75 children (average 57 months old)
Stout & Leckenby, 1988	Mode, tempo, melody, music versus no music	Recall, behavioral intent, attitude, emotion	Real and constructed	1,498 respondents (90 % female)
Witt, 1989	Mode, pitch, meter, rhythm, tempo, melody, style, instrumentation, duration of spot and music, known music	Recall, attitude toward ad and brand	Real and constructed	750 respondents
Tauchnitz, 1990	Emotional evaluation of music	Emotional evaluation of brand, brand awareness	Real and constructed	67 (?) students (average age 24 years old)

(*Continued*)

Table 1.1 (Continued)

Contribution	Independent variable	Dependent variable	Stimuli	Respondents
Tom, 1990	Hit music, parody of hit music, original music	Recall	Constructed	151 students
Stewart, Farmer, & Stannard, 1990	Exposure, time, cue	Recall	Real	2,856 respondents (18–54 years old)
Stout, Leckenby, & Hecker, 1990	Tempo, volume, mode melody	Attitude toward ad and brand, emotion	Real (?)	1,200 respondents (18–54 years old)
Gorn, Goldberg, Chattopadhyay, & Litvack, 1991	Music, information, music + information	Recall, belief, attitude toward ad and product, product choice	Constructed	176 elderly (60–84 years old)
MacInnis & Park, 1991	Fit, indexicality, involvement	Attitude toward ad and brand, emotions, attention	Constructed	178 undergraduate women
Yoon, 1993	Familiarity, liking	Attention, recall, attitude, evaluation of brand, skin conductance	Real	105 students
Hung, 1994	Congruity	Attitude toward ad and brand, brand perception, meaning	Real and constructed	569 students (in 2 experiments)
Middlestadt, Fishbein, & Chan, 1994	Music versus no music	Attitude toward ad and behavior, beliefs	Constructed	97 undergraduate students
Bozman & Mueling, 1994	Liked, disliked, neutral music, involvement	Attitude toward brand	Constructed	210 undergraduate students

Vihn, 1994	Emotional evaluation of music and visuals, attitude toward music and visuals	Emotional evaluation of ad and brand, attitude toward ad and brand, behavioral intent	Real and constructed	163 respondents (124 respondents 1–30 years old and 39 respondents 60+ years old)
Hitchon, Duckler, & Thorson, 1994	Ambiguity, complexity	Attitude toward ad and brand	Constructed	102 undergraduate students
Olsen, 1997	Music, silence, interstimulus interval	Recall, attitudes to ad elements	Constructed	744 (3 experiments)
Stewart & Punj, 1998	Exposure, time, cue	Recall	Real	745 respondents (18–54 years old)
Hahn & Hwang, 1999	Tempo, known background music, resource match	Recall, attitude toward ad and brand, emotion	Constructed	249 undergraduates (2 experiments)
Hung, 2000	Congruity	Meaning	Real and Constructed	134 students (25–44 years old)
Hung, 2001	Congruity	Music images and emotions, ad images and emotions, meaning	Constructed	102 students (18–22 years old)
Shen & Chen, 2006	Congruity, attention	Recall, attitude toward ad	Constructed	130 students (average 23 years old)
Alexomanolaki, Loveday, & Kennett, 2006	Jingle, instrumental music, music and voiceover, no music	Implicit and explicit memory	Real and constructed	95 undergraduates (18–30 years old)
Galan, 2009	Musical genre, tempo, congruity	Attitudes toward ad and brand, intention to buy, memorization, perceived duration	Constructed	491 students (17–25 years old)

(Continued)

Table 1.1 (Continued)

Contribution	Independent variable	Dependent variable	Stimuli	Respondents
Alexomanolaki, Kennett, & Loveday, 2010	Familiar, unfamiliar music	Memorization, association, perception of musical fit	Constructed	67 undergraduate students (18–37 years old)
Chou & Lien, 2010	The song's period and nostalgia, relevance of lyrics	Cognitive responses, affective responses, attitudes toward ad and brand	Constructed	276 Undergraduates
Yeoh & North, 2012	Musical fit	Brand choice, perception of musical influence	Constructed	90 students
Oakes & North, 2013	Classical music, dance music, no music	Brand image	Real and constructed	135 second-year undergraduate marketing students

television commercials on the financial success of an advertised product, indirect means must be employed to examine the effectiveness of advertising elements like music" (Bullerjahn, 2006, p. 216). More specifically, "it seems . . . clear . . . that music's effectiveness in television commercials is hard to measure and hard to verify. The results to date have provided a very mixed message" (Bullerjahn, 2006, p. 233). For example, in certain instances, music appears to increase communication effectiveness, whereas in other circumstances, music may decrease effectiveness for reasons that are occasionally unclear (see also Alpert & Alpert, 1991, p. 232; Craton & Lantos, 2011; Henard & Rossetti, 2014).

A plausible reason for this difficulty in studying the effects of music is the complexity of musical signification in commercials. Most important, music itself in commercials does not strictly have effects on viewers. Rather, music presents a wide variety of *potentials* to affect its audiences. It is primarily through music's particular association with its cotexts (see next section) that these potentials are specified and realized, such that music may be said to contribute to processes of signification, which are in turn offered for particular viewers to interpret. A detailed examination and declaration of the cotextualization of music is typically not provided in the contributions listed in Table 1.1, whereas this book aims to provide precise, detailed insights into the possible cotextualization of music and the potentials of musical signification.

1.3 ORGANIZATION

This book is organized into two main parts that highlight different aspects of a textual analysis. Each part begins with an examination of the case referenced above; based on this examination, more wide-ranging theoretical insights are discussed. This case thus presents a recurring theme or thread throughout the book. Figure 1.1 presents a simple illustration of the two analytical perspectives that inspired the organization of this book into two main parts: the contextual and cotextual perspectives. Both perspectives are necessary when analyzing music in commercials, although the division between contextual and cotextual perspectives is notional; that is, the distinction does not reflect an intrinsic quality of the phenomenon of music in commercials. Based on introductory accounts of the music in the Apple/The Blue Van case, I aim to demonstrate how separating the two perspectives can be useful for analytical purposes. Figure 1.1 illustrates that contextual perspectives are the most wide-ranging and can serve as a background from which to examine cotextual perspectives. The box presenting the primary interest of this book "Music in commercials" is foregrounded and indicated by dotted lines that are intended to illustrate that the examination of music in commercials is "saturated" by both contextual and cotextual perspectives.

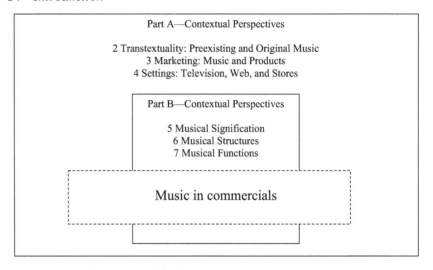

Figure 1.1   An illustration of the book's main perspectives

In the first part of this book, the perspective is contextual. I have chosen to present this perspective first because cotextual analysis is often largely dependent on contextual factors. This dependence is particularly evident when examining how the origin of music (a contextual issue) influences the processes of signification in a commercial (a cotextual issue).

On the most general level, the contextual perspective is informed by "a semiotic concept of culture" that can be specified as follows: "As inter-worked systems of construable signs . . ., culture is . . . a context, something within which they [construable signs] can be intelligibly—that is, thickly—described" (Geertz, 1973, p. 14; see the earlier definition of text). Here, the concept of context is used to identify the conditions of the text, for example, the premises for its coding and decoding. In a wider sense, context can be considered as a text's "natural habitat" (inspired by Mey, 1993, p. 181). Because this habitat comprises all living and environmental conditions, the contextual perspective is potentially far-reaching and is theoretically even endless. Consequently, the contextual perspective presented here does not pretend to be exhaustive, and I have excluded a number of issues apart from the already mentioned perspectives of production and reception, for example, the cultural historical preconditions for and developments of commercials as well as the changing spread, dominance and uses of media.

Inspired by the book's sample and existing research, three main issues have been chosen for the presentation of the contextual perspective. First, in Chapter 2, "Transtextuality: Preexisting and Original Music," I discuss the origin of music in commercials. Informed primarily by the notion of trans-textuality, I discuss how music in commercials textually relates to music outside the universe of a commercial. Throughout this book, I use various terms for the people who watch commercials (e.g., viewers, audience, users); however, in this part of the book, the term *listener* is predominant. Second, in Chapter 3, "Marketing: Music and Products," I discuss how music in commercials relates to marketing and the products and brands outside the universe of a commercial. Third, in Chapter 4, "Settings: Television, Web Ads, and Stores," I discuss the type of communicative context in which music in commercials belongs. I present commercials as a specific type of communication, and I discuss how music in commercials compares to music in other types of television programming and commercial settings.

In the second part of this book, the perspective employed is cotextual. The concept of cotext here refers to "that portion of text which (more or less immediately) surrounds it" (Mey, 1993, p. 184). In commercials, the textual elements (i.e., visuals, written words, music, and other types of sound in commercials) exemplify what are considered discrete analytical elements here. A cotextual analysis thus examines the relationships between these elements. Occasionally, cotext is used to refer to a monomodal text's elements that precede or follow the textual element of interest, such as a chapter, a paragraph, a sentence, or a particular word in a written text. The following is an example of this usage: "Co-text: text which precedes or follows that under analysis and which participants judge to belong to the same discourse" (G. Cook, 2001, p. 4). Relative to this example, it is important to emphasize that the present perspective also includes the synchronous relationships among text elements, that is, visuals, written and spoken language, and other sounds.

Accordingly, the cotextual perspective is potentially extensive. Even if this perspective may appear to be textually more delimited compared with the contextual perspective, it is nonetheless beyond the scope of this book to include all possible topics. Again, inspired by the book's sample and the available research, I have chosen three main issues to present the cotextual perspective. First, in Chapter 5, "Musical Signification," I discuss the issue of musical signification with a particular focus on how music relates to other textual elements. Second, in Chapter 6, "Musical Structures," I present the possible and typical structures of music in commercials. Third, in Chapter 7, "Musical Functions," I present the functions of music in commercials.

NOTES

1. For research aimed directly at producers of music in commercials, see, for example, Zager (2008). (For material related to jingles, see Chapter 6.) See also the practitioner-oriented literature in the recent field of sound branding (e.g., Bronner & Hirt, 2009; Groves 2011; Jackson & Fulberg, 2003; Lucensky, 2011; Treasure, 2011).
2. This and all further non-English quotes are translated by me.
3. Based on numerous cases and interviews with individuals in the business of music placement—creative directors at advertising agencies, licensing

managers, and musicians—Klein (2009) discusses the reasons that popular music in advertising has become "ubiquitous" (p. 1) and identifies the consequences for music, fans, the music industry, and music marketing.

4. TV 2 is a publicly owned television station in Denmark. The station began broadcasting nationally on October 1, 1988, thereby ending the monopoly previously exercised by the Danmarks Radio. The station primarily receives its funding from advertising revenues.

5. The month of April has been chosen because it represents a typical month in terms of the number of new commercials being broadcast and their use of music—for example, significantly fewer new commercials are broadcast during the summer (June and July), and in December, use of a particular type of preexisting (Christmas) music is widespread. Although April is arguably predisposed to specific products and soundscapes (e.g., birdsong in commercials for amusement parks and garden equipment), there is no reason to suggest that this tendency has a significant influence on the music appearing in commercials at this time.

6. I have searched for contributions that have demonstrated an interest in the effects of music in television commercials in the English, German, and Scandinavian languages. In addition, advertising research (along with the interpretive studies mentioned above) has contributed to this area with important quantitative, non-experimental studies (e.g., Murray & Murray, 1996; Olsen, 1994).

Part I
Contextual Perspectives

The first part of this book examines music in commercials from a contextual perspective. The purpose of this part of the book is to present what I believe are key features of the "natural habitat" of music in commercials. As noted in Chapter 1, contextual dimensions can be beneficial to consider before examining cotextual issues, although I do not suggest that this process of analysis should always be required.

Figure A.1 illustrates that in this part of the book, the focus is on music in commercials from a contextual perspective, with cotextual perspectives remaining in the background. Because the two perspectives are not mutually exclusive, cotextual issues are not entirely absent from the first part of the book. For example, the issue of "music–product relationship" implies the visual presentation of a particular product. However, the analysis of the specific cotextualization, structure, and function of music is not presented until the second part of the book.

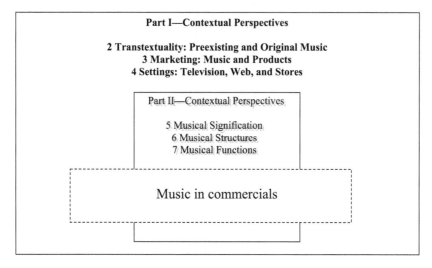

Figure A.1   An illustration of the primary focus of the first part of this book

The following section concentrates on the music "heard" in the case of Apple/The Blue Van. Subsequently, I spend three chapters discussing how music in commercials is textually related to music from outside the universe of commercials, how music in commercials relates to the market of products and brands outside the universe of commercials, and how music in commercials presents a specific type of communication that differs from other music on television and in other types of commercial settings.

THE APPLE/THE BLUE VAN CASE—I

On March 7, 2010, a commercial for Apple's iPad was broadcast for the first time during the Academy Awards presentation on the American network ABC. The commercial featured excerpts from the song "There Goes My Love" by the Danish band The Blue Van. The commercial synchronized the announcement of the release of Apple's new iPad on April 3, 2010, with the American rerelease of The Blue Van's album *Man Up*.[1] In weeks that followed, the commercial aired in America and throughout the world. Presumably, millions of viewers heard the music while watching the commercial. The presentation of the Oscars alone attracted 39.3 million American viewers. I refer to these viewers below, unless stated otherwise. In the following, I briefly introduce the background for this case from the perspectives of Apple and The Blue Van, respectively.

Apple

Apple Inc. is an American multinational corporation founded in 1976 that designs, develops, and sells consumer electronics. Apple is one of the world's largest information technology companies and mobile phone producers, and Samsung is one of its most significant competitors in the field of smartphones, for example (C. Jones, 2013). In 2013, for the first time, Apple became the world's most valuable brand (S. Elliott, 2013). Music appears to have played a role in Apple's attainment of this position. First, music is an integral part of Apple's products and services. For example, the iPod allows for personalized musical reproduction, the iPod Nano and the iPad allow for audiovisual reproduction of music (videos), and the iTunes Store (i.e., a software-based online digital media store) is one of the world's largest music vendors. Second, in the new millennium, Apple's market communication has been heavily infused with music. For an overview of some of the music used in Apple's stores, commercials, presentations, and other marketing materials, see Kudit (2014).

The commercial featuring The Blue Van's "There Goes My Love" is an example of how music has often featured prominently in Apple's commercials. More specifically, the commercial illustrates what appears to be one of several trends in the selection of music for Apple's commercials. The music is unknown to most viewers of the commercial. Moreover, stylistically, the music resembles the turn-of-the-millennium "garage rock revival" by bands such as The Strokes, The White Stripes, Jet, and the Yeah Yeah Yeahs—all of which have incidentally been used by Apple.

The reasons for this particular musical branding strategy are not evident; however, the strategy is arguably influenced by broader marketing conditions. Prior to the commercial mentioned earlier, Apple established connections with numerous emerging bands, some of which have realized vast commercial benefits from this exposure. For example, in 2003, a commercial[2] for Apple's iPod helped the Australian band Jet to achieve commercial success with the song "Are U Gonna Be My Girl." This particular commercial was part of what has been described as "one of the most effective marketing campaigns in recent times" (Doyle, 2011). The commercials of this campaign featured silhouetted characters passionately dancing to specific pieces of music while holding a white iPod that presents a significant contrast to the silhouettes and brightly colored backgrounds in tropical colors (e.g., lime green, yellow, pink, fuchsia, and bright blue). A more recent example comes from the placement of the song "1, 2, 3, 4" by Leslie Feist in a commercial[3] for Apple's iPod Nano. In 2007, this commercial helped make the song a commercial success (for further examples, see Blau, 2011; A. Elliott, 2010; Hampp, 2011; Terr, n.d).[4]

The Feist commercial indicates that garage rock is not the only musical trend in Apple's commercials. Arguably, at least two major trends are evident: "polished, cosmopolitan garage rock sung by leather-jacketed dudes and whimsical, cosmopolitan synth-pop sung by cute girls" (DiCrescenzo, 2011). Additionally, it is not only unknown, emerging bands that have been used by Apple. For example, in 2004, U2 appeared in a silhouette-styled commercial with excerpts of its new song "Vertigo,"[5] and in 2008, Coldplay appeared with excerpts of its song "Viva la Vida." The former is an example of how Apple has co-promoted the iPod and the iTunes Store during the silhouette campaign. Moreover, both commercials illustrate how an Apple commercial has helped secure commercial success for the newly released material of established artists. Overall, Apple has built a reputation for producing commercials that appeal to both the eyes and ears of consumers, promoting not only their own products but also music from various musical genres from both established and emerging artists.

The Blue Van

The Blue Van was founded in Broenderslev when its members were in the sixth grade. Subsequently, the band moved to Copenhagen, where they recorded two EPs. In 2004, the band signed with TVT Records, and in 2005, The Blue Van released its first full-length album, *The Art of Rolling* (TVT Records). Subsequently, The Blue Van produced another album, *Dear Independence* (TVT Records, 2006), and the band toured extensively across the United States, Europe and Japan, among other areas. For example, during

27 concerts in the United States (5) and in Europe (22), The Blue Van was featured as the supporting act for the Australian band Jet, which was highly successful at the time—not least because of the abovementioned placement of their music in an Apple commercial.

The song "There Goes My Love" was released on The Blue Van's third full-length album, *Man Up*. The song was released in Denmark on October 27, 2008, after the band had signed a new contract with Playground Music/Iceberg Records (TVT Records had been declared bankrupt earlier that year). The album received national acclaim; however, similar to the band's previous albums, this album was only moderately successful commercially. The album did not achieve top chart positions in Denmark and was not distributed internationally. Against this background, building a relationship with Apple was considered an exceptional opportunity for the band to finally experience positive affiliation and exposure. According to one band member, "Apple is known to focus intently on the quality of sounds in their commercials; there is no talk during the commercial, and the music is allowed to appear perfectly clean" (Christensen in T. Andersen, 2010). This idea fueled the band's vision of an imminent international breakthrough: "My guess is that big things are going to happen to us this year" (Christensen in Knudsen & Jensen, 2010). Journalists echoed this enthusiasm, and Apple's selection of "There Goes My Love" was unanimously celebrated. For example, as the local newspaper observed, with barely disguised regional and national pride,

> Denmark received one of the less significant awards at the Oscars last night [i.e., Best Live Action Short for *The New Tenants* by Joachim Back and Tivi Magnusson]. However, the Oscars recognition was not the only significant gift for Denmark. Apple broadcast its first commercial for the iPad, which likely resulted in greater success for these men from Broenderslev. The Blue Van's 'There Goes My Love' was then chosen by Apple to appear in the commercial. It doesn't get much better than this.
> (Knudsen & Jensen, 2010).

MTV commented, "'There Goes My Love' was just one out of many songs that Apple had in mind for their iPad commercial, so we congratulate (The Blue Van)!" (MTV Networks, 2010). Others remarked that "there is probably gold in this for The Blue Van" (Shaer, 2010) and that "this is not just about exposure but is also a pat on the back for artistic quality" (Christensen, 2014).

The reason that Apple chose "There Goes My Love" is not well documented (which is typical for this type of process, see, e.g., Lee, 2008). The Blue Van's manager could only guess what had prompted Apple's interest: "I do not know why The Blue Van is particularly suited for synch [licensing] compared to other bands—maybe it is because of the raw indie-retro sound" (Zähringer in Friis, 2010). The deal with Apple also followed an attitudinal U-turn by The Blue Van, as the band's guitarist explains: "The first time we got a synch offer in 2005 we were naïve and turned it down.

We did not want our music to be associated with products that had nothing to do with our music" (Christensen in Friis, 2010). Five years later, in 2010, music placements accounted for approximately 70% of The Blue Van's total income (Friis, 2010), and in promotional material, the band's music placement record was presented as one of its career highlights (see Iceberg Records, 2010). Nevertheless, according to the band's manager, The Blue Van appears to have maintained the criteria for the brands with which it would associate: "We would never had accepted licensing the music for washing powder—it would have been devastating for The Blue Van if they got famous as the 'washing-powder' band, even if we, no doubt, would have earned more on such a deal" (Zähringer in Hansen, 2011).

Before its association with Apple's iPad commercial in 2010, The Blue Van had some experience licensing its music. For example, in 2009, excerpts from the song "Silly Boy" from *Man Up* appeared in a Samsung commercial,[6] and other songs from that album had appeared in several television series. Table A.1 presents an overview of some of the most significant placements of The Blue Van's music.

In addition to the examples listed in Table A.1, songs by The Blue Van have appeared in promos including numerous program promos on ABC, FOX, and NBC (2010–2013) and trailers (e.g., for the film *Die Hard 5*, 2013). This list indicates that music licensing has continued to add to The Blue Van's income. Whereas the exact reasons for this promotional strategy are not evident, the selection of this strategy is arguably influenced by broader marketing conditions that appear to complement the conditions from the brand perspective. The economic environment in the music industry along with threatening career conditions appears to have made music placement acceptable and even necessary for up-and-coming bands during this period (Klein, 2009; Meier, 2011; Taylor, 2012). Compared with the risk of becoming a "washing-powder band," the probability of becoming known as the "iPad/Apple band" is of no concern to the band and its manager. Actually, the existence of "Apple awe" indicates that a band may strive to bond with a prestigious brand and find it thrilling to do so.

Evidently, as exemplified, the placement of their music in Apple commercials has previously helped up-and-coming artists to achieve commercial success. However, The Blue Van did not achieve such success. Although there was a brief increase in downloads of "There Goes My Love" (Friis, 2010), the increase was modest and short-lived and did not result in an international breakthrough. As commercial effects failed to materialize, the national media's enthusiasm for the band's association with Apple faded rapidly. The association with Apple may have helped The Blue Van to secure additional licensing contracts, as perhaps indicated by the subsequent variety of placements (see Table A.1). However, in general, the case illustrates that commercially promising, far-reaching distribution with a prestigious brand cannot alone predict the subsequent commercial effect of placed music. Although every band that has appeared in an Apple commercial has

Table A.1   List of significant placements of the music of The Blue Van.

Distribution	Media	Advertised product	Song placed
2006	Film	The Art of Crying	Various
2008	Television series	Count-Down—Die Jagt Beginnt (RTL)	"Man Up"
2008/2009 (United States)	Commercial	Samsung/T-Mobile TV	"Silly Boy"
2008/2009	Television series	*90210* (CBS), episode 11	"Man Up"
2009	Television series	*CSI:NY* (CBS), episode 511	"Man Up"
2009	Game	MLB '09 The Show (Sony Playstation)	"Man Up"
2009	Television series	*Free Radio* (VH1 Viacom Media Networks)	"Be Home Soon"
2009 (Canada)	Commercial	Telus	"Product of DK"
2009	Television series	*90210* (CBS), episode 19	"Silly Boy"
2010	Television series	*Mercy* (NBC)	"Man Up"
2010 (United States)	**Commercial**	**Apple iPad**	**"There Goes My Love"**
2010	Television series	NCIS: L.A. (CBS), season 1, episode 11	"Man Up"
2010	Game	Football league (NFL Enterprises)	"I'm A Man"
2010/2011	Television series	*Hellcats* (CW/ Warner Bros.)	"There Goes My Love"
2010/2011	Television series	*Royal Pains*, theme song (NBC)	"Independence"
2010/2011	Television series	*Royal Pains*, episode 1 (NBC)	"Be Home Soon"
2010/2011	Television series	*Shameless* (NBC)	"Silly Boy"
2011	Television series	*CSI: NY* (CBS), episode 717	"You Live, You Learn, You Die"
2011 (various states in the United States)	Commercial	Time Warner Cable	"Be Home Soon"
2011	Television series	*Entourage* (HBO), episode 802	"Man Up"

Distribution	Media	Advertised product	Song placed
2012 (North America)	Commercial	Red Lobster	"I'm A Man"
2012	Game	NHLPA Web Series (Fifth Ground Entertainment)	"There Goes My Love"
2012	Film	*Magic Mike*	"Love Shot"
2012	Television series	*Hard Times Of RJ Berger* (MTV), episodes 205, 208 (two songs), 212	"Love Shot," "I Can Feel It," "You Live You Learn You Die" and "Loser Takes It All"
2012	Film	*Fright Night*	"I'm A Man"
2012	Television series	*Inbetweeners* (MTV), two episodes	"There Goes My Love" and "Silly Boy"
2012	Film	*American Reunion*	"I'm A Man"
2012	Television series	*Dallas* (Warner Bros.)	"I'm a Man"
2012	Film	*The First Time*	"Silly Boy"
2012/2013	Film	*21 and Over* (Mandeville Films/ Relativity Media)	"Man Up"
2013 (various states in the United States)	Commercial	Time Warner Cable	"Be Home Soon"
2013 (mainland China)	Commercial	Kraft's Chips Ahoy	"I'm A Man" (re-recorded in 2013)
2013	Television series	*Free Radio* (VH1/ Viacom Media Networks)	"There Goes My Love"
2013	Film	*Living Legends* (Eurodialogue OOD)	"Love Shot"
2014	Television series	*Beauty and The Beast* (CBS), episode 27	"Would You Change Your Life?"
2014	Television series	*Degrassi* (CBS/ Paramount), season 12	"Love Shot"

experienced some effect in terms of interest and sales, the effects are frequently modest (see, e.g., Harding, 2008; Klein, 2009, p. 123). Obviously, no single factor can explain why The Blue Van's relationship with Apple did not have a more pronounced effect on the band's career. Possible factors may relate to live concerts, appearances on radio and television programs, record company promotion, professional reviews, interviews, viral activity by users (e.g., posting, redistribution, and debates on social media), and perhaps even the song's (possible lack of) catchiness and memorability in the ear of the listener. However, consistent with the present approach, I focus on textual matters in the examination of the case that follows. Specifically, presenting an important aspect of a contextual analysis, I examine how the excerpts of "There Goes My Love" placed in the commercial relate to the album version of the same song. The focus of the analysis is thus on "the music heard." Subsequently, as part of the introduction to the second part of this book, I examine the case from a cotextual perspective.

As is typical of music placed in commercials, only excerpts of "There Goes My Love" appear in the commercial. Moreover, the specific excerpts that do appear represent a restructuring of the song. Although the 30 seconds of music in the commercial appear uninterrupted and in an even rhythmic flow, the music does not actually match a continuous sequence of 30 seconds from the album version of the song. Table A.2 indicates how musical episodes (i.e., much of the intro, the break that marks a shift from the intro to the verse, and the first part of the chorus) are omitted in the commercial.

The resulting collage progresses from the verse to the chorus with a high proportion of musical episodes, including lyrics. Thus, the so-called individuality predominance factor[7] is high in the commercial. Furthermore, the lyrics are relatively open to interpretation, and a number of "open spaces" (Iser, 1974) must be "filled out" by listeners. Although a general reading may include the identification of a human relationship and interactions, listeners must make sense of the more detailed references, such as the references to "I" and "you" as indicators of the identity of the individuals in the song and the phrases "my love," "I'll have an answer," "take off your gloves," and "I'll let you try" as indicators of the nature of the relationship and its interactions. The lyrics of the album version of the song may strongly suggest a particular type of relationship and interaction (i.e., preparing to perform and performing fellatio), but because of the omission of the most suggestive phrases (see Table A.2), the excerpts used in the commercial do not clearly suggest such a reading. The actual cotextualization of the lyrics (addressed in the second part of this book) appears to afford a more circumscribed variety of possible readings.

In summary, Table A.2 illustrates that it is essential to consider the specific excerpts of the music placed in the commercial to fully grasp the potential signification of the song. A different combination of musical episodes from the album version of "There Goes My Love" (e.g., including the instrumental intro and more of the chorus at the expense of parts of the verse) would substantially alter the potential signification of the song in the commercial. This

Table A.2 "There Goes My Love"—the album version compared with the commercial version (lyrics courtesy of Mette Zähringer, Iceberg Records A/S; adapted from Graakjær 2014)

	"There Goes My Love" album version	"There Goes My Love" commercial version
Intro	8 instrumental bars (guitar 1 riff)	~~8 instrumental bars (guitar 1 riff)~~
	—	—
	8 instrumental bars (guitar 1 riff accompanied by guitar 2 riff, bass, and drums)	~~5 instrumental bars (guitar 1 riff accompanied by guitar 2 riff, bass and drums)~~
		3 instrumental bars (guitar 1 riff accompanied by guitar 2 riff, bass, and drums)
	—	—
	Break (episode marker)	~~Break as episode marker~~
Verse	*Be, Be the charming type,* *Take off your gloves and show what they hide,* *Please, please my naked wrists,* *With your hands and fingertips* *And please, baby get on your knees,* *Don't bare bare bare your teeth,* *I'll let you try,* *If you close your eyes,* *I'll have an answer for your ass!*	*Be, Be the charming type,* *Take off your gloves and show what they hide,* ~~*Please, please my naked wrists,*~~ ~~*With your hands and fingertips*~~ ~~*And please, baby get on your knees,*~~ ~~*Don't bare bare bare your teeth,*~~ *I'll let you try,* *If you close your eyes,* *I'll have an answer for your ass!*
Chorus	*"There Goes My Love,"* *"There Goes My Love,"* *"There Goes My Love," love love love love,* *"There Goes My Love,"* *"There Goes My Love,"* *"There Goes My Love," love love love love!* *Break (episode marker)*	~~*"There Goes My Love,"*~~ ~~*"There Goes My Love,"*~~ ~~*"There Goes My Love," love love love love,*~~ *"There Goes My Love,"* *"There Goes My Love,"* *"There Goes My Love," love love love love!* Break (episode marker)

observation also shows that a piece of preexisting music should not be considered merely "placed" in a commercial. The editing of the music is highly meticulous, and viewers who are not familiar with the song have no possibility of identifying its restructuring. The particular combination of musical episodes thus actually "produces" a particular version of a song, and I further illustrate this process at the beginning of the second part of this book.

At this point, I examine the contextual aspects of music in commercials beginning with the issue of transtextuality.

NOTES

1. The commercial can be accessed here: www.youtube.com/watch?v=R41NN PBqRCk.
2. See www.youtube.com/watch?v=mAxUIjJrFKQ.
3. See www.youtube.com/watch?v=8qP79rRzzh4.
4. There is no simple or objective measure of "commercial success." I use the concept here to indicate a sudden increase in the sales of a particular song immediately following the airing of a commercial in which excerpts of the song had been placed (for further details on the sales effects of the placement of "1, 2, 3, 4," see Powers, 2010).
5. The commercial can be accessed here: www.youtube.com/watch?v=54vgFVh OAF0.
6. See www.youtube.com/watch?v=9ptt7Z0bSjo.
7. That is, "a rough quantitative measure of the significance of 'individuality' in a musical piece, based on a reading of the dualism of lead vocal melody and instrumental accompaniment" (Björnberg, 2000, p. 358).

2 Transtextuality
Preexisting and Original Music

This chapter examines how music in commercials can be textually related to music outside the realm of the commercial and how this relationship can be analyzed. Musical signification in commercials largely depends on such textual relations:

> Music operates in television through a process of association or correlation with other texts: either musical works, which serve as syntactical objects of comparison, or through extramusical texts, such as images, words, or sounds through which a listener can draw common meanings.
> (Rodman, 2010, p. 39)

Several procedures for the examination of musical relationships exist, including the interobjective comparison method presented by Philip Tagg (for details on this method, see Chapter 5). However, this chapter is inspired primarily by the notion of transtextuality: "the ensemble of any type of relation, explicit or not, that may link a text with others" (Lacasse, 2000, p. 36; see also Stockfelt, 2006).

The transtextual relationship between music in a commercial and music from outside the universe of the commercial can manifest in various ways. At the most general level, two types of relationships must be recognized. First, the music in a commercial can appear to "quote" or "paraphrase" a particular piece of music outside of and prior to the universe of the commercial. In this case, the music from outside the commercial predates the music in the commercial, and this type of music is thus coined *preexisting music*. Second, the music in a commercial may appear not to quote or paraphrase a particular piece of music outside of and prior to the universe of the commercial. In this case, the music has had no previous existence, and because it originates from the commercial, this type of music is coined *original music*. While this distinction in the first place is made by the researcher—based on the researcher's accomplished knowledge of the music's distribution—the perspective of the listeners should be considered in the second place (see more below).

When analyzing music in commercials from a transtextual perspective, the first question to be examined is thus whether the music is preexisting or original. From the perspective of transtextuality, the distribution and, therefore, the possible reception and familiarity of the music are important. Hence, for a musical text to have existed, it needs to have been distributed. In many cases, "preexisting music from the perspective of distribution" equals "preexisting music from the perspective of production" (i.e., music composed as a self-contained product not intended to appear in a commercial). However, the two perspectives do not fully overlap: Whereas all distributed music has been produced to some degree and in some manner, not all produced music has been or will be distributed. Additionally, a piece of preexisting music (from the production perspective) may be released at the same time as the broadcasting of the commercial in which the music appears (e.g., in cases of cross-promotion or music–product partnership, see Chapter 3). Following this example, the music is preexisting from the production perspective, but it is apparently not preexisting from the distribution perspective (although it might be argued that the two musical versions coexist and are codistributed). In the following, I distinguish between these two perspectives when it is necessary to do so.[1]

The following sections are organized in accordance with these two types of musical relationships, and I discuss the significance and subtypes of both types in relation to music in commercials. I include the preceding case analysis and a number of supplementary cases.

2.1   PREEXISTING MUSIC

The presence of preexisting music in commercials is the exception rather than the rule. Examining some of the few available studies that include large-scale, randomly selected samples (e.g., Allan, 2008; Bjurström & Lilliestam, 1993; Greckel, 1987; Leo, 1999; Steiner-Hall, 1987), we find that the proportion of commercials that include preexisting music is only as high as 15%, and this finding also applies when considering the random sample for this book. Although commercials that include preexisting music are not dominant in terms of raw numbers, they have received considerable scholarly attention—perhaps because of the *attractiveness of particularity bias*, which arguably predisposes scholars to examine *unusual* (extraordinary, attention-grabbing) or extreme (see Chapter 1) cases at the expense of *usual* (ordinary, anonymous) cases. For example, regarding the use of art or classical[2] music, "for those who deal constantly with art music [e.g., musicians or musicologist], commercials which include art music are particularly salient" (Riethmüller, 1973, p. 78).

Within the experimentalist tradition (see Chapter 1), preexisting music is more or less explicitly included as an independent variable in studies that examine the effect of music that is "familiar," "liked," or "congruent" (e.g., Bozman & Mueling, 1994; Hung, 2000; Oakes, 2007; Tom, 1990; Yoon, 1993). Seminal experimental contributions to understanding the influence of preexisting music have been offered by authors working within the knowledge activation framework, such as North and Hargreaves (2006). Although those two authors do not explicitly focus on preexisting music, they claim that a fit between the associations attached to music and the values and attitudes attached to the product by consumers enhances decision making. This argument clarifies some of the motives for advertisers to select this type of music: "Sophisticated classical music in an advertisement for perfume," for example, may have a positive influence on consumers (North & Hargreaves, 2006, p. 113). The crucial point is that music activates culturally determined knowledge structures in the audience (for further experimental contributions to this "fit," see Areni & Kim, 1993; MacInnis & Park, 1991; Park & Young, 1986; see also Chapter 5).

The use of preexisting music in commercials has evoked at least two different responses by those who adopt interpretive approaches. First, a critical perspective has emerged. This perspective is often based on Marxist notions of ideology (e.g., Marx & Engels, 1970) and is inspired by Freudo-Marxist theories, such as those relating to "false needs" and "surrogate gratifications," which dominated the German intellectual climate during the 1970s (e.g., Haug, 1986). For example, the various publications by Motte-Haber (1972a, 1972b, 1973) are clearly informed by a Marxist perspective. She claims for instance that the use of classical music in commercials leads to the "destruction of musical meaning" (Motte-Haber, 1973, p. 178), transforms "art to the lowest stage of non-art" (1972a, p. 153), and leads to "musical illiteracy" (Gertich & Motte-Haber, 1987, p. 59; see also Fehling, 1980; Schmidt, 1983). These claims are not supported by empirical research—experimental or ethnographic—and concrete examples of the aesthetic mechanisms generating such dangerous effects are largely absent. Interestingly, perhaps illustrating the *attractiveness of particularity bias* noted in Chapter 1, the critique of the use of classical music in commercials appears to concern a small proportion of broadcast commercials: "Excerpts from the field of art music" are included in "one to two percent of all commercials" (Riethmüller, 1973, p. 78); for example, in the random sample for this book, classical music is deployed in 2% of the commercials from the April 2008 volume and 1% of the commercials from the April 2012 volume. Although a critical perspective can be found in more recent contributions—for example, the use of popular music in commercials has been discussed from a critical perspective (see, e.g., Burns, 1996; Savan, 1993; see also Allan 2005)—the concerns became outdated in the late 1980s. Moreover, such concerns do not appear to have had a significant influence on scholars in the Anglophone context, as illustrated by the following assessment: "The study of the effect of the 'secondhand use'—or abuse—of classical music in advertising has been almost entirely ignored" (Tota, 2001, p. 115).

The second perspective focuses on processes of musical signification. Whereas the critical contributions concern the implications of music in commercials for the appreciation of "ordinary" music (e.g., classical music), for the well-being of listeners and viewers, or for society at large, this perspective generally aims to understand and illustrate how preexisting music contributes to processes of signification. Parallel to the critical perspective, a considerable number of early German studies demonstrate how scholarly interest in music in commercials need not necessarily be informed by Freudo-Marxist theories. These studies have emphasized the importance of understanding *how* music in commercials actually works and describing *what* type of phenomenon this music is (e.g., Helms, 1981; Jungheinrich, 1969; Meissner, 1974; Riethmüller, 1973; Rösing, 1975, 1982; Schmitt, 1976). For example, the significance of Rösing's (1982) contribution is in highlighting the role of music in the construction of the overall meaning of an audiovisual message—a perspective that is explored more meticulously in subsequent research on popular music (e.g., N. Cook, 1994; Tagg, 2013). N. Cook (1994) thus investigated music in commercials to illustrate a point of general importance: the actual process of signification. By comparing the role of music in different commercials (one of which includes excerpts from Mozart's *Marriage of Figaro*), Cook argued that music has the potential to construct or negotiate meaning by interacting "with the story line, the voice-over, and the pictures" (1994, p. 30). Meaning thus "emerges" from interactions in specific contexts, a concept that is further developed by N. Cook (1998; see more on this perspective in Chapter 5) and by Hung (2000, 2001) using an experimental perspective (for further examples of interpretive approaches to preexisting music, see, e.g., Bonde 2009; Pekkilä, 1998; Rodman, 1997; Springer, 1992; Taylor, 2000; Tota, 2001).

Tota (2001) offers a particularly instructive discussion of the signifying potential of preexisting music, and I present key aspects of this investigation. Interestingly, contrary to most other studies of preexisting music, Toto is inspired by audience-response theory (e.g., Eco, 1979; Iser, 1974): the issue of how "model or implicit listeners/viewers" create meanings from the interplay between music and other sign systems. Tota examined how "a text is modified when its use radically changes in ways that the original author could never have even imagined" (2001, p. 116). For example, the use of *Carmina Burana* in a commercial for Guinness and the use of Mahler's Fifth Symphony in a commercial for Pasta Barilla clearly include neither the listeners whom the composers (Carl Orff and Gustav Mahler, respectively) could have had in mind nor the so-called ideal listening situation (Tota, 2001, p. 15). Throughout the work, Tota does not specify precisely which excerpts from the preexisting music are placed in the commercial. For example, the precise excerpts from Mahler's Fifth Symphony are undisclosed (as is the specific recording). However, from a text analytical perspective, it is important to specify the exact excerpt because different excerpts from Mahler's Fifth Symphony, for instance, lead to different potentials for signification (see more in the next section).

Although Tota focused on cases of relatively well-known classical music, the author's perspective is useful for understanding other types of music as well. Tota suggested that the analysis of preexisting music in commercials should consider three points in time (T1, T2, and T3), each characterized by a specific mode of reception. T1 refers to the reception of a given piece of music after its initial release, that is, its "existence" prior to its appearance in a commercial. T2 refers to the reception of an excerpt of the same music in a commercial, and T3 refers to the reception of the same piece of music encountered subsequent to and "outside" of the commercial (Tota, 2001, p. 117). Tota also suggested that we should imagine the progress of a piece of music over time as illustrating "a sort of 'career'" (2001, p. 115). This metaphor highlights the importance of a piece of music's previous distribution (T1) to the music's signification power in the commercial (T2), which in turn affects the future reception of this particular piece of music (T3). Listeners may thus attach the meanings associated with the commercial to those originally associated with the preexisting music; for example, "instead of feeling an infinite desire on listening again to Beethoven, the social actor may think of the taste of the new ice cream" (Tota, 2001, p. 117). This process of musical hybridization—or "contamination" (Tota, 2001, p. 113) or even "connotative hijacking" (Tagg, 2013, p. 184; see also Englis & Pennell, 1994)—can lead to different results regarding "the receptive experiences of different social actors" (Tota, 2001, p. 117). For example, for listeners familiar with a particular piece by Beethoven (i.e., who would be listening to Beethoven "again"), the result may be a feeling of dispossession (for an experimental study of similar effects, see Blair & Shimp, 1992). However, for listeners who are not familiar with the music, this result cannot occur because these listeners lack the T1 experience (see also Tagg, 2013, p. 184).

The significance of a listener's familiarity with a piece of music prior to its inclusion in a commercial can be further illustrated by reconsidering the case of Apple and The Blue Van. Whereas "There Goes My Love" does indeed predate the commercial—that is, the song was produced and distributed before it was included in the commercial—the song would have likely been unknown to most American viewers. Given that production has not led to wide-ranging international distribution and reception in this case, T1 is irrelevant, and T3 thus differs. For producers and band members, T3—including associations with the Apple brand (as indicated by the earlier discussed "Apple awe")—is the desired result. T2 is intended to propel the "career" of the song, the album, and the band, and it presents an opportunity to fundamentally bring the music "into (post)existence." A particular version of the song is thus "produced," and this version arguably differs from the version constructed by listeners who experienced the song prior to its inclusion in the commercial. Arguably, these listeners are led to associate the song's strong suggestion of a particular type of relationship and interaction (i.e., preparing to perform and performing fellatio) with the brand and the relationship presented in the commercial, which may in turn result in unanticipated (e.g., comical) readings from Apple's perspective. Because of the omission of the song's most suggestive phrases (see Table A.2), the excerpts used in the commercial do not clearly convey such a reading to viewers who hear the music for the first time in the commercial. To these listeners, the potential of musical signification is fueled by the style and genre of the song rather than its "opus"—that is, "the particular song by the particular band with the particular potential of signification" (in the second part of this book, I further explore the issue of musical signification).

This case indicates how processes of signification are dependent on the precise choice of excerpts of preexisting music that are used in a commercial. To determine such precise excerpts, it is necessary to be able to specify the "original" text or hypotext to which the music in the commercial refers. In the following, I discuss the issue of how the "original" text (Tota, 2001) can actually be specified.

On Specifying the Preexisting Music

As indicated, the examination of whether the music in a commercial is preexisting should be oriented toward distribution and, hence, possible reception. Sometimes this examination is a simple undertaking. For example, a commercial may include excerpts from a widely distributed (and therefore well known to both listeners and analysts) piece of music. Occasionally, however, such an examination becomes challenging. Of course, no listener or analyst is familiar with (the distribution of) all the world's music. Because the specific origin of a piece of music is not normally announced in the commercial—except when the music presents the product being advertised (see Chapter 3)—such problems inevitably arise when analyzing music in commercials compared with media such as films, in which the closing credits typically specify the music that has been used. Previous research has also noted this problem: "There are several instances of songs that cannot be determined in terms of whether they have been originally composed for the commercial [i.e., original music] or have been imported from somewhere else [i.e., preexisting music]" (Bjurström & Lilliestam, 1993, p. 73). Obviously, the inclusion or the absence of a brand and product name in a song's lyrics may indicate whether the music is preexisting (as indicated with respect to the Apple case). However, a number of electronic tools that could prove helpful in examining the possible prior distribution of music have emerged, including corporate websites, designated websites,[3] smartphone apps (e.g., Soundhound and Shazam), and YouTube. For example, The Blue Van's music is the topic of several user comments on YouTube. If these sources do not provide relevant information on the preexistence of the music, then it seems reasonable to suggest that the music is not preexisting. Moreover, if listeners have no experience with prior distributions of the music, then prior distribution cannot influence the processes of signification from the perspective of these viewers (as discussed from the perspective offered by Tota, 2001).

When determining the preexistence of music in commercials, questions arise with respect to how, when, and where the music existed prior to its appearance in the commercial. The answers to these questions would normally require (a) the specification of an "original" text—or a "hypotext" in Genette and Lacasse's terminology (see below)—and (b) the mapping of the possible "career" of the music prior to its inclusion in the commercial. For example, the case of Apple's placement of excerpts from "There Goes My Love" illustrates how a recording (i.e., the album version of the song) can present the "original" text, whereas the prior "career" of the song has been brief and insignificant. In this respect, the analysis of this case is relatively simple. However, the analysis is more complex in cases in which the preexisting music does not refer to a recording. According to Tagg (1979), the three primary modes of storage and distribution of sound are oral transmission, musical notation, and recorded sound (p. 34). To what extent these modes might be comparable to specific genres (e.g., folk music, art or classical music, and popular music, respectively) is not addressed in this book (see Talbot, 2000, for details on the possible specifications of musical originals and "works"); nonetheless, compared with "recorded sound," "oral" and "notational" transmitted music are more difficult to specify. For example, Mahler's Fifth Symphony is available in several recordings that differ in terms of tempi and dynamics. Thus, a transtextual analysis must rely on convention and the expected auditory structure of the particular piece of music (see Graakjær, 2009b, for an example of the use of an occasional song).

Additionally, it can be difficult to map the "career" of a particular piece of music, as Tota maintained: "In post-modern societies the destiny of the text is less predictable" (Tota, 2001, p. 121; see the following discussion). Experience with a piece of music prior to its appearance in a commercial may thus have a long history and include a wide variety of co(n)texts. For example, Tota explains how a listener's construction of meaning in a commercial that contains excerpts from Mahler's Fifth Symphony may be influenced by the music's prior appearance in Visconti's movie *Death in Venice* (Tota does not specify which excerpts were included). Subsequent placements of "There Goes My Love" present other examples. Thus, for example, listeners may attach the meanings associated with the song in the game NHLPA Web Series as well as the series *Hellcats, Inbetweeners,* and *Free Radio* to the meanings initially associated (for some viewers) with the music in the commercial (see Table 1.1).

These examples indicate that although a song's musical style and genre may inflect toward culturally and historically dominant or preferred meanings, listeners may have constructed dissimilar "musical careers" for particular pieces of preexisting music that will in turn influence their reading of the (music in the) commercial and subsequent placements in different ways. This view of listeners may help explain why preexisting music is not normally deployed as a musical brand; from a strategic perspective, the spread and the career of preexisting music are practically uncontrollable, which does not facilitate processes of musical branding. As noted, listeners may associate dissimilar meanings with the music and the brand, and some listeners may even feel a sense of dispossession (for more on musical brands, see Chapter 3). Moreover, perhaps unwillingly on the part of the producers and senders of a commercial, the same piece of preexisting music may appear in two (or more) simultaneously distributed and competing texts, resulting in a blurring of the potential power of signification. For example, "currently, the beginning of the opera 'Carmen' appears in two different commercials, one is promoting coffee, the other stockings. Is this a mistake by the advertising agency?" (Motte-Haber, 1972b, p. 148; for another example, see Tagg, 2013, p. 269). The significance of listeners' possible prior exposure to preexisting music is also emphasized by experimental researchers: "An effort was made to avoid potential confounds by finding a song that was not presently being used in 'real world' advertising" (Roehm, 2001, p. 53).

In the following sections, I further describe the concept of transtextuality with respect to preexisting music in commercials. Two specific types of transtextuality are introduced: intertextuality and hypertextuality.

Intertextuality

Intertextuality refers to the "actual presence of a text within another" (Lacasse, 2000, p. 37; see also Kristeva, 1980). The definition adopted here thus differs from more inclusive definitions, such as "a blanket term for the idea that a text communicates its meaning only when it is situated in relation to other texts" (Gracyk, 2001). All texts are positioned in relation to other texts, as the concept of transtextuality specifies. However, not all texts include a "quote" from a particular piece of music outside of and prior to the universe of the commercial. When a piece of music is "quoted," the commercial includes a particular musical excerpt that appears identical to (parts of) the musical text from outside the universe of the commercial. For example, in commercials that (cross-)promote music, such as the previously mentioned commercials promoting U2 and Coldplay (and the iPhone and iTunes), the music in the commercial is identical to the music available on the market. Any observable difference between the two versions would likely seem deceitful to listeners, who would expect to be able to buy the music on the market that they have heard "appetizers" for in the commercial.

In the case of Apple and The Blue Van, "There Goes My Love" is likewise "quoted." However, as illustrated in Table A.2, the music in the commercial does not match any continuous sequence of 30 seconds from the album version of the song. The resulting collage is not unusual when a piece of preexisting music is used. From a strategic perspective, the collage technique allows for different portions of the song to be included, for example, specific parts of the lyrics and the chorus (in a similar vein, commercials promoting a full CD or concert may present a collage or medley of several "hooks" (Burns, 1987) from more than one song; see Chapter 6 for more on the medley). This case inspires me to suggest that from the perspective of the textual analysis of musical signification, the determining feature of intertextuality is not a full identity with respect to the preexisting song and the "quote" applied in the commercial. Generally, the most relevant consideration is whether there is a "sameness of sounding" (inspired by Lacasse, 2000, p. 39) between the two versions of the music. If listeners cannot discern a difference between the two versions, then the difference is arguably inconsequential in terms of musical signification. For example, to ordinary listeners (those who are not experts on the recordings of this particular piece of music), it is of less importance whether Mahler's Fifth Symphony is presented in the recorded version conducted by Bruno Walter, Sir John Barbirolli, Pierre Boulez, Sir Charles Mackerras, or Simon Rattle (see Duggan, 2006, for an overview of some of the available recordings).

Thus far, the discussion of intertextuality has focused on the hypotext and "career" of a specified piece of preexisting music or "opus." However, the particular career of a piece of preexisting music is occasionally less significant than the musical type (style and genre) represented by that piece of music. For example, when a particular serenade by Haydn is quoted in a commercial for a women's fashion store, ordinary listeners will most likely not be able to identify Haydn as the composer and will likely not associate specific experiences with this particular piece of music (compared with the appearance of more widely distributed pieces of music, such as *Carmina Burana* or Mahler's Fifth Symphony). Listeners are more likely to be familiar with the particular type of music (i.e., calm and light Viennese classicism). Hence, the music presents potential for signification not primarily because of its "career" but because it presents a specific, widely distributed type of music (potentials of signification might help promote a store and its clothes as, e.g., serene and distinguished). For example, a particular "opus" could arguably be substituted with another piece of music of the same type without a noteworthy effect on the signification of the commercial (see Chapter 5 for an introduction to this analytical procedure, known as the commutation test). A similar reading could apply to the Apple/Blue Van case to some extent. From the perspective of listeners who are not familiar with the preexisting music, "There Goes My Love" may thus "opus-anonymously" have sounded like yet another song in the style of Jet or any other garage rock revival band. Notably, The Blue Van had previously performed in Jet's slipstream; in 2006, The Blue Van supported (opened for) Jet—an internationally acclaimed band at the time—at numerous concerts in the United States and in Europe. However, contrary to the music of Haydn, this song includes lyrics, and because the lyrics present a particularly strong potential for signification, "There Goes My Love" could not be substituted by another song of the same type without having a noteworthy effect on the signification of the commercial (see the second part of this book for more on the signifying potentials of the lyrics).

Hypertextuality

Hypertextuality refers to the construction of "a new text (hypertext) from a previous one (hypotext)" (Lacasse, 2000, p. 40). This new text could perhaps be regarded as a transtextually "in-between" text because elements of the music have both preexisted the commercial and been modified specifically for inclusion in the commercial (see, e.g., Magis, 2013). However, what is relevant from a text analytical perspective is that this music has a clear transtextual relationship with a specific "hypotext" from outside of the commercial. A particular piece of preexisting music has provided the foundation for the construction of a new text (i.e., "from a previous one"), and the potentials of signification are thus highly dependent on the prior distribution of the particular piece of music.

Whereas intertextuality is characterized by a musical quote, hypertextuality is characterized by a musical restatement or "paraphrase." That is, when a piece of preexisting music is "paraphrased," the commercial includes an excerpt that appears modified compared with (parts of) the musical text from outside the universe of the commercial. In simple terms, hypertextuality does not present a "sameness of sounding" but an "adjustment of sounding." Typically, this specific adjustment actively fuels the potential musical signification. The adjustment differs in scope and audibility.

In some instances, the new text paraphrases the structure of the previous text in a way that makes it difficult for listeners to detect the difference (i.e., to determine that the music presents a case of intertextuality or hypertextuality). Cases of such "sound-alikes" may be intended to evoke the potentials of significance of the specific "hypotext" without the costs of royalties or licensing fees. Therefore, the adjustment balances two concerns. The music must sound like the previous text to be able to evoke the desired potentials. However, the music must sound sufficiently dissimilar to the previous text to prevent possible lawsuits. For example, in an Ilva (Danish furniture provider) commercial from the April 2012 volume, the background music to the foregrounded voice-over closely resembles the groove from Lloyd's "Dedication to My Ex" (featuring André 3000)[4]—in the commercial, the instrumentation and harmonic progression are slightly modified, but the recurrent beat unmistakably resembles the preexisting song, which achieved a top 10 position on the Danish charts several months prior to its inclusion in the commercial. Although the preexisting music is clearly not quoted, the music in the commercial clearly evokes the popular spirit of the particular preexisting song.

In other instances, the new text paraphrases the structure of the previous text in a much more noticeable manner. This is illustrated by two types of hypertextuality, which seem particularly relevant to the analysis of music in commercials: parody and travesty.

The music in a commercial is rendered as a parody when it retains "the stylistic properties of the original text while diverting its subject" (Lacasse, 2000, p. 41). As previously indicated, it is rarely possible to unambiguously specify the "subject" of a piece of music. However, the previous career of the music, along with its lyrics, may present strong indicators of the music's subject. For example, a commercial (from the April 2004 volume) for Orange (a telecommunications company) includes excerpts (i.e., the groove and instrumentation) from the break-dance hit "(Hey You) The Rock Steady Crew" (by Rock Steady Crew; released in 1983). However, in the commercial, a Danish male performer presents a range of products offered in an intentionally awkward rap style (the rhythms and rhymes do not quite match). The music here contributes to a potentially humorous and ironic distribution of what would otherwise be dull product information (see also Tom, 1990).

The music in a commercial can be rendered a travesty in cases in which "the whole point is to serve up a well-known song in a completely different style: the melody and lyrics are the same, but they now have a new orchestration and vocal style" (Lacasse, 2000, p. 42). An example of such a travesty is found in a commercial (from the April 2004 volume) for a new attraction in Tivoli (an amusement park in Copenhagen): a roller coaster called The Demon. The commercial features excerpts from the beginning of H. C. Lumbye's "Champagne Galop."[5] In the commercial, the melody is the same as specified in the original score; however, it is accompanied by a hip-hop-style beat. In a subsequent commercial for The Demon (from the April 2008 volume), the melody is played by an electric guitar. This travesty illustrate the daring youth qualities of The Demon within the tradition of the old park; Tivoli was founded in 1843, and "Champagne Galop" was composed for its two-year anniversary in 1845. The use of that particular music thus illustrates an early example of a musical brand (for more on musical brands, see Chapter 3).

For either parody or travesty to function, listeners must be able to decode the musical adjustment. This decoding in turn presupposes that the music is familiar to the listener. If the "hypotext" is not known to listeners, then the "hypertext" cannot be construed as such, and the music may be (mis) interpreted as an example of "odd" original music. In this fashion, both cases of parody and cases of travesty appear to encourage listeners to pay attention to the music and the musical adjustment. Listeners may even feel "compensated" or "rewarded" for paying attention and for being able to decode the sophisticated and perhaps even "creative" or "humorous" use of music. Arguably, from a strategic perspective, the use of musical hypertextuality can be highly useful in constructing such reactions, along with the use of intertextuality. However, positive listener evaluations cannot be generally expected from the use of preexisting music, as indicated by the discussion and examples of feelings of "dispossession" and "contamination."

Thus far, inspired by the perspective of Lacasse (2000), I have focused on the textual relationship between the music in a commercial and preexisting music prior to and outside the commercial. From a text analytical perspective, this perspective is both important and necessary. However, this examination of the "music-to-music" relationship is insufficient when aiming to understand audiovisual text as music in commercials. Naturally, commercials are not only heard but also watched (with varying degrees of attention and concentration, as noted in Chapter 1). To illustrate the necessity of including an audiovisual perspective, let us reconsider the case of Apple/The Blue Van. When the relationship between the album version and the commercial version is examined exclusively from the perspective of audition, a case of intertextuality arguably transpires. However, when the music from the album version is compared with the way in which the music's subject is potentially diverted in the commercial from an (audio)visual perspective, a case of transtextuality (i.e., a parody) appears for listeners familiar with the song prior to its appearance in the commercial (see Chapter 5 for an examination of the relationships between music and moving pictures).

2.2   ORIGINAL MUSIC

As previously indicated, although scholars have been predominantly interested in the uses of preexisting music, most commercials include original music (i.e., music with no prior distribution outside the setting of the commercial). Thus, original music does not refer to a specific "hypotext," and it has had no prior "career." Original music is not necessarily composed for the purpose of appearing in a specific commercial; "stock music" originates from a stock of precomposed music available to commercial producers (see, e.g., Karmen, 2005). However, from the text analytical perspective offered in this book, the processes of production are less important than the processes of distribution and listeners' familiarity with the music. Nevertheless, the processes of production may help explain why some examples of original music in a commercial appear more distinct than others. Stock music is produced with no particular commercial, product, or brand in mind and is thus arguably prone to relatively insignificant musical expressions; hence, the music may be acquired by—and should be able to function for—"anybody." By contrast, music produced for a particular commercial, product and brand is designed for "somebody" in particular, and this purpose may inspire relatively distinct musical productions, including musical brands (see Chapter 6 for more details on musical distinctiveness). Musical brands also illustrate how original music can be analyzed from the perspective of transtextuality. However, whereas the transtextual analysis of preexisting music focuses on the relationship between the commercial version and a hypotext from outside the universe of a commercial, transtextual analyses of musical brands require an analysis of relationships within the universe of the commercial. For example, the musical brand associated with Intel has been consistently used in commercials since 1994, and its jingle has been updated on numerous occasions. Additionally, the musical brand for McDonald's introduced in September 2003 has changed considerably during the campaign (see Chapter 3 for more information on musical brands, Intel and McDonald's).

Whereas original music has had no distribution prior to its appearance, a type of "post-existence" may follow a piece of music's appearance in a commercial. Certainly, this post-existence does not occur on a regular basis; for example, compilations of original music from commercials are not common relative to the more typical compilations that include preexisting music.[6] However, significant examples can be provided. For example, after having appeared in a commercial for Coca-Cola, the song "I'd Like to Teach the World to Sing" was widely distributed in the United States and Britain as an "independent" song in two versions—one by The Hillside Singers and one by The New Seekers. The songs represented a type of "de-coked" version of an original song used for the commercial; for example, the original version included the lyrics "I'd like to buy the world a Coke" (see Klein, 2009, p. 83, for further details).

Pastiche

Generally, the relationship between original music for a commercial and music from outside the commercial can be described as a pastiche: "An author of a pastiche identifies and assimilates a particular set of stylistic features in order to create an entirely new text displaying the stylistic configuration in question" (Lacasse, 2000, p. 44). Although original music does not refer specifically to a particular hypotext, it does refer generically to similar types of music from outside the commercial. A pastiche is arguably characteristic of popular music in general, and scholars have identified, for example, an "extensive use in popular music of borrowings—the importance of 'tune families', the reliance on common-stock models, formulae, grooves and riffs, the privileging of variation over variety" (Middleton, 2000, p. 60; see more on grooves in Chapter 6). Pastiche may be particularly well suited for the analysis of (original) music in commercials.

Thus, the style and genre of the music will often play a central role in musical signification, as it has been proposed that "the signification of commercial music has do to with the uses of fixed clichés" (Steiner-Hall, 1987, p. 56). N. Cook (1994) asserts that the rise of postmodernism has altered musical practice: "Traditionally, musicians compose with notes, rhythms, and perhaps timbres. Only with postmodernism has the idea of 'composing with styles' or 'composing with genres' emerged" (N. Cook, 1994, p. 35; see Wüsthoff, 1999, and Miller, 1985, for examples of traditional compositional procedures). This claim is followed by this statement: "But composing with styles or genres is one of the most basic musical techniques found in television commercials" (N. Cook, 1994, p. 35), thus implying that the practice of advertising and marketing itself may have historically presaged the coming of postmodernity. Similarly, it has been argued that "marketing represents the essence of the ongoing transition to postmodernity. In other words, the postmodern age is essentially a marketing age—there is an *identity* between marketing and post-modernity" (Firat, Dholakia, & Venkatesh, 1995, p. 48; see also Rutherford, 1994, p. 6). Additionally, L. Andersen (2001) registers changes in the functioning of music in commercials caused by postmodern culture: such music becomes more inclined to irony, parody and pastiche, and intertextual references become more pronounced. Taylor (2000) presents yet another illustrative example by analyzing a style—"world music"—rather than an opus. Taylor discusses how an authentic, non-Western musical style is being used in commercials to represent an idealized image of exotic environments. The author notes that in this particular style, commercials more often use originally composed music resembling an authentic preexisting style rather than the "real stuff." Music thus contributes to the creation of a "hyperreal simulacrum," that is, a copy for which there is no "original referent" (Baudrillard, 1994).

According to the transtextual perspective, music in commercials does not exist in a "musical vacuum." Inevitably, music in commercials relates to music from outside the universe of commercials. The examination of music in commercials from a transtextual perspective should begin by specifying whether the music has any relationship to a particular hypotext from outside the universe of the commercial. If such a hypotext can be specified (i.e., if the commercial includes "preexisting music"), then the next step is to examine the precise excerpts from the text presented in the commercial and how these excerpts may be modified in the commercial version compared with the hypotext. Two types of transtextual relationships can be observed—intertextuality and hypertextuality—and the latter can be further differentiated as one of two types—parody or travesty. If a particular hypotext cannot be identified (i.e., if the commercial includes "original music"), then the examination must consider the style and genre of the music, which are captured by the concept of pastiche.

From the perspective of distribution and listeners' familiarity with music, various subtypes of music can be proposed. The following subtypes are based on the preceding discussion and characteristics of musical expressions in the sample of commercials used for this book. These subtypes should be viewed as an illustration of the significance of distribution and listeners' familiarity and can be used to inspire a detailed mapping of transtextual relationships. When considering preexisting music from a transtextual perspective, one can observe the following three subtypes:

1. **Preexisting known opus music:** The hypotext is known to the listener, and the specific "career" of the musical text hence influences the potentials of musical signification.
2. **Preexisting unknown opus music/"postexisting" music:** The hypotext is not known to the listener and the style, and the genre and possible lyrics included influence the potentials of musical signification. However, because of distinct exposure in the commercial, the inclusion of lyrics that do not include a product or

brand name or a former practice of using preexisting music in commercials for the given product or brand may cause the listener to expect the music to exist outside the universe of the commercial. The listener may search for the music and thus contribute to creating the music's "postexistence."

3. **Preexisting genre music:** The "hypotext" is not known to the listener; thus, the style, genre and possible lyrics influence the potentials of musical signification. The listener does not contribute to the creation of music's "postexistence."

Likewise, when considering original music from a transtextual perspective, one can observe the following two subtypes:

4. **Original genre music:** The music originates from the commercial (selected from a stock or composed specifically for the commercial) and relates to music outside of the commercial via pastiche. The style, genre, and possible lyrics influence the potentials of musical signification.

5. **Original opus music:** The music originates from the commercial (typically composed specifically for the commercial) and relates to other music, such as a hypotext in the form of the release of a musical brand, within the universe of the commercial. The potentials of musical signification are influenced by the style, genre, and possible lyrics as well as the previous "career" within the universe of commercials for that particular brand.

What and how music is "known" in this typology rely on the knowledge structure of the general public as well as more specific (e.g., individual or subcultural) constructions of musical "careers" for specific pieces of music and musical styles. Thus, different listeners may construct a commercial's potential for musical signification in different ways. For example, listeners (and analysts) may find it difficult to distinguish between Types 3 and 4, and the Apple/Blue Van case has illustrated how some listeners may hear Type 1 while others will hear Type 2.

Whereas the preceding has focuses on the relation between music in the commercial and music from outside the commercial, in the next chapter, I focus on the relations between music in commercials and marketing and products.

NOTES

1. Because of the primary significance of distribution for the purposes of this book, I have generally refrained from using, for example, the concept of "pre-composed music" (see, e.g., Collins, 2008, p. 18). "Predistributed music" presents an attractive alternative, but I have also refrained from using this

concept because of the present focus on "the specific existence of the distributed music" rather than "the (industrial and technological) processes of distribution" in terms of, for example, the channels, contracts, and participants involved.

2. Both here and in the following text, classical music is used to refer to musical art that is produced or rooted in the traditions of Western music (both liturgical and secular; see Tagg, 1979, p. 34).

3. For example, www.soundsfamiliar.info, www.inthe80s.com/adsmusic/index. shtml, www.werbesongliste.de/werbesongs.html, www.songtitle.info, www. songofthesalesman.co.uk, www.whatsthatcalled.com, www.uktvadverts. com, www.reklamemusik.dk, www.squidoo.com/tv_commercial_music, www. kulturblog.com/2005/08/cool-songs-and-tv-commercials/, http://oldies.about. com/od/theculture/a/asseenontv.htm, and http://commercials.tuneforums.com/.

4. The music can be assessed here: www.youtube.com/watch?v=ZsycXtkC4z8.

5. A version of the music can be heard here: www.youtube.com/watch?v=M4Q 83mJLtm4.

6. For example, *Commercial Breaks—The Essential Sound of TV Advertising* (2001), *Commercial Grooves—Nostalgic Tracks from TV Adverts* (2004), *Various Artists/Classics From Ads* (2007), *As Heard on TV* (2007), *TV Ad Songs* (2008), and *Guinness 250—Music from the TV Ads* (2009).

3 Marketing
Music and Products

This chapter focuses on how music in commercials relates to marketing and products outside the universe of a commercial. Marketing refers broadly to the activities involved in creating awareness of a company's products or services. More specifically, marketing includes the process of communicating the value and characteristics of a product, service, or brand to customers for the purpose of selling. In this context, music can play the role of (a) the product, that is, *musicproduct* (or the *marketing of music*); (b) an accompaniment to the presentation of a nonmusical product, that is, *productmusic* (*marketing with music*); or (c) a combination of (a) and (b), in which the promotion of the music product coincides with the promotion of a nonmusical product, that is, *music–product partnership*.

3.1 MUSICPRODUCT

In commercials, a musicproduct essentially refers to music that is promoted as available on the market either as a self-contained product or as a part of (i.e., textually embedded in) another product, such as a film. From a transtextual perspective (see Chapter 2), a musicproduct manifests as preexisting music and has an intertextual relationship with music from outside the commercial. The marketing process is thus directed toward fostering awareness of the availability of the music and communicating its value and characteristics. The intertextual relationship with music outside the commercial normally ensures a true and fair view of what listeners can expect from the music available on the market.

Music marketing has traditionally involved numerous parties, such as record labels, public relations firms, music managers, music publishing companies, entertainment agencies, music distribution firms, and entertainment lawyers. All these parties strive to promote music airplay, publicity, concerts, and sales of units in various formats, and they fundamentally contribute to shaping the creation, circulation, and consumption of popular music genres and cultures, as demonstrated by Negus (1999). Depending on the available media and forms of distribution, a wide variety of promotional materials has been effectuated during the process of creating awareness and communicating the values and characteristics of the music. Promotional materials include both nonauditory (e.g., album covers, print advertising, posters in magazines, banners on websites) and auditory/audiovisual materials.

In commercials, the listener will typically be introduced to excerpts from the music in the form of an edited assortment of musical highlights and hooks from a particular song or album (see Chapter 6 for more on the medley). Apparently, the promotion of musicproducts in commercials can have significant effects on music sales. For example, in a random week (i.e., Week 30 of 2008), the six best-selling albums in Denmark had all been promoted in commercials.[1] Interestingly, when considering the effects of radio airplay, exposure does not appear to have a similarly significant effect, according to a study finding no overlap between the 10 best-selling and the 10 most played artists nationally in 2004 (Bay, Gudnitz, & Jahn, 2005, p. 13). Perhaps continuous exposure to particular pieces of music on the radio can substitute for actually purchasing that music (see, e.g., Liebowitz, 2004). Arguably, this substitution capability has not always been the case (see, e.g., Wallis & Malm, 1988), and changing marketing conditions in the music (and the media) industries may have set the tone for new trends in musical marketing (see more in the following discussion).

3.2   MUSIC–PRODUCT PARTNERSHIP

The term *music–product partnership* refers to self-contained music that is available on the market and appears in a commercial promoting a nonmusical product. In this setting, the values and characteristics of both the music and the nonmusical product are concurrently produced and promoted, which is what characterizes the "partnership" or the process of "cross-promotion." Because the music is available on the market, it is more or less predisposed to becoming a desired product itself. The music of music–product partnerships thus typically presents cases of *licensing* or *music placement*, referring to the placement of excerpts from a piece of preexisting music in a commercial for a nonmusical product (see the introduction and Klein, 2009). From the perspective of transtextuality, the music is thus preexisting.

The cross-promotion or "mutual fertilization" of music and products has a long history. For example, within the closely related field of music usage in films, music placement has been highly influential. Original songs (i.e., songs produced for a particular film that were unreleased prior to the promotion and distribution of the film) have not only been used but also have occasionally enjoyed widespread success on the music charts. Examples of such songs include "Laura" (for *Laura*, 1944), "Rain Drops Keep Falling on My Head" (for *Butch Cassidy and the Sundance Kid*, 1969) and "(I've Had) The Time of My Life" (for *Dirty Dancing*, 1987). Since the 1950s, motion pictures also have regularly included significant preexisting music (Romney & Wootton, 1995; J. Smith, 1998). The use of well-known preexisting music in traditional Hollywood productions appears to have been considered taboo—"well-known music of any kind was thought to carry associational baggage for the spectator, and not only was this potentially distracting but these associations might also clash with those established by the narrative" (J. Smith, 1998, p. 164). However, the inclusion of preexisting music in films became increasingly common from the 1980s onward, as reflected in recent research.[2] In addition, soundtracks from motion pictures are often found on the charts of top-selling albums (e.g., Brophy, 1999, p. 10). Given this background, it is surprising that studies of product placement have largely ignored music.

Whereas product placement—that is, a practice that deliberately aims to benefit from the promotional opportunities provided by exposing a commercial product in an attractive, "natural" setting where it is used and valued by admirable and ordinary people alike for its seemingly unique qualities—has attracted much attention from marketers, media researchers, and consumer advocates, the issue of music placement in media products has largely remained unexplored (see J. Smith, 1998, 1999, and Holbrook, 2004, for rare exceptions). Music is not mentioned in histories of product placement in movies (e.g., Segrave, 2004) or in textbooks that define and discuss the phenomenon (e.g., Clow & Baack, 2004; Fill, 2002; Galician, 2004). Illustrative of this neglect is the analysis by Galician and Bourdeau (2004) of product placement in the 15 top-grossing motion pictures of 1977, 1987, and 1997. The authors carefully identify 546 instances of product placement, but somewhat disappointingly, the analysis does not consider music. All the placements identified (i.e., products "seen," "mentioned," and "used") obviously refer to *visual* commodities such as cars, cigarettes, and beverages. This neglect by researchers could be caused by the mistaken belief that music primarily belongs to the realm of (popular) culture rather than to that of private enterprise (see Graakjær & Janzten, 2009, for further discussion and examples).

There has long been a connection between the advertising and music industries. For example, Taylor (2012) describes how a musical band played an important role in a company that sponsored a radio program in the 1920s (the *Clicquot Club Eskimos*, 1923–1926). By the 1960s, members of rock bands were sometimes introduced to the public as jingle musicians to "get them accustomed to studio work before . . . making a record as a band" (Taylor 2012, p. 133). During that same era, established performers such as Aretha Franklin, Ray Charles, and Johnny Cash each performed a version of a soft-drink jingle. Until the 1980s, it was not unusual for commentators to characterize music in commercials as "pale, watered-down derivations of hit records" (Taylor, 2012, p. 172). Beginning in the 1980s, however, the licensing of preexisting music or "real songs" became "increasingly common" (Taylor, 2012, p. 144; see also Karmen, 2005; Wallis & Malm, 1988).

During that period, it seemed reasonable to suggest that "today's hit music presents tomorrow's advertising music" (Bjurström & Lilliestam, 1993, p. 95). Recent developments have emphasized the possibility that "today's advertising music" can become the "hit music of tomorrow" (e.g., the commercials featuring the music of Feist and Jet).

Music can play a more or less significant role in music-product partnerships. Whereas the Apple/The Blue Van case appears to illustrate how music can play a less significant role (i.e., the music is not announced in the commercial) other examples can illustrate how music can appear on center stage and be released at approximately the same time as the commercial. Occasionally, this process resembles the promotion of music. For example, as indicated above, in September 2003, McDonald's launched an unprecedented global brand campaign that included the slogan "i'm lovin it." An essential part of this campaign was the broadcast of commercials with appearances and vocals by Justin Timberlake in more than 100 countries.[3] At the time, Justin Timberlake had achieved great commercial success. For example, his first solo album, *Justified* (2002 on Jive), had reached top charts worldwide, and he was already a triple MTV Video Music Award winner. For the campaign, McDonald's used excerpts from a new Justin Timberlake song, "I'm Lovin' It," which was concurrently promoted as a self-contained song (i.e., with no mention of McDonald's) in a music video broadcast for the first time in September 2003 on MTV.[4] It appears that this music is preexisting from the production perspective but not from the distribution perspective (see also Klein, 2009). Subsequently, the song was released on an EP and made available for download, while McDonald's continued to use Justin Timberlake as a celebrity endorser. For example, McDonald's sponsored Justin Timberlake's first concert tour, the 2003–2004 *Justified World Tour Lovin' It Live*, which reached North America, Europe, and Australia (see Chapter 6 for more information on McDonald's musical brand).

The Apple/Coldplay case presents another illustrative example. Coldplay's album *Viva la Vida or Death and All His Friends* was first promoted in May 2008 in a commercial for iTunes.[5] The commercial included excerpts from the song (and the title track from the album) and the following announcement: "Viva la Vida—Coldplay. Exclusively on iTunes." During the following month, beginning on May 7, the song was available for preorder exclusively on iTunes, and beginning on May 25, the song was available for downloads, again exclusively via iTunes. The album was not released on Parlophone until June 11. The commercial clearly promoted both iTunes and the new song (and album) by Coldplay, and the band realized a significant commercial benefit from the arrangement. For example, "Viva la Vida" was iTunes's best-selling song of 2008, and the song became the band's first number one single in both the United States and the United Kingdom.

As indicted, these cases exemplify how music (i.e., an artist and a song) can gain explicit exposure in music–product partnerships. Occasionally, however, the music is not explicitly announced in the commercial (see, e.g., the commercials featuring the music of The Blue Van, Jet, and Feist). These commercials appear to illustrate a particular type of music placement, that is, the placement of excerpts from a piece of preexisting music by an unannounced and (to most viewers) *unknown band* in a television commercial for a nonmusical product. Although there is little information on the actual prevalence of and possible increase in the use of preexisting music in commercials (as noted in the introduction), recent developments appear to have effectively set the tone for a specific mode of music placement that apparently extends to other media settings, including films (see the earlier discussion), television programs (e.g., J. Brown, 2001; Stilwell, 1995, 2005), service settings (e.g., Graakjær, 2012), and computer games (e.g., Collins, 2008).

As marketers and corporate brands "are exploring more emotion-based, cultural, and lifestyle-oriented marketing strategies in an effort to break through promotional clutter, speak to consumer 'identities,' and compete for 'cool'" (Meier, 2011, p. 403), advertising agencies "are forced to search out more esoteric tracks that are still perceived as pristine," including "music from the distant past, from obscure genres, and from independent bands that are known to only a few thousand fans" (Holt in Meier, 2011, p. 411). Correspondingly, given the general lack of radio outlets (and effects), for such bands and the cost of "primary promotion"—for instance, music videos or commercials that primarily promote music in the form of a musicproduct—music placement in commercials offers an attractive opportunity for up-and-coming bands in an Anglophone context (see Stevens, 2011, for a somewhat dissimilar development in Japan) to reach a large audience that might otherwise be unreachable. Moreover, the old structures of the music industry are collapsing. For instance, new methods of musical access—such as Spotify, Pandora, and Shazam—have emerged, and accusations of "selling out" have lost significance and have become increasingly rare. With the current "decrease—to negligibility—of the difference between 'advertising music' and 'music'" (Taylor, 2012, p. 1), it is not unusual for audiences to enjoy, pay attention to and search for music that has been featured in commercials using previously described tools. Apple presents an illustrative case: "From August 2007 to January 2008, U.S. consumers conducted nearly 1 million queries for iPod related commercials or the underlying music" (Seeking Alpha, 2008).

From the perspective of a non-musical product, placed music imports the potentials of musical signification to characterize the product. The relationship with the "hypotext" is that of either intertextuality or hypertextuality, and in both instances, the potentials of musical signification are closely linked to the advertised product. For example, the music of Justin Timberlake helps

McDonald's produce a specific youth-and lifestyle-oriented brand image. In the iPod commercial, the Jet song "Are U Gonna Be My Girl" helps illustrate how the product can be easily and safely used for energetic dancing and musical enjoyment. Similarly, in the commercial for the iPod Nano, the excerpt from the music video to "1, 2, 3, 4" by Leslie Feist illustrates how the product can be used for the efficient and pioneering reproduction of audiovisual musical texts. Although the music of neither Feist nor Jet is (an integral part of) the product being advertised, the music plays an important role in depicting the product.

From the perspective of the music, affiliation with a particular product can help to characterize and promote music. Depending on the particular product and its cotextual exposure, the music may be associated with specific emotions, attitudes, lifestyles, and practices of use. The results of these associations may include a renewed interest in "known opus music" or to increased interest in "unknown opus music" for up-and-coming (e.g., Jet and Feist) or well-established (e.g., Coldplay and Justin Timberlake) artists. For example, the partnership with McDonald's guarantees Justin Timberlake worldwide exposure for his new song and awareness of his upcoming world tour, and the associations with Apple's iPod and iPod Nano help cultivate the status of Jet's and Feist's music, respectively, as products in a market outside the universe of the commercial. The example par excellence is Moby's album *Play* (1999), in which all 18 songs were licensed for music placement in various settings. These placements appear to have strongly contributed to sales (see Allan, 2005; Klein, 2009, p. 66, Taylor, 2007).

However, in addition to the characterization and promotion of the music, the desire to associate with a non-musical product (i.e., a prominent brand) may involve more fundamental issues of musical production. As Apple and other brands contribute to the more or less transitory popularization of specific bands and genres (e.g., Feist and Jet), they also conceivably influence production (e.g., the song structure and lyrics) prior to the process in which music is placed in a commercial. One indicator of this dynamic is that during the 2000s, it became increasingly common for record labels to hire strategic marketing executives whose job is to seek brands and media outlets for music placement (Taylor, 2012, p. 209). Consequently, demands for "appropriate placement music" have been made explicit; for example, "in demand, often requested synch-friendly music has lot of edit points, good breaks" (Reinboth, 2011; see also Klein 2009). "There Goes My Love" appears to accidentally illustrate these requests (see more in the following discussion), allowing for "temporal alignment" between the music and moving pictures, although this alignment may not be unusual with respect to television commercials. Furthermore, this case will illustrate how polysemantic lyrics with "open spaces" can allow a brand to "colonize" the semantics of song lyrics. This process appears to present a paradoxical, implicit request that exotic placement music must not signify anything in particular (e.g., specific persons, periods, places, or events). The process also suggests that previous general characterizations of music in commercials must be reconsidered; "the musical structure must be based on the principles of simplicity, intelligibility, and clarity" (Steiner-Hall, 1987, pp. 56–57). However, further research is needed to clarify the extent to which more or less explicit "requests" actually affect how music is structured in the first place and how different media "request" different structures, such as commercials versus computer games (Collins, 2008), films (Greenspan, 2004), or music radio airplay (Percivel, 2011; see also Klein, 2009, p. 77). Whereas the actual effect on music structure is difficult to specify, *brand dropping* (Lehu, 2007) illustrates a more obvious example of how a brand's "requests" can affect music. Contemporary hip-hop music appears to presents the most conspicuous marketing case; for instance, "McDonald's . . . offered rappers $1 per radio play of songs that mentioned the Big Mac" (Klein, 2009, p. 137). However, the phenomenon is by no means recent: according to Lehu, the Eagles' "Hotel California" (1976), for example, had paid placement for upmarket brands such as Mercedes and Tiffany (Lehu, 2007, p. 171). Additionally, Gregorio and Sung's (2009) longitudinal analysis of 3,476 top 10 songs from 1955 to 2002 reveals "an increase in brand mentions over the five decades, with a noticeable spike beginning in 1995" (p. 218).

3.3 PRODUCTMUSIC

Productmusic essentially refers to original music (i.e., music not available as self-contained music on the market) that accompanies the promotion of a nonmusical product. Two types of productmusic can be distinguished based on a piece of music's distinctiveness (for more on [in]distinct music, see Chapter 6) and its association with a nonmusical product.

First, productmusic can appear indistinctly, with no specific association with a particular object. Such music will not significantly accompany the promotion of a product or brand for a longer period. Moreover, this music appears indistinct in the sense that it has no hooks (Burns, 1987) and is usually deployed in the auditory background of a voice-over, for example. From a transtextual perspective, this type of indistinct productmusic corresponds to original genre music (see Chapter 2).

Second, productmusic can appear to be distinctly and exclusively associated with a particular corporate brand via systematic inclusion in the brand's various commercials. In other words, music is distinct when it is significantly prominent as a textual element within the commercial compared with musical expressions of other commercials. From a transtextual perspective, this type of *distinct productmusic* or *brandmusic* (see the following discussion) corresponds to original opus music. A "systematic inclusion" of the music indicates that the music is produced and deployed in a process that can be described as *music* (or, more inclusively, *sound*) *branding*—the strategic use of sound (e.g., music) for branding purposes. This type of marketing with music typically involves sound designers and practitioners in the field of sound (or audio) branding. Ideally, from a marketer's perspective, a musical brand (*brandmusic*) should meet most, if not all, of the following criteria (inspired by, e.g., Groves, 2011, p. 169):

- Distinctiveness: The music is clearly distinguishable from other music.
- Recognizability: The music is readily identified, recalled and associated with the brand.
- Flexibility: The music is operational regardless of the musical setting and the technical availability of dissimilar auditory "touchpoints," such as commercials, websites, telephone waiting lines, and physical service and sales settings.
- Consistency: The music is activated on all touchpoints and across different concurrent campaigns.
- Continuity: The music is workable through various periods.
- Semantic and syntactic "fit": The music corresponds to the attributes and values (semantic) of the product or corporate brand and to the structure of the logo and slogan (syntactical).

The brandmusic for Intel Inside, which was produced by Walter Werzowa, presents a case to illustrate these criteria. For example, the blend of marimba and xylophone sounds is arguably associated with a "high-tech corporation" (semantic fit), and the ascending melodic intervals of a fourth and a fifth corresponds to the accentuation of the syllables in "In-tell in-side," while being synchronized with the animated visual presentation of the logo (syntactical fit). Moreover, although this brandmusic has been used for many years,[6] the jingle has been modified slightly on numerous occasions (i.e., it has recognizability, continuity, and flexibility). This last feature indicates that the analytical perspectives of transtextuality can be deployed "internally" within the universe of commercials for a particular brand. The changing structures of the jingle for the McDonald's campaign *i'm lovin' it* also illustrates this feature (see more in Chapter 6).

As noted, from a transtextual perspective, brandmusic typically manifests as original music. The use of preexisting music (i.e., self-contained music available on the market) could undermine the desired distinctiveness and recognizability of this music. Preexisting music is thus normally deployed for the promotion of products, a marketing process that typically extends over a limited period, whereas brandmusic is linked to other brand elements, such as logos and slogans, over a longer period. Some of the previously mentioned scholarly contributions on the use of preexisting music in commercials appear to illustrate this point. Thus, an excerpt from Bob Seger's "Like a Rock" is apparently used primarily to promote a particular Chevy truck rather than

Chevrolet as a corporate brand (see Rodman, 2010), and the excerpt from Mozart's *Marriage of Figaro* is apparently used primarily to promote the new Citroën ZX 16v rather than Citroën as a corporate brand (see N. Cook, 1994). Note the following recommendation from a practitioner's perspective: "Real brand music should not portray just a temporary position, but rather the core values of a brand" (Groves, 2011, p. 174).

When we consider the Apple/The Blue Van case from the perspective of brandmusic, "There Goes My Love" is used primarily to promote the iPad rather than explicitly promoting the Apple brand. As an indication, the song and the band were used by Apple in only one commercial, and they have since appeared in other media settings. For example, the Samsung/The Blue Van case illustrates that the band has also promoted one of Apple's most significant competitors. Additionally, based on the specific "opuses" included, Apple has continuously changed the musical accompaniment to its commercials. However, the use of "There Goes My Love" may have supported the Apple brand on a more general level. Although the commercial did not clearly add to the reputation of Apple as a "tastemaker, doing for bands what Oprah Winfrey has done for books" (Lee, 2008; see also Barnhard & Rutledge, 2009), the following three brand effects may be observed. First, the selection of the song adds to Apple's reputation in pursuing esoteric songs that may be perceived as unspoiled to most listeners. Second, the style and the genre of the song correspond to one of the musical types already associated with the Apple brand. The song thus presents a particular type of branding based on a musical type (i.e., style and genre) rather than an "opus." Third, the specific deployment of the song in the commercial appears to uphold Apple's reputation for "focusing intently on the quality of sounds in their commercials," as declared by a band member.

The partnership between McDonald's and Justin Timberlake presents an illustrative example of musical branding in commercials. The partnership between McDonald's and Justin Timberlake ended in 2004, and henceforth, Justin Timberlake no longer appeared in commercials for McDonald's, although excerpts of his song "I'm Lovin' It" continued to appear in the commercials. Most significantly, as the campaign has progressed, the *parapapapa* part of the song has emerged as the musical brand for McDonald's. In commercials, the musical brand in the format of a jingle (see Chapter 6) appears at the end of the commercial as an accompaniment to the slogan and logo signature.[7] This case is unusual because the musicbrand originates from a piece of preexisting (or at least codistributed) music. However, because the partnership with Justin Timberlake was not long term and because the song "I'm Lovin' It" was not a commercial success as a self-contained song, the *parapapapa* jingle could persist as the musical brand of McDonald's. Whereas most listeners will likely associate the jingle with McDonald's, arguably only some listeners will associate this music with Justin Timberlake.

3.4   MUSIC AND PRODUCT CATEGORY

In this section, I extend the examination of relationships between music and products to include the issue of product category: Are specific product categories particularly well suited for music (or no music), music placement, or specific musical styles and genres? The literature offers no consensus on how these questions should be answered. For example, some observers generally reject the idea of any particular relationship between a product category and the use of music: "No product is especially well suited to music treatment, except perhaps musical products such as records, music videos, stage shows, rock concerts, and symphonic and operatic productions" (Book, Cary, & Tannenbaum, 1984, p. 25). Other observers propose a number of specific relationships. For example, Bjurström and Lilliestam (1993) observe that "classical music"—which is found to be deployed "quite often"—is used for the promotion of expensive, high-class products: "Classical music signifies quality, timelessness, and good taste" (Bjurström & Lilliestam, 1993, p. 83; this observation appears to correspond to the preceding example from North & Hargreaves, 2006). More generally, the authors suggest the following: "Products for which the style is important, e.g., clothes, are usually promoted with the inclusion of significant music. In contrast, more neutral products, e.g., food, will include neutral or insignificant music" (Bjurström & Lilliestam, 1993, p. 83). Another illustrative example concerns the use of music in commercials for the financial products of banks and insurance companies, among others. The promotion of such products has been highlighted for its lack of music, with the following explanation: "The absence of music suggests a pseudo-competence and respectability, which would be compromised by the inclusion of music" (Leo, 1999, p. 42; for a similar observation, see Helms, 1981). Additionally, "feel-good pop music [is] normally employed to sell fast food" (Klein, 2009, p. 124), and "a product category that consistently licenses pre-existing music for its television commercials is automobiles, and for many consumers the car is where the majority of music listening occurs" (Klein, 2009, p. 80; for a similar observation, see Allan, 2008, p. 410).

Although these examples illustrate a tendency within a specific sample from a specific place and time, I suggest that products do not have a "natural connection" (Klein, 2008, p. 3) or generic qualities that generally predispose them to particular types of musical promotion (see the following discussion). This argument may be illustrated by the example of (fast) food, which is associated with both "neutral, insignificant music" (Bjurström & Lilliestam, 1993) and "feel-good pop music" (Klein, 2009). In addition to differences in sampling—that is, Bjurström and Lilliestam analyze a larger sample of randomly chosen commercials broadcast in Sweden in 1992, whereas Klein relies on an (undisclosed) selection of cases based on an information-oriented selection of commercials broadcast in the U.K. in the 2000s—the apparent lack of consensus between the two observations could be explained by the dynamic position of food as a product category. Compared with the sample used in this book, commercials for food indeed include significant "feel-good pop music" in some cases, for example, the song from the earlier described *i'm lovin' it* campaign for McDonald's. However, food commercials are not significantly more likely to include "feel-good pop music" than are commercials for other products.

The use of music in commercials for financial products provides another example of the dynamic positioning of specific product categories. Thus, in the sample for this book, commercials for financial products include more music than in most other categories, and the music often appears distinctive. For example, in the April 2004 volume, both Nordea and Danske Bank (i.e., the two largest banks operating in Denmark) launched new campaigns, and both the initial commercials and subsequent commercials contained music that played a significant role in promoting and branding the banks (Graakjær, 2010). Again, the lack of consistency between the two contributions—that is, the sample of this book and those of Steiner-Hall (1987) and Helms (1981)—is likely influenced by differences in samples, but the position(ing) of banks may have also changed in recent times.

Products can be associated with music in a more specific sense. Music can thus be deployed to demonstrate the functions of a particular product, such as by illustrating the effects of a product's use (as one of ten functions of music in commercials by Steiner-Hall, 1987; see Chapter 7). From this perspective, some products—such as TVs and technology for private musical reproduction (e.g., see the silhouette commercials for Apple mentioned earlier)—may appear to be more prone to using music than others—such as laundry detergent and cereal. However, because practically all products produce sound when handled (e.g., washing machines, cereal, cars, water bottles) all product sounds can potentially be musicalized or structured in a way that conforms to musical (e.g., rhythmical) norms for music (see the introduction).

The examples suggest that a "product category" cannot universally be referred to as a stable and determining factor for the appearance of music in commercials. Equally important, a particular type of music cannot be universally associated with a particular (type of) product category. Arguably, specific preexisting "opuses" may be particularly well suited for placements in commercials for specific products. An example from the sample for this book involves a commercial for a Danish supplier of eyewear, Synoptik (from the April 1996 volume), which contains excerpts from the song "I Can See Clearly Now" (by Johnny Nash, 1972). The song is deployed in such a way that the metaphorical implications of the lyrics yield a much more literal meaning in the commercial. Similarly, in a commercial from the April 2012 volume for a brand of children's chocolate, Kinder Maxi, excerpts from the song "Yummy, Yummy, Yummy" (by Ohio Express, 1968) are used and parodied (e.g., they are sung by a chocolate bar), and the career of the song incidentally includes numerous humorous appearances in the television shows such as *The Simpsons* and *Monty Python's Flying Circus.*

These examples illustrate that "advertisers are often drawn to choruses that represent the messages they are trying to convey" and that advertisers can sometimes be "incredibly literal" (Klein, 2009, p. 106; see also Henard & Rossetti, 2014).[8] However, musical styles and genres are not universally associated with specific product categories. For example, in the sample used in this book, the use of classical music is not exclusively associated with "expensive, high-class" products, although one example is apparent: the deployment of an original composition of classical music in a commercial from the April 2012 volume for Bang & Olufsen (a Danish company that designs and manufactures audio products). Throughout the two most recent volumes of the sample, excerpts of different types of preexisting classical music are used for the promotion of beer, a bank, a mobile phone company, a national lottery, a skin conditioner, and a product to prevent nail fungus, among other products. This finding indicates that the spread and signifying potentials of musical styles and genres change according to cultural and historical settings (see, e.g., Leo, 1999, p. 37, and Blake, 2007, on classical music; see also Taylor, 2000, 2007, for an examination of "world music" and "electronica," respectively). Moreover, the specific piece of music and the exact cotextualization of the music significantly influence processes of signification. For example, some pieces of classical music are better known and more popularized than others, and an excerpt from a piece of classical music may be humorously or ironically used in a commercial. For example, in a commercial from the April 2008 volume for Carlsberg, an excerpt from the beginning of Richard Strauss's *Also Sprach Zarathustra* contributes to the ironic staging of an overpowering, novel product that appears to set the agenda for renewed (hu)man existence.[9] Finally, as indicated by the discussion on music placement, commercials do not merely adapt to and reflect passing trends in music. Commercials also contribute to the spread and production of signifying potentials of particular musical "opuses" and thus to specific musical styles and genres.

Generally, because both convergence and divergence present essential dynamics of promotion (see Chapter 4), we should expect only temporary relationships between product categories and musical styles and genres. For example, if many commercials begin to include the same type of music because of the popularity and well-disciplined potentials of signification for this particular type of music (i.e., a process of convergence), then producers might be encouraged to use other types of music or even no music (i.e., a process of divergence). In this view, the suggestions for particular relationships should be considered usable as snapshots of a trend at a particular place and time. I have shown how wider contextual issues may affect the use of music (or musical styles and genres) in commercials. For example, products for which "style is important" could include all products, not least the competitors' products that are functionally equivalent to one another (i.e., parity products).

In this chapter, relationships between music and advertised products have been examined. Three basic types of music–product relationships have been presented. Similar to the presentation of the types of transtextuality (see Chapter 2), the three types are observed based on the literature and the characteristics of musical expressions in the sample of commercials used for this book. To further illustrate this presentation, the same piece of music may be positioned in different ways in different commercials (e.g., as a musicproduct in one commercial and as placement music in another). For example, in addition to appearing in a commercial from the April 2004 volume for Riberhus (a Danish producer of cheese), an excerpt from Chicago's "If You Leave Me Now" (*Chicago X* from 1976) is also part of a medley in a commercial from the April 2012 volume for a CD (Café Hack, Sony Music Denmark). Moreover, a single commercial may include more than one of the three types—such as indistinct productmusic and brandmusic or brandmusic and music placement—the latter is exemplified by the Samsung/T-Mobile commercial featuring brandmusic for Samsung and T-Mobile using the placement of The Blue Van's "Silly Boy."

NOTES

1. That week's chart of best-selling albums in Denmark can be assessed here: www.hitlisterne.dk/default.asp?w=30&y=2008&list=a40.
2. For research that focuses more on the issue of preexisting music compared with previous studies of music used in motion pictures (e.g., Gorbman, 1987; Kalinak, 1992; Prendergast, 1992), see, for example, Smith (1998), Mundy (1999), Kassabian (2001), Inglis (2003), Reay (2004), Lannin and Caley (2005), Donnelly (2005), and Powrie and Stilwell (2006).
3. The first commercial for the campaign broadcast on TV 2 can be viewed here: www.youtube.com/watch?v=dI-xHMM8wXE. At the beginning of the campaign in some locations (e.g., China), Justin Timberlake was replaced by a local pop star.
4. The music video can be viewed here: www.youtube.com/watch?v=-IHcp8Pl_X4.
5. The commercial can be viewed here: www.youtube.com/watch?v=O3mYc1m3 lsM&feature=related.
6. The jingle was used for the first time in 1993; see an early version here: www.youtube.com/watch?v=XVhRK-YmG2M.
7. The following examples illustrate how the original *parapapapa* expression has come to appear instrumental—that is, without vocals—and varied according to the musical cotexts of the particular commercials with respect to melodic, rhythmic, and harmonic structure: www.youtube.com/watch?v=vntnlfnXr7s and www.youtube.com/watch?v=OtWRCIkFl00.
8. Of course, some lyrics appear to be more prone to promotional (re)use than others are. Perhaps not surprisingly, Louis Armstrong's "What a Wonderful World" is one of the most popular pieces of music for advertisements, whereas a song such as AC/DC's "Highway to Hell" has not, to my knowledge, been featured

in a commercial for cars or children's candy. AC/DC has appeared in commercials for brands such as Gap (i.e., an excerpt from the song "Back in Black" in a commercial from 2007: www.youtube.com/watch?v=T_K-GxEk3K0) and Nike (i.e., an excerpt from the song "Rock'n'Roll Ain't Noise Pollution" in a commercial from 2006: www.youtube.com/watch?v=volIlLCZ3nM).

9. See the commercial here: www.youtube.com/watch?v=0W7QN-oYrtg. This particular piece of music has been used widely in commercials. For example, Tagg refers to "the start of Richard Strauss's Also Sprach Zarathustra in ads for fabric softeners, office machinery and mobile phones" (Tagg 2013, 184). Stanley Kubrick arguably began an "audiovisual popularization" of this particular piece of music when it was used in his film *2001* (from 1968) to "underscore aspects of overwhelming importance relating to the universe and human existence" (Tagg, 2013, p. 184).

4 Settings
Television, Web, and Stores

In this chapter, I present commercials as a specific type of communication. Moreover, I discuss how music in commercials compares to music in other types of television programs and to music in other commercial settings. The chapter therefore aims to explore music in commercials as a particular type of music on television and as a particular type of advertising music. First, I introduce commercials as a communicative genre.

4.1 COMMERCIALS

In this section, I describe the characteristic of commercials and the context in which they appear (Jantzen & Stigel, 1995; Rutherford, 1994; Stigel, 2001). Of course, not all commercial channels around the world are comparable to the Danish Channel TV 2, and the characteristics and contexts of commercials are dynamic because of broader developments within the advertising and media industries (e.g., the advent of new technology and media). However, I suggest that TV 2 presents an illustrative example of the context of (music in) commercials for the purposes of this book. Additionally, the random sample of commercials for this book has been selected from TV 2 (see the introduction).

From a textual perspective, commercials are audiovisual expressions with a normal duration between 10 and 60 seconds, most typically 30 seconds (see, e.g., the Apple/The Blue Van case). Therefore, musical expressions in commercials will normally be shorter than musical expressions in films and music videos, for example, despite the overlap in musical functions between these genres. Commercials are heterogeneous in the sense that they include and blend virtually every mode of address and genre known from other programs on television, such as news, documentaries, films, music videos, game shows, reality shows, and sports. However, this "parasitic" characteristic is a common characteristic of advertising in a more general sense: "They [ads] borrow so many features from other genres that they are in danger of having no separable identity of their own" (G. Cook, 2001, p. 39; see also Rutherford, 1994, p. 68). Commercials can thus be regarded as miniaturized versions of television programming in general. Music may play an essential role in this respect. For example, in a commercial from the April 2012 volume for VVS Eksperten (a Danish plumbing supplier), stereotypical "news music" is deployed to underscore a commercial's imitation of a news program (for more on news music, see, e.g., Deaville, 2009; Leeuwen, 1989; Tagg, 2013, p. 512, and see the following). Hence, music in commercials represents a wide variety of styles and functions. Across this heterogeneous configuration, commercials share an explicit reference to a world of objects—products, services, and brands—outside the universe of the commercials. Commercials typically promote objects that are characterized by some degree of novelty and considerable sales volume.

From the production perspective, commercials must compete with one another and with the announced programs to attract the attention of viewers who may be distracted. This necessity places the commercial under a specific type of pressure. Viewers must be inspired to take an interest and cognitively "participate" in what is presented in the commercial. Inspiring this interest is a considerable challenge today, given the increasing availability of commercial-free content online and recording devices that give viewers the ability to skip commercials (see, e.g., Bollinger & Wang, 2013). Generally, both convergence and divergence are essential dynamics of commercial promotion. To ensure clarity and comprehensibility, commercials must conform to conventions of modes of address to some degree (i.e., a dynamic of convergence). By contrast, to be prominent relative to other commercials and to attract the attention and interest of viewers, commercials must divert from these conventions to some extent (i.e., a dynamic of divergence). Measured in terms of cost per second, the production and the distribution of commercials make this content one of the most expensive types shown on television (see, e.g., Rutherford, 1994, p. 11).

From the distribution perspective, commercials are typically broadcast to a relatively large and wide audience (regional, national, or international). Normally, a particular commercial is broadcast on TV repeatedly for a limited time (i.e., several times per day, per week, or perhaps per month). This rate of recurrence typically reflects the topical nature of the advertised product and arguably resembles the television distribution of music videos: "The fact that popular videos are repeated so often gives them a forum for exposure that is more similar to television commercials than to entertainment programming" (Lull, 1992, p. 12). Finally, from the perspective of a TV channel, commercials present "alien" texts that are not easily controlled despite the channel's attempts to exercise some influence on the production and distribution of commercials (see the following for more information).

From the recipients' perspective, commercials are viewed as uninvited during the channel flow. Additionally, commercials are transitory in the sense that they will "disappear" as soon as they have been transmitted—an observation that illustrates "the 'ephemerality' of the medium of television" (Deaville, 2011, p. 8). However, some commercials may be found, stored, and remediated on, for example, producers' websites or YouTube, where viewers can search for particular commercials and the music therein. The Apple/The Blue Van commercial presents an example of a commercial that is accessible and available for comment on YouTube. Moreover, Apple illustrates how a brand can encourage viewers to view and search for commercials on YouTube.[1] YouTube has also become a frequently used avenue for the distribution and reception of music videos, and music videos are among the most popular types of content (Burgess & Green, 2009, p. 50). Moreover, both commercials and music videos are parodied by You-Tube users, thus illustrating the participatory culture in which consumers can actively participate in creating and circulating new content (Burgess & Green, 2009). The creation and circulation of new musical content can also be observed in face-to-face interactions. Music from commercials can thus appear in the context of everyday social discourse when, for example, viewers latch on to a musical phrase and transform its meaning in an effort to influence social relationships (see, e.g., Alperstein, 1990).

4.2 MUSIC ON TELEVISION

Certainly, turning on a television set implies tuning in to some type of music. For example, music helps to contextualize the setting of fictional programs, to regulate the mood of a program's participants and viewers and to signal breaks and continuity during the flow of a program. Music also helps to sell commodities, including the commodity of music itself: artists, albums, and events. This selling occurs both during commercial breaks and in regular programs. The latter is selling in disguise, for example, in the form of product placement and "puppet programming," that is, cases in which information or entertainment programs serve as puppets for commercial purposes and are not controlled by the official presenter or channel (for more on this issue see Graakjær & Jantzen, 2009b). As Frith (2002) observed, "music is omnipresent on television, in short, but the television experience is rarely just about music" (p. 280).[2]

The fact that music appears in practically every television genre is often neglected in studies of television and popular music (Negus & Street, 2002, p. 210; see also Frith, 2002). As stated by Donnelly (2005, p. 110), "the most prominent academic texts that have looked at television programmes—such as John Ellis' *Visible Fictions* [1992] and John Fiske's *Television Culture* [1988]—always fail to deal with the music." Additionally, the few significant contributors in the field have observed that "TV music has been virtually neglected as an area of serious inquiry" (Tagg, 2006, p. 113) and, more recently, that "television music has had difficulty establishing itself as a serious area for academic study" (Deaville, 2011, p. 7; see also Kassabian, 2013b). However, as indicated, music has a significant presence in television programming: one study, for example, reports that music is present in 37%

to 70% of programming time (Tagg, 2013, p. 35). In the following, I intend to position music in commercials in the context of television programming.

Television is in the business of informing and entertaining audiences. However, television is also in the business of delivering viewers to the political system and to private enterprise, thus legitimizing the money spent to maintain broadcast services. To succeed in this field, channels must attract and retain viewers, which is the primary purpose of channel music: It attempts to increase awareness of future programs (e.g., teasers) or to convince people to continue to watch a channel while commercial breaks interrupt a favored show or television drama (e.g., bumpers). Both recurrent channel music and the music used in those programs that serve as anchors in the flow of programming thereby emphasize the invariable and perpetual qualities of the station or network. In doing so, channel music contributes to the routinization and perhaps even ritualization of watching television (e.g., Selberg, 1993). This music thus eases viewers' orientation and decision making regarding which channel to choose as the primary channel to watch or simply "where to feel at home."

Channel music essentially refers to music that is organized by a channel itself and therefore is unique to that particular channel. This music also has the objective of selling, but its commercial circuits are less obscure than those of the previously mentioned puppet programs and product placement. The channel deploys music to attract and maintain its audience's attention for the purposes of 'selling' advertisers to the audience or to render the audience measurable, thus contributing to the channel's political legitimacy. The music thus has the distinct promotional purpose of drawing attention to upcoming programs or profiling a program or channel. Compared with the "alien" music of commercials, this music is directly controlled and organized by the channel. In the following, I aim to provide an overview of different types of channel music and to discuss the promotional functions of this music for programming. Two basic subcategories of channel music can be observed: music in "nonprograms" and music in scheduled programs.

Music in "Nonprograms"

Television is scheduled in increasingly precise time slots. In the era prior to deregulation and (predominantly commercial) satellite television, only a few programs had a fixed place on the daily, weekly, or monthly schedule, such as the evening news or children's programs. In countries where only public broadcasters operated, the remainder of the schedule was loose, allowing time for programs of varying length and even for longer intervals without scheduled programs during the evening hours. The commercialization of European television in the 1980s changed that situation, intensifying inter-channel competition for programs and audiences. The program schedule became standardized, with many more scheduled programs (especially news), earlier and later "prime-time" programming and many programs with a standard length of 25 or 50 minutes. Between these scheduled programs, the time slot contains commercial breaks and brief intervals that advertise upcoming events on the channel.

These brief intervals can be labeled "nonprograms." These programs are not featured in newspapers, magazines, or programming news. When examining television schedules from the perspective of viewers, these non-programs appear to be unimportant padding—they are anonymous (not mentioned or specified) and appear to be merely constituting a pauses between programs. From the channel perspective, the value of the padding is quite different. Padding is the material that enables the channel to amuse, attract, and retain the audience, thereby contributing to the channel's commercial goal of delivering a sufficient number of viewers to its advertisers. Accordingly, the aim of these nonprograms is not simply to "waste time" in a mildly pleasant way while nothing of real importance to the viewers happens. In fact, the importance of padding is arguably indicated by the sheer amount of time that is devoted to nonprograms during the flow of TV (for more on television flow, see, e.g., Williams, 1974). Thus, television flow has been increasingly dominated by "bits of information that make promises for more to come" (Stigel, 2004, p. 29). Moreover, as a possible result of stylistic spillover effects on other types of programs, "we are dealing with more and more self-reference within the range of programs" (Stigel, 2004, p. 29; see also Hicketier & Bleichert, 1997). Such measures are expressed through different types of "promos," which are commercials that refer internally to the channel and/or to the programs that the channel provides to its viewers. Promos promise that although nothing is currently occurring, something interesting and relevant is about to occur (in 5 minutes, tomorrow, or in 1 week) on the same channel.

Promos approximately (see modifications discussed later) correspond to music in the extradiegetic space as termed by Rodman (2010): "Extradi-egetic space is the realm of television that narrates outside the television's narrative programs"; "operating in extradiegetic space, some TV networks and studios use musical mottos to identify themselves" (p. 54). However, "music functions on television do not always fall discretely within the three spaces of television," and "musical functions change over time as new codes of television are negotiated between viewer and producer" (Rodman, 2010, p. 59). The most common types of promos are the following:

- *Bumpers*: short lead-ins and lead-outs surrounding a program and thus smoothing the breaks between the scheduled program and commercials (e.g., a sponsor announcement; Bjurström & Lilliestam, 1993; Rodman, 2010)
- *Teasers:* longer presentations of a program that will be broadcast in the near future but not immediately following the teaser. The music

accompanying this type of promo often originates from the intradi-egetic space, that is, "the story world . . . of a particular TV show." This music, typically an excerpt from the theme music for a particular program, "calls attention to the characters, emotions, settings, and objects in the diegesis without actually being in the diegesis" (Rodman, 2010, p. 54). As noted previously, the music of The Blue Van has appeared in the form of teasers.

- *Channel idents:* short-duration logo presentations that identify the channel (Brownrigg & Meech, 2002)
- *Listings:* stilstill shots, sometimes animated, of the programs to be broadcast at a particular time of the day, often associated with *channel idents*

In addition, *fillers*—a non-scheduled program used to fill unforeseen "gaps" in the flow—can appear. This type of promo is somewhat different in that it presents a profile of the channel as a brand but does not directly correspond to the daily or weekly schedule or to specific programs.

Promos have the specific aim of directing the audience's attention to the listed programs, which in turn direct the viewers' attention to another type of unlisted program: commercials. As indicated, from a flow perspective, commercials are alien elements that advertise a product that have no obvious relationship to the channel or to its programs. Both commercials and promos are in the business of identifying and promising a desirable future experience or product, but they differ in that they identify different future scenarios. Promos point to a future experience in the present world of the channel by identifying what is being broadcast currently or in the near future, whereas commercials point to a future appropriation of products in the absent (but perhaps "real") world of the market.

The music used in promos and commercials differs in style and function. Commercial music is quite diverse in terms of its presence, distinctiveness, and origin. Conversely, music in promos is nearly always distinctive and originally composed. The inclusion of (distinctive) music is related to the general functions of promos, which structure the flow of television in both syntagmatic and paradigmatic ways. Promos sequence the flow from a "horizontal" perspective by occurring regularly and repeatedly and from a "vertical" perspective by signaling, calling, and enabling recognition and association. The music in promos is crucial: It smoothes breaks and pauses, and it highlights current and coming programs in the service of frequently absent-minded or distracted "viewers" (or more aptly, "listeners"). Apparently, the idea of promos is "what is out of sight must come in the ear." Because all viewers potentially are "listening" even when they are not looking at the screen—for instance, they may attend to other tasks while the television remains on—music can cause viewers to return their attention to the screen. Music therefore functions as a sort of "umbilical cord" between the viewer and the screen, ensuring that the viewer does not miss upcoming programs. To a regular viewer, promos may be easily recognizable and differentiable even when listening is only peripheral: Distinctiveness entails differentiation, and repetition entails recognition and association.

The musical interface controlled by the channel (i.e., bumpers, channel idents, and listings) is important in contexts of numerous channels, each attempting to maintain and provide *identity* while addressing viewers fond of zapping and, when not zapping, preoccupied by other tasks (i.e., not looking at the screen). Compared with previous uses of fanfare-like themes, channel music (and especially channel idents) has become more "fun-fair"-like (Brownrigg & Meech, 2002). The result is reportedly "more fluid and musically more sophisticated forms" with "not one monolithic version, but a series linked both in vision and sound" (Brownrigg & Meech, 2002, p. 352f). Promo music is rarely preexisting and is thus unlikely to be or to become a product, although borderline cases can be identified. In such cases in which all or most of a channel's musical interface is standardized (or styled) by one specific artist, the product is arguably apparent through the (style of the) artist being promoted, if not the exact music used.[3] Furthermore, teasers can present musical products by including excerpts of complete title tunes (which often become products themselves) that will be heard in the actual program.

Music in Scheduled Programs

The increase in competition among channels has intensified the attention that broadcasters direct toward scheduling. The urge to create structure in the flow of weekly programming that is both interesting and recurrent and thus easily recognizable and memorable has divided the "prime-time hours" into distinctive parcels of programs. On public service channels, this practice has led to a remarkable increase in news programs that serve as daily anchors in the weekly schedule. The ability to produce interesting and reliable news coverage has become an important aspect of inter-channel competition for viewers because building a loyal news audience propels the share of viewers who watch commercial breaks before and after the news or who remain tuned in for the subsequent evening schedule. Selecting relevant items from the continuous flow of news; presenting them in a comprehensible, credible, and interesting manner; and continuously upholding distinct criteria for the selection and presentation of news are thus of seminal importance in meeting viewers' expectations and thus in profiling the program and the channel. The use of visual and sound logos assists in emphasizing this profile. In this respect, music is often utilized to create program idents (approximately corresponding to the intradiegetic music described earlier) that distinguish a channel's programs from its competitors' programs.

Because news has become such an important type of program both for anchoring the schedule and for profiling a channel's identity, the use of music in creating a distinctive signature is especially noticeable. An analysis of the first 23 seconds of the most popular Danish news program (TV 2's 7 o'clock *News*) shows how music functions to combine all the program's visual and sonic elements during its introduction (Graakjær, 2004). Music establishes an underlying coherence among these various aspects, thus producing not only a continuous sequence leading to the first news item of the evening but also a new sense of unity that is clearly distinguishable from the visual and sonic impressions remaining from the preceding programming (namely, a brief sequence of "nonprograms" after the commercial breaks). The function of music is therefore primarily syntagmatic: It informs viewers that a *new* program is about to begin and that this program differs from the previous programs in the schedule, as the music simply sounds different. However, this music simultaneously serves a paradigmatic function: It informs the viewers that the *same* program that they usually watch at this hour is about to begin, because the music sounds similar and is therefore easily recognizable, implying that the news program will resemble the programs in previous days, weeks, months and years. Moreover, this music is paradigmatic because it differs from the sounds that accompany the news programs of other channels. This music sounds distinct, implying that the program is distinct from its competitors.

Beginning with a pronounced kettledrum and quickly (after 5 seconds) developing into something resembling a reveille motif, the music of *News* has many of the "fanfare"-like qualities that characterized the channel idents in television's earlier years (Brownrigg & Meech, 2002).[4] Also involved is the musical-structural feature that appears to have been a defining trait of news music for quite some time, namely, the "music of the telegraph." Musically phrased through rhythmic staccato attacks in alternating rapid succession, this music resembles "morse-coding" (as well as teleprinters and stammering), and it is associated with speed, excitement, and urgency, all seminal aspects of the news (and several other genres, such as live sports; see Tagg & Clarida, 2003, p. 487; Leeuwen, 1989). Of course, the purpose of this composition is to signal that something new and important is about to occur, thus creating a rupture in the flow of the channel and alerting the viewer to pay attention. Additionally, within news programs, musical expressions occasionally highlight that something new is about to occur in the form of the "stinger, which is a newly composed musical theme to accompany graphics and narration for major ongoing stories" that "announces the item to follow" (Deaville, 2009, p. 614).

This signaling emphasizes the syntagmatic function of this music. Subsequently, this signal is transformed into a sound structure that resembles the style of late romanticism, thus indicating that the program is serious, dramatic, and emotionally engaging. This style indication emphasizes the paradigmatic function of music. This evening's program has the same qualities and standards as the program from last evening, but these standards are used or expressed differently (and, by implication, "better") than on the competing channel's news program. Underscoring the program's profile—and by implication, that of the entire channel—is that "late romantic" music is arguably considered both sophisticated and relatively easy to digest (i.e., it is not overly academic). The news is relevant (serious and important) and interesting (entertaining and involving), thereby marking its distance from adversaries who allegedly either deliver relevant news in an uninteresting manner (e.g., DR1) or deliver interesting but irrelevant news (e.g., commercial satellite channel programs that focus on celebrities and [their] scandals).

Music thus serves to promote the importance of this particular program relative to other programs on the same channel and to similar programs on other channels. In the case of pronounced program music, the composition may thus affect intra-and inter-channel profiling. Program music signals to the audience that something different from the rest of the flow will be presented (intra-channel profiling). This signaling is the presentational function of music working on the syntagm of the flow. Compared with the three main functions of "title music" (see Tagg, 2013, p. 555), this function includes both reveille ("Wake up! Something different is about to start!") and mnemonic ("A particular, identifiable and recurrent . . . production is about to start.") functions. Simultaneously, the presentational function informs the audience that this program differs from other examples in the same genre (inter-channel profiling) and that the difference in programming is consistent: This particular episode of the program will represent the same distinct qualities as episodes from previous evenings. This representational function of music frames a program as different from the programs offered by competitors, and it is comparable to the preparatory function ("something of a particular type . . . is about to start" (Tagg, 2013, p. 555). Different items and other news anchors, presenters, journalists, and new sources may exist; however, the program consistently provides a unique blend of seriousness and wit and of perspectives and methods of reporting (form) in a perpetually shifting world (content).

The discussion has illustrated that, indeed, "the dominant use of music on television, one might conclude, is to sell things" (Frith, 2002, p. 282). Music in commercials is "surrounded" by other types of commercial music that promote and characterize a channel (typically in the form of extradiegetic promo music), a program (typically in the form of intradiegetic program ident music) or even the music "itself" in cases of "puppet programming" or music placements (typically in the form of diegetic music). These environmental conditions for music in commercials further add to the pressures to which commercials are subjected.

4.3 MUSIC IN WEB ADS AND STORES

Fundamentally, advertising involves attracting the attention of possible consumers. In Latin, the term *advertising* means "to turn toward" (*ad vertere*), and sound is arguably privileged for this purpose: consumers may look in the other direction, but their ears cannot easily be redirected, let alone closed. Indeed, sound may encourage consumers to "turn toward" a commercial message. The shouting of the medieval public crier (Dyer, 1982, p. 15) and comparable historical instances—such as commercial announcements sung by street vendors (see, e.g., Bridge, 1921; see also the example in Mukarovsky, 1979, p. 11; see Chapter 7)—illustrate that sound has long played a pivotal role in attracting the attention and interest of consumers. The announcements sung by street vendors can be regarded as symbolic of commercial newcomers. For example, it is also characteristic of television (and radio) commercials that music appears rather unexpected and uninvited and that it has the purpose of catching the attention and interest of "passing" customers for whom the purchase of goods is not the primary purpose of being "there."

In the following, I aim to contribute to the understanding of music in commercials as a particular type of advertising music. It is beyond the scope of this chapter to deeply examine all the facets of music in advertising; thus, I concentrate on two settings: music in web ads and music in stores.[5]

Music in Web Ads

Internet users are almost inevitably exposed to commercial messages, such as sponsored text links in search engines, animated banner ads, billboards, advertorials, pop-ups, and commercial websites. Although web advertising includes a wide variety of expressions, there is a general conception that web ads should be regarded as a relationship or structural connection between an embedded web ad (e.g., a banner ad) and its linked website (the *target ad*) (see, e.g., Janoschka, 2004). Based on the available scholarly studies that include larger sample of web ads (e.g., Fiore & Kelly, 2007; Jensen & Helles, 2007; Tsang, 2007; Jessen & Graakjær, 2010), the general impression is that web ads do not often include music or even sound (which has inspired the more inclusive reference to "sound" here rather than the more exclusive category of "music").[6] There are several possible reasons for this lack of sound (see the following discussion), and some have argued for future change. For instance, "the lack of sound on the vast majority of websites is part of its [the Internet's] unfulfilled potential . . . we are still in the 'silent' era' of the Web, but 'talkies' are not far away" (Jackson & Fulberg, 2003, p. 7), and "increasingly, music is beginning to appear on high-end product sites, such as race cars, fashion houses, and real estate developments" (Kassabian, 2013b, p. 99). Indeed, from a diachronic perspective, an increase in web ads that include sound is observed by Jessen and Graakjær (2010), who compare a sample of ads from 2004/2005 to a 2008/2009 sample. In this context, I introduce the conditions of music in web ads to the extent that they can be examined at the time of this writing.

With respect to the conditions of sound, the Internet differs considerably from television. Whereas television arguably presents sound relatively independently of user activity (i.e., sound is mutable, but it usually emerges when the television is switched on), sound on the Internet is more likely to be dependent on (i.e., a result of) user activity in various ways. Television presupposes speakers and sound—televisions have always been produced with integrated speakers—whereas the Internet has arguably been conceptualized and used as a visual form of media with less focus on sound technology from both producers and users. Thus, it can be argued that the use of sound on the Internet is not characterized by either consolidation or familiarity, most likely related to the perspectives of both the sender (e.g., designers' inattention to the potential of sound) and the channel (e.g., the technology generally allows reproduction of sound only to a certain degree of complexity).

Sounds in embedded web ads are rare; for example, a study of 1,246 ads indicates that sound is included in fewer than 5% of ads (Jessen & Graakjær, 2010, p. 542). When sounds are present, they are typically activated by the user's mouse, for instance, by a mouse-over (a relatively deliberate activity) or by clicking on the ad. Such instances are typically formatted as embedded audiovisual videos of various periods, and they often resemble television commercials (thus presenting a case of an "unchanged" representation of the television commercial in another medium; Bolter & Grusin, 1999). However, in web ads, a user can manipulate a video in different ways (revealing a dimension of "improvement"; see Bolter & Grusin, 1999): If the mouse does not remain on the ad, then the video will often be interrupted, only to begin again when the cursor hovers over the ad—a design that facilitates user activities (most likely not intended by senders) such as scratching (the reactivation of a video in brief intervals).

Because the user's activity triggers the sound rather than the reverse, this "silent" and only potentially auditorily embedded ad presents, at first sight, a peculiar audiovisual advertisement phenomenon. *Attracting attention* is not the sound's primary function, contrary to the almost archetypal function of sounds in advertising in general. Rather, the sound emphasizes and sustains attention, prompting the user either to leave the mouse where it is (for videos) or to click. Embedded ads appear to be predominantly visual expressions (pictures, texts, and sometimes animations), attracting attention through various sorts of eye catchers (e.g., colors and movements) or verbal imperatives. Only when the mouse has unintentionally moved over the ad is it sensible to consider sound to be capturing attention, which is most obvious in cases of the sound at the beginning of a video (e.g., a musical expression resembling the earlier mentioned "bumper" in television programming, which is also a good example of a scratchable video).

When considered in relation to the characteristics of its medium and genre, a silent, embedded web ad may not be regarded as peculiar after all. Internet users appear more likely to experience sounds in ads as an intrusive and negative element than television viewers do.[7] This tendency can likely be explained by the Internet's status as a *pull* media, in which the user typically expects and experiences a high level of control over information (e.g., one searches the

Internet). Television commercial sounds are also occasionally considered uninvited and disturbing (see, e.g., Schafer, 1977, p. 268). However, the sounds of television programming play an important role in establishing both continuity (the unbroken and overlapping sequence of events) and breaks (the abrupt highlighting of present or upcoming events)—that is, useful, if not directly attractive, features of television programming matching distracted viewers. A particular attribute of embedded web ads compared with television commercials is that they appear synchronous with the noncommercial material on a website; for example, there are no interrupting "bumpers." Synchronous television advertising typically occurs through more integrated and subtle music placements and puppet programming within programs. Accordingly, automatically activated sounds from an embedded web ad can compromise the user's focus and expectations of control.

With respect to the destinations of embedded web ads (i.e., commercial websites not devoted to music), sound and music occur more frequently and are more varied compared with the embedded web ads themselves, although a large majority of websites do not include sound. A study of 798 websites indicates that fewer than 10% of sites include sound on their main pages (Jessen & Graakjær, 2010, p. 542). Although that study potentially neglects to consider important content elsewhere on the website, the main page is "the minimal unit that defines a website; it is the part that users are most likely to encounter, thus, arguably, it is the most salient and important part to analyze" (Herring, 2004, p. 6). For example, Apple's main page[8] does not include sound, and a survey of national McDonald's websites has indicated that sound occurs on 6 of the accessible 80 websites[9]—in all 6 instances, versions of the *i'm lovin' it* jingle (see Chapter 6) are included in the soundscape.

The advertising messages on websites do not occur synchronously with noncommercial materials (contrary to the case of embedded web ads), and the text is ready for "reading" and exploration either immediately following the initial click or subsequent to an introduction. Websites without an introduction will usually feature sounds and music independent of user activity (apart from the initial arrival to the website). In some ways, this context is similar to numerous incidents of everyday life in which music is nearly inescapable, such as when dining, waiting in line, or shopping (for more information on music in stores; see the following discussion). On websites featuring music that begins and continues without user activity, repeated musical expressions are predominant. Groove and sound appear to dominate over melodic curvature and harmonic progression (which can also be characteristic of the musical format of groove in television commercials; see Chapter 6). From a syntagmatic perspective, this type of music may be considered "circular" (or elliptical) rather than linear (Björnberg, 2000). Accordingly, a website's supplementary music differs from the music in shops in that the latter normally consists of longer lasting culminating progressions with tuneful pieces of music. Conceivably, this situation reflects the difference between the decision to "stay on a website" versus to "stay in a shop": in shops, the stay is normally sequenced in a relatively well-defined manner (shopping is arguably organized according to a script; Schank & Abelson, 1977), whereas a stay on a website is typically characterized by a non-predetermined exploration or visit of shorter duration and can end at any time without consequence. Only rarely do commercial websites provide immersive spaces to be explored, typically involving the user entering a first-person perspective from which a three-dimensional space can be experienced. Here, music functions through the psychological and physical positioning of the user, and sounds in general will appear with varying degrees of importance to the narrative structure. For example, sounds can aid a user in creating a narrative structure by functioning as markers and signals of the user's choices and movements. Herein lies a substantial difference from media such as films and commercials. In commercials, the media text is predefined, and there is no opportunity to construct a viewer sub-flow in the text, as is possible on some websites and in some computer games, which reflects a more general condition of Internet use (i.e., a high level of user activity and control).[10] Compared with commercials, many website menus are characterized by no or only small visual movements (apart from possible user-generated movements). In such cases, music functions to assure the user that he or she is online and to counteract the potential (unwanted) boredom that could be attributed to a website and its product.

With regard to the origin of music, no clear tendency is shown, but one interesting occurrence must be addressed briefly. Preexisting music that is often relatively unknown to ordinary users is sometimes part of the appeal of certain commercial websites. Considered a type of co-promotion of music and product, this phenomenon has also been prevalent in television commercials (see Chapter 3). However, a website adds new dimensions by providing information instantaneously and concurrently. The co-promotion of music and jeans (e.g., Levi's, GAP, and Mustang) provides an illustrative case ("music to wear"). For example, the Mustang website has played and provided instant access to "rock musicians with equal amounts of talent and potential. Yet unknown to the majority, this can change rapidly."[11]

Some auditory phenomena that arise as a result of user activity are comparable to those previously discussed in relation to embedded web ads. For instance, sound effects can be heard as a result of a mouse-over in which the sounds become indices of the objects viewed, and sound and music are parts of audiovisual expressions, such as the "unchanged" (or perhaps slightly improved) remediation of television commercials. Mouse-over-activated videos have somewhat different conditions on websites compared with their status in embedded web ads: auditory phenomena are not necessarily "up front" (loud and sudden)—as in many mouse-over-activated embedded ads—because the attention of users can be presupposed and therefore need not be captured. In addition, remediated television commercials do not impede user activity; in fact, they can be considered types of promos that are sometimes initiated on a website without additional user activity.

Furthermore, audiovisual expression can be embedded into the design of a website—for example, as part of a collage—thus reflecting a relatively sophisticated refashioning of television commercials. Along with a website's auditory phenomena, a range of features is typically accessible through clicks that provide optional constituent elements (e.g., puzzles, games, menus, immersive scenarios).

Figure 4.1 presents an overview of the functions of sounds in embedded web ads and in the linked target ads in relation to various modes of user activities (i.e., reading, navigating, and editing). According to Finnemann (2001), digital texts are characterized by modal shifts between different modes of reading, representing "a discontinuous process, included as part of the reading process" (p. 44). Addressing digital texts in general, Finnemann distinguishes among three modes of "reading": (a) the reading mode, that is, "reading 'as usual' (including skimming)"; (b) the link mode, that is, "navigating and browsing"; and (c) the editing mode, that is, "interactive behavior changing the future behavior/content of the system" (Finnemann, 2001, p. 43). Thus, these three types of user activities can describe the ways in which users read or engage with web ads and possible sounds, namely, reading, navigating, and editing.

When the functions of sounds in web ads are considered in relation to these three modes of user activity, the following is characteristically observed. In the *mode of reading*, the user merely listens to and watches a commercial video or simply reads a written text in a banner ad. This reading mode is similar to that encountered during viewers' reading of television commercials (although the level of attention may differ); therefore, the functions of the sounds—and thus the possible music—are somewhat similar to those presented by music in commercials (see Chapter 7). With

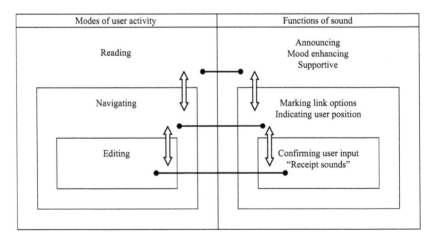

Figure 4.1   Functions of sounds in relation to modes of user activity (adapted from Jessen & Graakjær, 2010, p. 547)

respect to the function of sounds in the mode of reading, I highlight three functions: the supportive, mood-enhancing, and announcing functions. The announcing function of speech (in the form of a presenter, a testimonial, a voice-over, or a dialogue) tends to be less dominant, whereas the supportive and mood-enhancing functions of object sounds and music appear to be more widespread. The term *supportive* is used to denote a predominantly structuring and underlining function of sound, generally based on the assumption that sound will be subordinate to the visual part even more so on the Internet than on television (see the discussion of media-related conditions of sound). The term *mood enhancing* is used to refer to the usual function of music and object sounds in visually uneventful periods, and in this context, sound functions as a relatively unspecific moderator of the experience of a web ad (similar to the experience of being in a store with music; see the following section). Sounds with a supportive function arguably point *into* the audiovisual expression—for instance, by emphasizing movements and bridging scenes—whereas sounds in an uneventful visual setting are more likely to point *out from* the media text, identifying and positioning the user as someone who needs to make a move.

Unlike the "simple" reading of content in the reading mode, the mode of navigating clearly involves a more active and tactile contribution by the user, typically involving moving or clicking the mouse to browse parts of the ad's content using the provided links and menus. In sum, in the navigation mode, we can identify two dominating functions of sound. First, sounds function as an indication of the user's position, for instance, by using different music in the different levels of an ad's composition. In such cases, the sound emphasizes the location of the user by connecting specific music or incidental sounds with specific "spaces" or levels in the ad's structure; accordingly, the sound underlines where the user is or should be. Second, sounds function as a marker of link options, both directly in the form of sound effects or exclamations and indirectly in the form of circular, repeated sounds that urge the user to navigate.

Finally, in the editing mode, the user contributes input that has some type of effect on the content or appearance of the ad. Examples of editing could include the marking of radio buttons and checkboxes as means of choosing preferences (e.g., the color of a car, the settings of a game) or the submission of information to the system by completing forms with numbers and words (e.g., sending orders and contact data). In this mode, sound functions primarily as confirmation of the user's input. In contrast to navigating mode, in which sounds normally function as motivating activity, the sounds in editing mode are relatively *confirmatory* in that they function as "auditory receipts" that highlight the result of an activity.

The linked black dots in Figure 4.1 indicate that the given modes of activity are typically associated with particular functions of sound. For example, when in editing mode, receipt sounds are predominant. Moreover, the vertical arrows indicate that the mode of user activity frequently shifts.

Music in Stores

Music in stores essentially presents a supplemental tool that contributes to the proper "atmospherics" for shopping: a deliberate design that generates "specific emotional effects in the buyer that enhance his purchase probability" (Kotler, 1973/1974, p. 50).[12] Music at commercial sites is forced on the shopper, and it is likely—at some level and more or less consciously—to influence the consumer's current level of arousal, mood, cognition, and actual behavior (e.g., product choice). Moreover, apparently analogous to the alleged development of the use of music in commercials, the use of preexisting popular music in stores has recently increased. For example, "background music in public spaces was once a subtle counterpoint to daily life, but attention-hogging foreground music has taken its place . . . Hints at this change surfaced in 1984, when . . . Muzak's then-president Tony Hirsch mentioned a new plan to broadcast 'original artist music', or 'foreground music'" (Lanza, 2013, p. 622), and

> several features of that music [i.e., music in stores] have undergone radical changes in the past twenty-five years. First of all, it now mainly . . . consists of songs by original artists, whereas it once was almost all popular songs and classics rearranged for lush strings.
>
> (Kassabian, 2013a, p. 84)

In the following, I consider a particular case, that is, the music deployed in the youth clothing store Abercrombie & Fitch (A&F), which illustrates the characteristic functions of music in stores.[13]

The musical style of A&F is remarkably homogenous, which appears to be a result of the selective screening of preexisting music to include on the store's playlist.[14] The store's music presents itself as a pop-flavored variant of electronic/dance music, influenced by the synth pop of the 1980s (e.g., Rick Astley) and the dance music of the 1990s (e.g., CeCe Peniston). The music's motorial flow (Björnberg, 2000, p. 357) is characterized by a high density and regularity of sound events or beats. Consequently, the dynamics of the music are relatively high and constant, and the music allows for impressions such as that of "thumping dance music" with "a throbbing beat" (Barreneche, 2006, p. 186) and "head-pounding music" presenting a "disco-grade boom" (Anthes, 2010, p. 40). Variations in the standardized playlist are manifested through the sex of the singer (male or female), the degree of transtexuality (whether the song represents a hypertext), seasonal distinctions, and song lyrics. With respect to song lyrics, emotional appeals and references to revealing and enraptured states of mind characterize the lyrics of the choruses throughout the playlist. The hook lines of the choruses generally reflect a comparatively high level of emotional intensity, and the voice of the singer tends toward "intoned feeling" (Middleton, 1990, p. 231).

Loud music does not constitute the only welcome to A&F's setting. People leaving the building leave a trail of a powerful perfume that significantly penetrates the otherwise-muddling olfactory impression. Moreover, a young man typically welcomes guests in the reception area with a smile and a trim, naked upper body. He and a model-like woman will greet consumers with an American-accented "Hey, how's it going? [or Hey, how are you?]—Welcome to A&F," and consumers are asked to have their photographs taken with the young man. In addition to the reception area, the store is characterized by a series of interconnected rooms, stairwells, and narrow corridors. There is no clear demarcation of where to go or where specific clothes can be found. For example, there are no apparent signs indicating where to find men's and women's wear, and numerous mirrors challenge the sense of direction. The store is poorly lit, and its interior is marked by dark wooden tables, shelves, floors, and roofs. Except for step lights on the stairs, bright spotlights are the only source of light directed at the clothes on the shelves, on the tables, and in the glass showcases. Furthermore, the store is characterized by a décor reminiscent of A&F's history as a provider of apparel for Ivy League sports and outdoor activities. Thus, the décor includes palm-like plants, a giant moose head hanging on the wall, a sculpture of a young naked man, and wall paintings of young muscular men with naked upper bodies rowing, boxing, fencing, and playing cricket and tennis. Because one cannot see outside of the store, a visit to the store leaves one with no particular sense of the external environment. Similarly, the sense of time is suspended because neither daylight nor clocks are present; only the range of clothes and music may hint at the time of year. The store assistants are all young, sylphlike beauties (apparently a result of careful screening; Mitchelson, 2007) dressed in figure-hugging clothes that are sold in the store. These employees tirelessly greet customers and sometimes even dance. The position of shop assistants in key transition places and rooms entails that customers' personal space (following Hall, 1967) will necessarily be invaded. Furthermore, because the music is so loud, intimate space must be invaded when customers need to seek help from assistants.

Presenting an extreme case (see the introduction), A&F's music clearly illustrates three typical functions of music in stores: an "architectural function," a "psychobiological function" and a "knowledge-activating function" (inspired by, e.g., North and Hargreaves, 2006; Sterne, 1997).

The architectural function of music refers to how music guides the experience of spatiality. Music functions as "sonic architecture" by being played in a space in which consumers are moving around (Groom, 1996; Sterne, 1997). At the entrance of A&F, I observed that the store's music appears to function as a selective permeable structure that "allows" some people to pass, while others are "refused" passage. Thus, I term this structure an invisible "social membrane."[15] In particular, the loudness, motorial flow, and style of the music effectively "select" potential customers to ensure that the in-store clientele and A&F's brand remain "clean." To some people, the occasionally physically open doors to the street are symbolically closed, which reflects how music can mark boundaries, instantiate impermeability, and effectively discriminate among customers.[16] Other examples of such segmentation functions of music can be identified by the use of specific music to repel unwanted clientele. For example, "after consulting a psychologist, a branch of McDonald's in Southampton is to replace chart hits with classical music to calm yobs who plague its customers. Instead of Eminem, they will hear artists such as violinist Nigel Kennedy playing Vivaldi and Mozart" (The Observer 2002; for further examples of music's ability to repel particular social groups, see Goodman, 2010; Johnson & Cloonan, 2009; Sterne, 2005).

Inside A&F, the unvarying distribution of music from speakers throughout the store functions to link the interconnecting rooms. The music creates an impression of coherence and continuity when moving from one room to another. Whereas the music in A&F functions to erase physical boundaries between sections, music can also mark boundaries in places where no clear physical separation is visible. For example, in shopping malls, the music that is played in each separate store signals that the consumer is about to enter a "new planet" within the mall's universe (which resembles the "indicating user position" function of some website music; see Figure 4.1). Moreover, in A&F, the music enables transfers from the public sphere and the private realm. The loud music allows for privacy in public; for example, couples' private conversations are concealed. However, the music makes anonymity and aloneness seem bearable. Most significantly, the music provides a resource for self-projection (see the following discussion), which is augmented by the cocoon-like experience created by the distribution of music throughout the store. The music thus sounds equally loud regardless of where customers are located, which conveys the impression of being immersed in a disconnected universe and escaping from the real world. Clearly, the nightclub prompts add to this experience (see the following disucssion).

The A&F case aptly illustrates how in-store music can indeed function as an auditory foreground (see the earlier reference to "attention-hogging foreground" music). However, preexisting music, including lyrics, may also function in an auditory background. For example, in an Apple Store,[17] preexisting music can act as an auditory background for other sounds, such as instructions and discussions of the functions of Apple products. Unlike what is offered to consumers at A&F, verbal communication between consumers and assistants is crucial to the service offered at an Apple Store. Consequently, the volume of the music is balanced to ensure that speech sounds may be easily foregrounded. Meanwhile, the music is sufficiently loud to be recognized and consciously enjoyed by listening (and sometimes humming) consumers. In general, the music assists in encouraging a positive mood in the store. To this end, the playlist includes current popular hits combined with older "pop classics," such as "The Sweetest Taboo" by Sade (1985) and "Learning to Fly" by Tom Petty and the Heartbreakers (1991). The range of musical styles in the Apple Store thus appears to be broader than the musical styles of their commercials; in other words, the musical style brand of Apple's commercials does not appear to extend to Apple's stores.

The psychobiological function refers to the ways in which music can influence the mood and arousal level of customers (see, e.g., Milliman, 1982; P. Smith & Curnow, 1966). Contrary to emotions, mood is a longer lasting, less intense and non-specific tone of feeling (Davies, 2001) that is not affected by a single stimulus. Music thus contributes to mood by generating an ambience in combination with other props in the store (e.g., the odor and the subdued lighting). In that respect, music for shopping resembles some of the uses of music on websites (see the earlier discussion) and most (but not all) film music, whose function is largely to convey the "right" atmosphere to a movie's audience. Mood enhancement can operate in two distinct directions—either reducing or increasing the level of arousal—and at A&F, the function of the music is clearly to increase the level of arousal. Evidently, its music creates an upbeat atmosphere in combination with nightclub prompts (see more the following discussion). The loud, fast, and dense motorial flow of the music appears to promote (Leeuwen, 2005, p. 4) a bodily response in the form of dance activity. Customers may "identify with the motor structure, participating in the gestural patterns, either vicariously, or even physically, through dance or through miming vocal and instrumental performance" (Middleton, 1990, p. 243). Indeed, most of the customers whom I observed would at some point participate in rhythmic entrainment, which refers to how people more or less consciously attempt to align their bodily processes with recurring aspects of musical rhythm (see Clayton, Sager, & Will, 2004; DeNora, 2000; Phillips-Silver, Aktipis, & Bryant, 2010). Here, it is crucial that the music contributes to the creation of an upbeat atmosphere of excitement and excess that may, for example, stimulate customers to position themselves in front of large mirrors in extraordinary garments and enticing postures similar to the heroes and heroines of pop culture ringing in their ears.

The knowledge activation function refers to the ways in which music at A&F can function as a resource for sense- and decision making as well as self-projection (see, e.g., Areni & Kim, 1993; North, Hargreaves, & McKendrick, 1999). The premise for this function is the existence of a more or less elaborate knowledge—or conceptual frame—of the music. Perhaps such a conceptual frame is part of the "admission fee" for entering A&F: If an individual is not familiar with the (type of) music being played, then he or she is somewhat "lost" in the first place. If the musical domain of A&F can be framed, then the frame can be utilized in facilitating decision-making processes by inference. Eventually, this framing can lead to a reframing in which a new conceptual domain has been endowed by—or *blended* with (Fouconnier & Turner, 2002)—the qualities and attributes of the music. At A&F, this process may occur in the following simplified manner: "This is dance pop music, dance pop music is joyful, sensual, and danceable, and

I like it (conceptual frame); these clothes belong to the music (via the models, the "clothes" actually "dance" to the music), so I will buy the clothes (inference). These clothes are joyful, sensuous, and danceable, so they are good for a night out with my friends (blending)." Although this reasoning may seem unsound, most customers typically act with imperfect knowledge under relatively strict time constraints, which leads to rapid decision making.

Conceptual blending theory can further illustrate how music contributes to positioning A&F as a unique location and brand. Thus, A&F arguably presents an emergent structure produced by a blend of at least two conceptual input spaces: the "night club" (e.g., model-like assistants who dance and flirt, a darkened environment without directional signs, mirrors, stair-step lighting, and a powerful scent) and an exhibition hall and "exhibition" (e.g., spotlights on showcases, sculpture, historical wall paintings, monitoring assistants at key transition points and "art(ifacts)" (clothing) meticulously on display). The input spaces share elements from the same abstract, generic space: an "indoor commercial setting" where visitors orient themselves toward objects on display for sale. The influence of music is essential in structuring A&F as a "nightclub-like youth clothing store."

To indicate the influence of music, the substitution of particular music with an alternative soundscape would conceivably allow other structures to emerge. For example, "no music" would most likely enhance the experience of an exhibition, whereas natural sounds (e.g., the sounds of running water, wind in the trees, and birds chirping) would perhaps prompt the impression of a safari or labyrinth to be explored (for more on this type of commutation testing, see Chapter 5).

The blended space of A&F exhibits a range of elements, some of which are more congruent that others. For example, the store's specific odor— Fierce, described on the website as "the clean scent of fresh citrus"—seems congruent with its music in some respects: It presents the "scentmark" of the location and is powerful throughout the entire store. Moreover, scents dominated by citrus potentially increase the level of arousal (Mattila & Wirtz, 2001). Experimental studies of "the interaction of environmental cues" in stores (Spangenberg, Grohmann & Sprott, 2005) have highlighted the commercially beneficial effects of such types of congruency. For instance, "playing fast-tempo music had a more positive effect on approach behaviors when the store was scented with grapefruit (high-arousal scent) than with lavender . . . When the stimuli in the environment act together to provide a coherent atmosphere, the individual in the environment will react more positively" (Mattila & Wirtz, 2001, p. 286), and "consistency between an ambient scent and music in a retail setting leads to more favorable evaluations of the store, its merchandise and the store environment" (Spangenberg et al., 2005; for similar conclusions, see Morrison, Gan, Dubelaar, & Oppewal, 2011; for more on "congruency" in commercials, see Chapter 5).

However, other elements or environmental cues are not congruent, such as pop dance music in contrast to the historical wall paintings and the meticulous display of clothes. Thus, visitors need to search for meaning and attempt to situate the objects of the setting "in relation to a horizon" (Nattiez, 1990). The setting thus invites customers to "create a story" using the available semiotic resources (Leeuwen, 2005). By referring to a state of mind ("How's it going?") rather than a specific goal to be obtained (e.g., "How can I help you?"), the sales assistant's form of address reinforces such an invitation. Arguably, customers not only "create their own story" but also participate in "staging the story" inside the store. In this respect, music appears to play a pivotal role. The blending aspect of A&F's setting may thus be perceived as creative and exiting: a new insight can be attained, or a new network of associations can form. An important implication of this association is the probability of A&F's brand "colonizing" the particular (style of) music played. Music can then become invested in A&F's brand, which shows not only that there is music in A&F but also that A&F is "in the music."[18]

This example also suggests that the music in A&F facilitates self-projection; hence, "individuals may engage in activities that permit them to self-project into a particular role or character," which may in turn "help them construct fantasies and augment reality" (Hirschman, 1983, p. 64). Thus, A&F's music enables customers to project themselves from the immediate present in the store to alternative times, places, and perspectives. That function is dependent on the preceding transfers from the public sphere and the private realm. The use of preexisting songs enables customers to project themselves into the past. For example, the song "Never Gonna Give You Up" may prompt customers to listen with a sense of nostalgia and associations with personal memories. Moreover, the store's musical style allows customers to project themselves into future settings where such music will be heard. For example, when a person thinks of spending a night out with friends, he or she projects him- or herself into the future and another setting (e.g., a nightclub). Similarly, A&F's music is used to project oneself into the setting in which the clothes are expected to pass the following test: "do the clothes 'resonate' and 'sound' right?" (for a similar analysis based on interviews with customers, see DeNora & Belcher, 1999). Moreover, customers can imagine themselves "clubbing in Barcelona" (as specified in the song Barcelona), thereby imagining (homo)erotic fantasies s(t)imulated by the alluring models and, in particular, the naked torsos of young men. In addition, the pervasiveness of musical covers or hypertexts means that the first-person singular is occasionally relatively vague. For example, this vagueness arises when a comparatively anonymous singer substitutes for the celebrated Rick Astley. As a type of open (or blurred) space (Iser, 1974), the first-person singular is then prone to be filled (or made distinct) by self-projecting customers. For example, customers can project themselves into a third-person perspective while placing the assistant in the first-person perspective. This type of projection is facilitated by the intimacy described in the songs, and the projection is further stimulated by the assistants' constant greetings. The music is then used as a resource to create an imaginary close and intimate, albeit momentary, relationship with the assistants while moving around the store. The darkened environment and the pervasive perfume effectively set the scene for customers to imagine intimate relations.

The preceding sections can help illustrate that music in commercials presents a particular type of advertising music. For example, normally a visit to a store will result in prolonged bodily experiences with whole pieces of music compared to the more transitory exposure to music(al excerpts and appetizers) in commercials. This arguably implies that, although not irrelevant for the understanding of the functions of music in commercials, listeners are more disposed to rhythmic entrainment in stores than in front of the television. The examination of sounds on websites has additionally made clear that music in commercials occur independently of user activity (apart from tuning in, that is); on websites, music and other sounds usually appear because of a user's activity most significantly in the user modes of navigating and editing. This illustrates a characteristic feature of music in commercials. Whereas users visit a website or a store, that is, users "arrive there" to for example search and browse, viewers are "confronted by" commercials that usually appear uninvited and hence in a sense unexpected. In other worlds, the "outside world" of products and brands seek out the viewer, whereas the user seeks out products and brands on websites and in stores. The process of "seeking out" viewers implies that significant functions of music in commercials are to contribute to attract the attention of and making contact with viewers who are neither "on" (a website) or "in" (a store), but merely "in front of" (a screen).

In addition to the chapter's previous discussion on commercials as a specific type of communication, and how music in commercials compares to music in other types of television programs, this illustrates that music in commercials is subjected to a particular type of pressure. Music in commercials has to contribute to, for example, compete with other (music from other) commercials and (the music of) other types of programming during the television flow. This particular pressure partly lays the foundation for the presentation of the formats and functions of music in commercials in the second part of the book. To approach an understanding of how music in commercials functions, that is, what the music "does" in commercials, it is thus necessary to have considered the relevant "duties" developed by this particular pressure.

The first part of the book has hence "set the scene" (or, perhaps more appropriate, the screen) for an examination of music in commercials from a cotextual perspective. The first part of the book has thus specified aspects of the "natural habit" of music in commercials, that is, some of its living and environmental conditions. Specifically, the first part of the book has illustrated how music in commercials is situated in an environment of various musical expressions, advertised products, and media settings. In Chapter 2, "Transtextuality: Preexisting and Original Music," I have specified how to analyze the relations between music in a commercial and music from

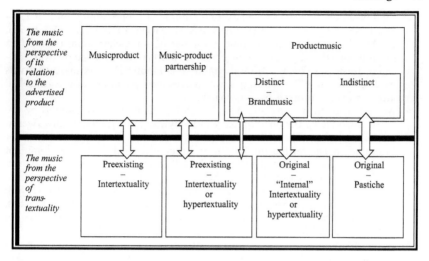

Figure 4.2 Overview of music in commercials from the perspectives of transtextuality and relation between music and product (the narrow arrow indicates that this particular relation is less prevalent)

outside the commercial. From this perspective, we can learn that music in commercials does not exist in a musical "vacuum" and that the relations to music from outside the commercial for example lay the foundation for the music's contribution to processes signification in the commercial. In Chapter 3 "Marketing: Music and Products," I have specified how music in commercials relates to marketing and products outside the universe of the commercial. From this perspective, we can learn that music in commercials can relate to products categories in various ways, and that music can play different roles in the context of marketing. We also learned that the distinctions of music from the perspective of its relationhip to the advertised product appear to correspond to the distinctions of music from the perspective of transtextuality. Figure 4.2 provides an overview of some of the most significant relations.

The following second part of the book takes a closer look at how musical signification, structures, and functions can manifest in commercials.

NOTES

1. See, for example, www.youtube.com/user/Apple.
2. For a study that examines music as the apparent "key ingredient" of television, see Linz (1985). Linz distinguishes between three categories of programs based on how music is situated within a program, that is, music programs, programs with music, and programs about music. Interestingly, the proportion of music that qualifies for one of the three categories amounts to less than 10% of the

total programming time based on two months of programming time in 1984 and 1985 on three German channels (ARD1, ARD3, ZDF; Linz, 1985, p. 92).

3. In Danish television, an example is the use of somewhat sophisticated jazz grooves for DR2 (by Thomas Blachman). Another Danish example was "calendar music" (1970–1973) by the modern composer Per Nørgaard that was used on DR1 in 1973. This music was played during pauses but was cancelled after a storm of protests by angry viewers.

4. According to Brownrigg and Meech (2002), this music was inspired by the music introducing the film company in Hollywood movies (especially Twentieth Century Fox). The authors argued that this fanfare was replaced by softer "fun-fair" music during the 1980s, and they identified three new dominant forms of sound in channel idents in the UK: a softer musical style, a dance-music style, and the use of sound effects other than music.

5. For research on music in radio commercials, see, for example, Julien (1985); Sewall and Sarel (1986); Blair and Shimp (1992); Berland (1993); Kellaris, Cox, and Cox (1993); Brooker and Wheatley (1994); Olsen (1995); Roehm (2001); Zhu and Meyers-Levy (2005); and Björnberg (2009).

6. Additionally, only a few experimental studies on the use of sound and music in web ads exist; for rare examples, see Cheng, Wu, and Yen (2008); and Redker and Gibson (2009).

7. See Nielsen's list of the most-hated advertising techniques on the Internet. Automatically activated sound is rated very negatively (see www.useit.com/alertbox/20041206.html).

8. See: www.apple.com/dk/ and www.apple.com/.

9. The websites were assessed via this link: www.aboutmcdonalds.com/mcd/country/map.html.

10. For studies of the appearance and functions of music in computer games, see, for example, Collins (2008).

11. Retrieved from: www.mustang.dk.

12. As indicated in the introduction, two research paradigms have emerged within the field of music in advertising, which also applies to music in stores and service settings. For qualitative-oriented studies within musicology, social theory, and communication studies, see, for example, MacLeod (1979), Radano (1989), Jones and Schumacher (1992), Tyler (1992), Groom (1996), Sterne (1997), DeNora and Belcher (1999), Lanza (2004), Owen (2006), Forsyth and Cloonan (2008), and Kassabian (2013b). For quantitative, experiment-oriented studies within (social) psychology, market, business and consumer research, see, for example, the following reviews: Turley and Milliman (2000), Oakes (2000), Lam (2001), North and Hargreaves (2006), Garlin and Owen (2006), and Allan (2007b). See also Areni (2003a, 2003b) for studies of managers' (implicit) theories of how music affects physical commercial settings.

13. The following observations from A&F are based on my own exploratory and open-ended observations on June 1, 2011, and November 14, 2011, in the Copenhagen store and on August 3, 2011, in the London store. My own observations are supplemented by published observations by market analytics, journalists, and former assistants (see Anthes, 2010; Barreneche, 2006; Mitchelson, 2007; Schonberger, 2011) and by videofilms from within several A&F stores on YouTube (e.g., www.youtube.com/watch?v=yoka8Xfl1ts and www.youtube.com/watch?v=-nKM3Z7oI2Y&feature=related). See Graakjær (2012) for a more detailed examination of the particular case from the perspective of critical discourse analysis.

14. The music has been chosen by Randy Schläger of the American retail-environment company DMX (see www.dmx.com/services/music/designer-profiles/randy-schlager and www.anfplaylists.com/about). For examples

of the music played at A&F, see BWO's "Barcelona" (www.youtube.com/watch?v=IDt-CoMY1cc) and a cover of Rick Astley's "Never Gonna Give You Up" by Audiostarz (featuring Pablo Cepeda) (www.youtube.com/watch?v=RlGs6X9Ue2g).

15. This metaphor is inspired by Goffman (1983), who uses it to indicate permeability in the relationship between the interaction and institutional order.
16. Apparently, the musical membrane is accompanied by other types of implicit selection criteria. For example, disabled people in wheelchairs cannot move around in the store because of its narrow corridors and lack of escalators. A&F has also been associated with explicit discrimination in relation to both the hiring and firing of assistants (Pidd, 2009). Even media personas have been subjected to A&F's selection processes (and innovative branding strategies; Clifford, 2011).
17. The following is based on personal observations in the Apple store in Barcelona in the afternoon of April 25, 2014.
18. This is quite literally true of the song "Summer Girls" by LFO (released in 1999), which features the brand name prominently in the chorus ("I like girls that wear Abercrombie and Fitch"; see Gregorio & Sung, 2009). Currently, A&F is marketing 'its' music on YouTube by providing playlists of the store's music accompanied by promotional footage (see, e.g., www.youtube.com/user/anfplaylists#p/u).

Part II
Cotextual Perspectives

In the second part of the book, I examine music from "within" a commercial, and I focus on how music relates to the other textual elements of the commercial. Figure B.1 illustrates that in this part of this book, the cotextual perspective is foregrounded, while the contextual perspective presented in the first part of this book is backgrounded.

To introduce the perspectives of the second part of this book, I begin by reconsidering the communicative genre of advertising (see Chapter 4) now with a focus on the formats that emerge as a result of the commercial's cotextual organization. Subsequently, I reconsider the Apple/The Blue Van case from the perspective of cotextuality. I concentrate on the music "seen," including a focus on how the music is organized in relation to the visual text elements of the commercial. In the succeeding three chapters, I (a) discuss the issue of musical signification with a particular focus on how music relates to other text elements, (b) present the typical structures of music in

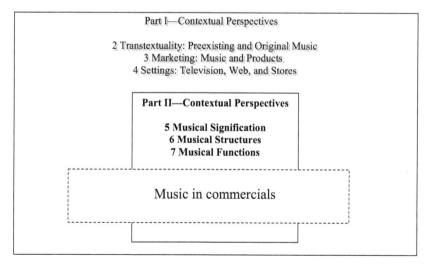

Part I—Contextual Perspectives

2 Transtextuality: Preexisting and Original Music
3 Marketing: Music and Products
4 Settings: Television, Web, and Stores

Part II—Contextual Perspectives

5 Musical Signification
6 Musical Structures
7 Musical Functions

Music in commercials

Figure B.1   An illustration of the primary focus of the second part of this book commercials, and (c) examine the variety of functions that music serves in commercials.

To introduce to the genre formats of commercials, I include the categorization presented by Stigel (2001), which is based on how the viewer is addressed and positioned. Although music has not played a significant role in the construction of this categorization, the categorization is clearly relevant to understanding musical structures and functions in commercials (see Chapters 6 and 7).

On the most general level, Stigel (2001) distinguishes two modes of address. First, viewers can be addressed in a direct and factional way, and three formats are specified: presenter, testimonial, and voice-over. Second, viewers can be addressed in an indirect and fictional way via two formats: drama and montage. A sixth format, voice-over+, includes features of both types.

The factional formats address viewers directly, and it is immediately evident that "somebody from the commercial" wants to inform, demonstrate, document, or persuade them. Somebody, an "I," is thus presented, and the viewer is addressed in the second person, "you," in various forms of simulated interaction (see, e.g., Horton & Wohl, 1956): the situations are presented as a shared "here and now" and in the co-presence of something being shown and said. The factional formats differ in how the "I" is presented. In the *presenter* format, the "I" is presented visually. The "I," an alleged representative of the producer, addresses the viewer through direct eye contact while the advertised product is presented both visually and verbally. In the *testimonial* format, the "I" provides a testimonial to the camera. The "I," an alleged "representative" of product users, addresses the viewer either through direct eye contact—a typical setup for a *celebrity endorser*—or through "indirect" contact—that is, making eye contact with an unseen interviewer positioned adjacent to the camera. The voice of the presenter and the testimonial—sometimes in the form of singing apparently not uncommon for commercials in the 1950s and 1960s (see Kilpiö, 2001; Rodman, 2010)—are both diegetic; that is, the voice originates "from the story world of the text itself" so that the voice is apparently heard by both actors and television listeners (Rodman, 2010, p. 53). In the *voice-over* format, the "I" is presented auditively and is "hidden" from the screen. The voiceover is thus intradiegetic in that it "calls attention to the characters, emotions, settings, and objects in the diegesis without actually being *in* the diegesis" (Rodman, 2010, p. 54).

These formats not only illustrate dissimilar "carriers" or "containers" of content but also present an implicit meta-message along these lines: "Hey, listen up. I am addressing you right now. I am here to inform you about something exceptional and important, and I want you to take specific action as soon as possible." These factual formats bear an obvious resemblance to factual television programming formats, and a news program would normally illustrate all three modes of address. For example, similar to the role of a news presenter, the trustworthiness and authority of the "I" is crucial to the ability of the factual format to document and persuade viewers.

As indicated, voice-over+ presents a mixture of both factual and fictional aspects. Similar to the voice-over format, the direct aspect is anchored in the speaking voice. However, contrary to the voice-over format, the visual part does not merely portray what is being said. In fact, the visuals have a life of their own, and the two levels interact to produce a third level to be inferred, hence the adfix "+": "The voiceover+ format consciously exploits the semantic differences, the disparities and different capacities of the symbolic systems (visual and verbal, abstract terms vs. concrete exemplars) in order to produce structured gaps and imbalances to be filled out for the audience" (Stigel, 2001, 334). From the perspective of music use, a type of "+" function arises when commercials include excerpts from a piece of pre-existing music with lyrics that do not have any obvious relation to the visual dimension of the commercial. Often in such cases, the viewer must fill in the gap or combine the two (music and visuals). The deployment of "There Goes My Love" in the Apple commercial presents an example of what could be termed a "musicover+."

The necessity for viewers to become involved (i.e., to infer and experience meaning) generally characterizes the fictional formats. Apart from the possible accompanying music, there are no intradiegetic constituents that explain or specify what is being shown in such a commercial. The two fictional formats differ according to the following dimensions. In the *drama* format, a story is performed by characters in relation to other characters or phenomena within the universe of the story. The performance unfolds in a (row of) scene(s) or a setup and is structured by the laws of narrative and continuity. The viewer must infer what is occurring by activating expectations and schemata for situations, scripts, characters, settings, and cause-and-effect rules. The viewer is thus encouraged "to participate in the little story being played out on the screen" (Rutherford, 1994, p. 69). In the *montage* format, a lyrical, associative, and thematic organization is presented based on repetition and formal sameness/opposition (regarding, e.g., characters, settings, lights, shapes, colors). The montage creates a universe of emotion and original impressions through rhythmic and visual linking and through the organization of visual material and music.

The fictional formats also imply a specific meta-message: "Actually, I'm not really addressing you. You are supposed to experience and figure out yourself what is meant. Kindly and discreetly . . ." Fictional formats may lead viewers to experience "a little jolt of pleasure . . . from working out the mystery of what the ad wants to say" (Rutherford, 1994, p. 69). The fictional formats bear some resemblance to other types of television content, such as films (drama) and music videos (montage; see Englis, 1990), although music videos in particular come in many forms other than montages (see, e.g., Frith, 1988 and more recently Korsgaard, 2013; Vernallis, 2013).

Since TV 2 first began the national transmission, commercials have become increasingly aestheticized: "The aspect of 'the how' of communication tends to predominate 'the what' of communication," and the aesthetic aspects "predominate other aspects such as the referential or informative" (Stigel, 2001, p. 329). Conceivably, this development reflects the pressure that commercials are placed under in their immediate environment (see also Chapter 4): Commercials appear en bloc—that is, together with other commercials—and as a break from regular programming, typically for a period of 3 to 5 minutes. The commercials are not announced on television listings; however, "bumpers" (see the following discussion) announce the coming (and ending) of a commercial break during the flow. This break appears either during programs or between programs; because of national legislation, the latter has been characteristic of commercials on Danish TV 2.

The aesthetization tendency generally manifests in a commercial's appeal to and reliance on viewers' active experience, including their imagination and preknowledge. It is doubtful whether this development reflects a universal trend, but the type of aesthetization described here has been observed in other European countries (see, e.g., Kloepfer & Landbeck, 1991). Simultaneously, commercials in the United States appear to have been dominated by factual formats (i.e., "lectures," see Wells, 1989). In Danish commercials in particular, "several concepts within the formats of drama and montage were maintained, varied and elaborated during the 1990s" (Stigel, 2006, p. 313). Most significant, an increase in the voice-over+ format has been observed. In association with these developments, the average duration of commercials has increased from approximately 10 to 15 seconds to approximately 25 to 30 seconds (Stigel, 2006, p. 313).[1] Although the duration itself is not necessarily indicative of aesthetization, longer commercials have greater potential for the presentation, variation, and elaboration of formats and modes of address. For example, in view of the previous discussion on the placement of music in commercials, the presentation of musical excerpts and highlights (e.g., excerpts from both the verse and the chorus) requires time. In addition, commercials have increasingly begun to refer to their own established symbols, canons, and phrases, thus expressing a type of meta-communication and self-referentiality (Stigel, 2006, p. 315ff.; see also L. Christensen, 2001); for an example of this phenomenon, see the description of the Orange commercial in Chapter 2. Arguably, the channel can also contribute to these developments. For example, commercials are rated and awarded various prizes, and viewers are explicitly encouraged to vote for the best commercials (see, e.g., Morgan, 2012).

THE APPLE/THE BLUE VAN CASE—II

When examining the cotextualization of the music in a commercial, one may find it useful to create an overview of the commercial. Table B.1 presents such an overview of the commercial for the Apple/The Blue Van case. The table highlights the sequential organization of the text elements of the commercial, and I suggest that this overview can serve as a model for

Table B.1   Outline of iPad commercial featuring excerpts from "There Goes My Love" (adapted from Graakjær 2014)

Episode	Demonstration	Announcement		
Seconds	0–25	26–27	28	29–30
Shot	0–21	22	23	24
Visuals	A montage of 21 shots of an iPad handled repeatedly by at least two different adult users (i.e., a male and a female).	A black iPad on a white background is presented via slow camera movement (i.e., a dolly in) toward the iPad. The illustration of iPad functions is accelerated.	The text "April 3" appears quickly, first in blurred, enlarged type at the periphery of the screen and then in medium-sized, sharpened type at the center of the screen, written in black letters on a white background.	The text/ graphic "[Apple logo] iPad" is presented.
Music(no other sounds)	Excerpts (see A.2) of the intro and verse of "There Goes My Love."	An excerpt from the chorus of "There Goes My Love."		

other commercials, although other commercials might necessitate modification (e.g., an additional row to include the possible appearances of "object sounds" and voiceovers). Table B.1 presents a rough outline of the commercial, which should be supplemented with (a) an actual viewing of the commercial, (b) other tables (see Tables A.2 and 5.1), and (c) the more detailed descriptions that follow.

As indicated in Table B.1, the commercial includes two primary episodes: the "demonstration" and the "announcement." During the 21 shots of the demonstration, a computer tablet is seen being repeatedly handled by adult users sitting on a chair at a table in what appears to be a living room. The first shot shows the tablet on a table, and a person picks up the tablet. Based on its design, the tablet is recognizable as an Apple product. The users are anonymous: the tablet is presented primarily in close-up shots from the users' point of view (POV). The handling of the tablet includes various fingertip movements. For example, the users' fingertips tap, swipe, drag, pinch and flick on the screen. The users' handling causes the iPad's content to change rapidly. For example, during the 21 shots of the demonstration, users are portrayed as managing websites, books, pictures, films, and e-mails. Whereas the setting of the users and the iPad presents continuous visual elements throughout the 21 shots, different users handle the iPad at different times. As indicated by their different clothing, at least two different users (a male and a female) appear. There is no further visual anchoring of time, place, or narrative. During the three shots of the announcement, the setting changes from what appears to be a living room to a white background that is unspecified in terms of time and space. Against this background, a tablet is first displayed free from users' handling. The tablet is presented via slow camera movement (i.e., a dolly in) toward the tablet, and the illustration of iPad functions is greatly accelerated to the point that the viewers cannot distinguish among the specific types of content on display. Second, the date "April 3" is shown. Initially, the text appears blurred in enlarged type at the periphery of the screen; subsequently, it appears in medium-sized, sharpened black type at the center of the screen. Underneath this text, another line of text ("Apps from App store") is announced in small gray type. Third, the Apple logo is revealed in combination with a name (iPad) in the same medium-sized, sharpened black type as the date.

In view of the commercial formats presented previously, the Apple/The Blue Van case presents a montage. The organization of the commercial as a "demonstration" episode is largely based on repetition and the formal sameness of, for example, the characters' handling of the device and the setting. There is no narrative structure and no explicating voiceover. The viewer must infer that (a) the users' handling of the tablet presents a host of functions of the tablet, (b) the tablet is a new Apple product, (c) April 3 is the product release date, and (d) iPad is the product's name. To most viewers, this inference would not have been troublesome. At the time, Apple had already built a reputation for announcing products before they were available, and various (commercial and user-generated) discourses from outside the universe of that particular commercial had plausibly already paved the way for interest in a "forthcoming product by Apple" by the name of "iPad."

On the surface, the music may appear to contrast with the demonstration. For example, the clothing and the setting do not reflect the hair and clothing style that are normally associated with the musical style presented by "There Goes My Love." Additionally, the pictures are displayed in a bright, clear style that appears to contrast with the rough sound quality of the distorted guitar and the almost screaming quality of the lead singer's voice. However, the music intersects with the visuals in various other detailed ways, and the following observations can be made.

On the most general level, the music binds together the frequent visual cuts and assists in the production of two main episodes. Thus, the music's introduction and verse are heard as a user (followed by other users) picks up and handles the iPad (see shot 0–21 in Table B.1), and the chorus co-occurs with the announcement (see shot 22–24). The fast pace of the iPad's changing contents parallels the relatively busy groove and high density of the musical impulses. Furthermore, the relatively fast-paced shot cutting is concurrent with the relatively busy style of the music, and the acceleration—fast-forward motion—of the presentation of the iPad content (see shot 22) is concurrent with a drum roll that is also in synch with a dolly in. There are no obvious synch points between the cuts and the musical beat until the cut to the last shot (from 23 to 24), which is remarkably in synch with the musical break. Additionally, the first beat of the bar tends to synch with the movement of the user's hand and with the changes on the iPad display. For example, a sliding finger movement is in synch with the hook line "There goes . . ." at the point of transition to the chorus.

Except at the beginning of the commercial, vocal phrases with lyrics prevail; throughout the commercial, specific words co-occur with specific content on the iPad and aspects of the users' handling of the iPad. A POV of the iPad in close-up from the users' perspective is predominant (21 of 24 shots), and the music is consistently heard at a high level throughout. From the production perspective, the music is clearly intradiegetic. For example, the music develops in an even rhythmic flow that is unaffected by the frequent cuts of the diegesis. However, the close-up of both the POV and the point of audition (POA) may suggest that the music is actually heard (as a private diegetic feature) by iPad users (see the following discussion).

The lyrics of the song appear to present a highly significant musical contribution to the commercial message. As indicated previously, the original lyrics strongly suggest a particular type of relationship and interaction, but the actual cotextualization of the lyrics appears to afford a more circumscribed variety of possible readings. A decisive visual feature in this respect is the prevalent first-person POV that allows the viewer to identify with or self-project into the user perspective. By introducing the open spaces of "I" and "You," the lyrics thus offer two possible positions into which viewers can project themselves (Hirschman, 1983).

When the viewer is positioned as "you," the lyrics function as a type of voice- or musicover that comments on the visual presentation of the ongoing "viewer activities." Apple, representing "I," identifies the viewer as having the potential to become "the charming type." Consequently, the process of becoming a charming type is presented by the call to prepare ("take off your gloves," "I'll have an answer," and "close your eyes") to handle the iPad ("I'll let you try")—which is aptly illustrated by the users' bare hands and fingers. The hook line "There Goes My Love" functions as a declaration of love while implying some other type of user activity. "There goes" both suggests that the users have learned the craft of handling the iPad and suggests that the users are going "there" (i.e., to an Apple Store) on April 3. In this reading, the viewer is generally positioned as highly individualized ("you"), as privileged ("let you try"), as lovable ("my love"), and as intensely enjoying the product ("close your eyes").

When the viewer is positioned as "I," the lyrics function as a type of internally oriented music directed toward him or her ("be the charming type" and "take off your gloves") or toward Apple/the iPad ("be the charming type" and "my love"). Thus, the first-person POV is arguably accompanied by a first-person POA. The latter is offered by the constantly high volume of music and by the synch points between the users' finger movements and the musical beat (see Table 5.1). Additionally, the phrase "I'll have an answer" is concurrent with the shots of the user apparently using his or her email on the iPad. These features appear to suggest that the user is hearing the music through the iPad (or perhaps an iPod). In other words, the music may appear to be a (private) diegetic feature of the presented universe, although the constant volume and the even rhythmic flow of the music do not strictly match the frequent cuts of the moving images and do not correspond to the rapid switching of the users who are presented visually. Again, the hook line is a declaration of love—but it is inverted: "I love Apple/the iPad." The almost-screaming vocal quality and high-pitched melody suggest a deeply felt, exalted declaration. Additionally, the phrase "there goes" implies that the iPad functions well and that it will be available on April 3 for "me" to have.

The two possible viewer positions illustrate the various potential significations that the lyrics of the song bring to the commercial. The lyrics present a symbolic resource that viewers can use to make sense of the commercial. Because the lyrics and their relationship with the visual presentation are ambiguous, viewers can alternate between positions and even construct alternative significations. For example, viewers may interpret "There Goes My Love" as Apple's ("my") presentation of "the little precious new iPad" ("love") ready to stand on its own feet. However, the positioning of the viewer as either "I" or "you" appears to be the most significant. Both positions imply an intimate emotional relationship between the viewer and Apple/the iPad. The illusion of intimacy is further fueled by the depiction of the iPad in human terms and the persistent "caress" of the users' fingers.

In summary, the particular fit between the music and the moving pictures characterizes the imaginative users, the brand, and the product (see more in chapter 5).

The account of the specific cotextualization of (the excerpts from) "There Goes My Love" indicates that although the song provides the only sounds in the commercial, it actually appears disconnected from the visual setting. First, the music is not explicitly presented by the band members performing the song, as was the case when the music video for Feist's "1, 2, 3, 4" was excerpted in a commercial for the iPod Nano. Arguably, highlighting the performer of the music in a music video places the artist and the song in an appealing position in the commercial (for a similar reading, see DiCrescenzo, 2011). Second, the music of The Blue Van is only vaguely integrated into the visual setting as a (private) diegetic feature. By contrast, in the commercial featuring Jet's "Are U Gonna Be My Girl," the song makes a much more pronounced appearance as an observable private diegetic feature. In that commercial, black silhouettes of human beings dance to music that is unmistakably ringing in their ears through an iPod. In that case, the iPod users are effectively embodying the act of listening to the song.

The music thus plays an essential part in establishing a visual style in the commercials with Jet and Feist through the dancing bodies and the excerpt from the music video, respectively. Because the use of music (for listening and dancing) and mediation (a music video) are explicitly demonstrated, viewers are strongly encouraged to engage with the music, its creators, and its users. No such encouragement occurs during the iPad commercial. Additionally, although "There Goes My Love" intersects with the visual structure, the music appears to be only marginally related to the product and to the Apple brand. Although the iPad is not primarily a technology for music reproduction, The Blue Van's music could have been presented during the iPad commercial as a product. In fact, music is only marginally illustrated through the iPad via a glimpse of a Doors album cover toward the end of the montage. If the commercial is understood as a type of "iPad demonstration video"—a reading encouraged by the visual demonstration of the iPad functions—then the music may even be distracting to viewers who are attempting to determine the iPad's functions.

From a text analytical perspective, the inexplicit, somewhat disconnected and perhaps even distracting appearance of "There Goes My Love" in the iPad commercial may help to explain why The Blue Van did not benefit from its relationship with Apple. At a minimum, this case illustrates how commercially promising, far-reaching distribution with a prestigious brand cannot alone predict the subsequent effects of music placement. Moreover, this case illustrates that collaboration between corporate brands and musical artists—what may appear to be a "happy marriage"—is actually characterized by a power imbalance. As this case shows, "brands today are in a position to set the terms, the rules, and the price" (Meier, 2011, p. 402) in licensing contracts. This case also illustrates how bonding with a brand can lead to textual restructuring of the music placed in a commercial. Rather than appearing "perfectly clean" as envisioned by the band, the music in the commercial is "tainted" by the selection, reorganization, and visualization of the musical episodes, which can result in changing the (potential) meaning of the lyrics. Thus, Apple is not merely responsible for *placing* the song in the commercial; Apple is *producing* a particular version of the song through the commercial. The particular version of the song allows Apple to appeal to viewers and potential iPad users on an intimate level by suggesting an emotional relationship, whereas the viewers' relationship with The Blue Van is depicted as more shallow—the band is "used and thrown away" as Apple continues to search for more esoteric and unspoiled tracks.

NOTE

1. This argument is based on samples of unique commercials broadcast for the first time. Conceivably, samples of commercials based on actual broadcasting (including repetitions and hence doublets) would paint a somewhat different picture. Furthermore, recent developments may have laid a foundation for shorter commercials (see, e.g., Anand, 2013; Fredrix, 2010).

5 Musical Signification

The preceding case analysis has highlighted a number of relationships between the music and the visual elements of the Apple/The Blue Van case. In this chapter, I examine these relations from a theoretical perspective. I introduce the issue of musical signification in commercials (i.e., the processes of signification that include music). Musical signification is complex, and this book does not propose to present and discuss musical signification in general. I agree with N. Cook (2001), who does "not mean to imply that there should, or could, be a grand unifying theory of musical meaning" (p. 176). In the following, I highlight perspectives that I find particularly helpful for understanding musical signification in commercials. The purpose is to outline how the process of signification of music in commercials can be understood as "at the same time irreducibly cultural *and* intimately related to its structural properties" (N. Cook, 2001, pp. 173–174). Following this position, it would be misleading to think of music as "*having* particular meanings";[1] rather, music "has the potential for specific meanings to emerge under specific circumstances" (N. Cook, 2001, p. 181). From the perspective of this book, such "circumstances" include the "context" (as announced in the introduction and examined in the first part of this book) and the "cotext" (the subject of this second part of this book), and commercials present a "specific" circumstance for the process of musical signification.

Theoretically, this portion of the book is informed by what I view as supplementary approaches to the textual analysis of popular music and audiovisual media, most notably, the approaches of Middleton, Cook, and Tagg and Clarida. Although Middleton focuses on auditory texts, I am inspired to consider both primary and secondary aspects of signification in analyzing the audiovisual text of a commercial.[2] Following Cook, who focuses on the analysis of "musical multimedia," I am primarily inspired to examine "iconic relationships" (N. Cook, 1998, p. 76) between music and motion pictures at the level of primary signification (additionally, Cook's perspective is arguably relevant to the examination of secondary signification; see the following disucssion). Furthermore, I include a sign typology developed by Philip Tagg from studies of music in television series to account for secondary signification (Middleton, 1990; Tagg, 2013).

In the work of Middleton (1990), primary and secondary signification is offered as an alternative for two related concepts (i.e., denotation and connotation) originating from the study of linguistic signification. Whereas denotation and connotation apply to the analysis of symbols of language, these concepts (particularly denotation) appear to be unsuitable for the study of musical signification: "denotation in the sense in which the term is used in linguistics is rare in music . . . there is no system of objective references to concepts and perceptions concerning the 'outside world'" (Middleton, 1990, p. 220). As Middleton concludes, "to avoid any difficulties attaching to the term 'denotation,' let us call this ground [structural semantics implicated in the musical form itself] the level of primary signification" (1990, p. 200).

5.1   PRIMARY AUDIOVISUAL SIGNIFICATION

Analysis at the level of primary signification is concerned with "structure, which is closely tied to the syntactic form" (Middleton, 1990, p. 222). The analysis further refers to "a 'structural semantics,' which would consider the meaning of units and parameters in terms of their relationships with other units and parameters and in terms of their positions on various 'axes' referring to binary oppositions or continua" (Middleton, 1990, p. 222). In the context of audiovisual analysis, "oppositions or continua" and "relationships of units and parameters" are examined at the intersection of music and moving pictures. Inspired by Cook (1998), this analysis of intersections is primarily guided by a search for "iconic relationships"—a type of relationship that "in multimedia overwhelmingly outnumbers others, and of these by far the most important are those that involve time" (p. 76). For example, Chion (2009) has highlighted synch points as "a moment in an audiovisual sequence where there is a marked synchronous encounter between a sound event and a visual element . . . The frequency and placement of synch points . . . help create meaning" (p. 268). N. Cook offers the more wide-ranging concept of a "parallelism of process" to highlight this "most perceptible and immediate of all cross-media configurations" (1998, p. 77). A temporal perspective is highly relevant to the textual examination of audiovisual texts: "Synchronization is an absolutely central element in achieving congruency between sound and image and thus is crucial in achieving the dramatic effects of the synergy of sound and image" (Donnelly, 2014, p. 25). Furthermore, this perspective appears to be particularly relevant to the study of television commercials, which are "just about the most temporally constrained form of artistic production in existence" and must therefore "exploit the most efficient means of communicating meaning fast" (N. Cook, 1998, p. 16ff.; see also Chapter 4). Through the temporal alignment of the two media, it is suggested that specific aspects of the music and the moving pictures belong together. N. Cook emphasizes the importance of the level and type of analysis: "The starting point for analyzing musical multimedia . . . is similarity" (1998, p. 80). Cook's approach in this respect is arguably consistent with Middleton's suggestion that we avoid "rush[ing] to interpretation" at the level of secondary signification (Middleton, 1990, p. 220; see also N. Cook, 2001, p. 173).

To generate this level of analysis, I provide a framework that is illustrated in Table 5.1. Table B.1 presented the structure of the commercial from a time-based perspective, whereas Table 5.1 specifies the structural relationship between music and the moving pictures based on five dimensions or "axes."[3] Whereas the five visual dimensions (presented in the left column of Table 5.1) appear to be relatively discrete, an auditory expression (presented

Table 5.1 Intersections at the level of primary audiovisual signification as exemplified by the Apple/The Blue Van case (adapted from Graakjær 2014)

Visual dimensions	Observations of intersections	Auditory dimensions
Content	Generally, the fast pace of the iPad's changing contents corresponds to the relatively busy groove and high density of musical impulses.	Sound structures
	Except at the beginning, vocal phrases with lyrics prevail; throughout the commercial, specific words co-occur with specific content on the iPad and aspects of the users' handling of the iPad.	
	The first beat of the bar tends to synch with the movement of the user's hand and the changes on the iPad display. A sliding finger movement is in synch with the hook line "There goes . . ." at the point of transition to the chorus.	
	The acceleration—fast-forward motion—of the presentation of the iPad content (see Shot 22 in Table B.1) is concurrent with a drum roll.	
Camera movement	There is no camera movement apart from the *dolly* in on the acceleration of the iPad activity and the functions on display (see Shot 22 in Table B.1). The *dolly* in is concurrent with a drum roll.	Sound movements and developments
Picture perspective (point of view POV)	A close-up POV of the iPad from the user perspective is predominant (21 out of 25 shots), and the music is heard at a consistently high level throughout. From the production perspective, the music is clearly intradiegetic, although the close-up of both the POV and POA could suggest that the music is actually heard (as a private diegetic feature) by the iPad users.	Sound perspective (point of audition/POA)

(*Continued*)

Table 5.1   (Continued)

Visual dimensions	Observations of intersections	Auditory dimensions
Sequencing of shots	Relatively fast-paced shot cutting (typical of the montage format)[1] is concurrent with the relatively busy style of the music. There are no obvious synch points between the cuts and the musical beat until the cut to the last shot (from 23 to 24, s Table B.1), which is remarkably in synch with the musical break. As examples of parallelism of processes, the intro and verse are concurrent with a user picking up and handling the iPad (see the diegetic episode shot 0–21 in Table B.1), and the chorus concurs with the section presenting the brand information (see the non-diegetic episode Shots 22–24 in Table B.1)	Sequencing of sound structures
Picture/ visual quality	Pictures are displayed in a bright and clear style that appears to contrast with the distorted and rough sound quality of the distorted guitar and the almost-screaming quality of the lead singer's voice	Sound quality

[1] A total of 21 shots occur in 25 seconds, with an average shot length of 1.19 seconds, which is less than average according to existing analyses of larger samples of commercials, for example, MacRury (2009, p. 226).

in the right column) may intersect with multiple visual dimensions. Thus, there are no unambiguous analogies that describe the relationship between visual and auditory expressions. At a minimum, the present framework does not pretend to provide this type of analogy; instead, its aim is more modest in stimulating analytical observations. The table may also be interpreted as a response to Cook's apparent invitation to "find a systematic way of modelling the relationship between music and pictures" at the level of "interplay of structurally congruent media" (1998, p. 159).

In Table 5.1 I present what I believe are the most significant interplays or intersections at this level of analysis.[4] The left and right columns present the corresponding audio and visual dimensions, respectively, whereas in the center column, I insert the observations made during the previous account of the Apple/The Blue Van case.

Table 5.1 aims to examine the relationships between the visual and auditory dimensions of the commercial. The table certainly appears capable of representing a case such as the Apple/The Blue Van case. However, in most other commercials, the auditory dimension is not exclusively musical: Other types of sound will appear, including speech and voice-over. Table 5.1 should thus indicate the possible appearances of different types of sounds, and a closer examination of the auditory cotextualization of music would require an examination of the more detailed intersections of music and object sounds, for example. One approach to addressing this issue would be to examine the intersections of music and voice-over based on the dimensions listed in the right column. This examination could include the sequential interactions between sounds as well as the layering of sounds. I will return to exploring the relationships between sounds with respect to commutation tests (see also Chapter 6 on musical structures).

5.2   SECONDARY AUDIOVISUAL SIGNIFICATION

The intersections observed in Table 5.1 illustrate how the specific excerpts of a piece of preexisting music can be organized in the visual setting of a commercial. Such intersections help to propel secondary signification—music-based associations to nonmusical structures (Middleton, 1990, p. 220ff.) that are occasionally referred to as "meaning." As indicated in the introduction to this chapter, the relationship between primary and secondary signification is not unambiguous. For example, Middleton (1990) observes that "on the one hand, a single 'connotater' may be made up of several signs on the primary level. On the other hand, whatever the size of a connotater, its content (what is connotated) is always, in theory, of infinite size: that is, the range of possible associations is endless" (p. 233). Although what is connoted is theoretically endless, the given "circumstances" (i.e., the context and cotexts of music) appear to afford a more circumscribed variety of possible meanings, which is arguably referenced by Middleton as follows: "It seems likely, that in practice there are, inscribed in the musical form and in its cultural history, *limits* to the transmutation of meaning" (Middleton, 1990, p. 54; see also N. Cook, 2001, p. 177). Rodman (2010) makes a related point in his discussion of musical style topics, that is, "traditional musical formulae passed from one generation to the next" (p. 117). Rodman argues as follows: "The topic is subject to interpretation (through a potentially unlimited number of interpretants), but because of its correlation with the visual objects on screen, and because of its alliance with the indexicality (a 'pointing to') of an extramusical object or idea, the number of interpretations is limited" (p. 117).

Arguably, the conceptual blending theory (see Chapter 4) resides at the level of secondary audiovisual signification. From this perspective, Table 5.1 presents a method of detecting and distinguishing the generic space's "common attributes" (N. Cook, 2001, p. 181, Rodman, 2010, p. 42) or "enabling similarities" in the absence of which there would be no perceptual interaction between the music and moving pictures.[5] Both music and moving pictures carry "potential signifiers for interpretation within a semantic field," and "while the text helps shepherd the viewer to select the preferred meaning, it is up to the viewer to pull these correlations from the text and interpret the text" (Rodman, 2010, p. 42; see N. Cook, 2001, p. 181ff., for an example of an application of this perspective to a commercial). In the following, I detail the signification process by specifying the potential signifiers of music using the sign typology developed by Philip Tagg.

In general, the sign typology illustrates how particular musical features relate to the external world, and musical sounds are regarded as representing nonmusical states or "nonmusical structures" (Middleton, 1990, p. 223). Tagg's approach is based on the general hypothesis that "commonly shared musical meanings (relations of musical signifiers to signifieds) do exist within a given culture" (Tagg & Clarida, 2003, p. 106). Empirically, this hypothesis is tested on a series of reception tests from 1979 to 1985 in which more than 600 respondents were exposed to the title music (which was apparently unknown to the respondents) from 3 to 10 television series (see Tagg & Clarida, 2003, p. 115ff.). The respondents were informed that they were about to hear "short pieces of music that have been used in film or on television," and they were subsequently asked to write down on a piece of paper "whatever you think could be happening on an imaginary film or TV screen along with each tune you hear" (Tagg & Clarida, 2003, p. 118). This process of free induction led to numerous visual-verbal associations, and Tagg aims to examine "whether those associations had anything in common and, if so, what" (Tagg & Clarida, 2003, p. 112). Compared to the functions of television music mentioned in Chapter 4, Tagg examines the preparatory function of music; if, for example, the respondents were familiar with the music in advance, then Tagg would test the mnemonic function of that particular music. Generally, Tagg finds a high degree of intersubjective consistency in the visual–verbal associations reported by the responses and therefore aims to study "the various ways in which responses to music relate to the musical structures of the pieces eliciting those responses" (Tagg & Clarida, 2003, p. 94). The sign typology is used (and in part developed) to comprehend the relationships between musical structures and human associative responses. However, because the empirical procedure "cannot directly tell us which part of the music relates semiotically to which part of which response" (Tagg & Clarida, 2003, p. 95), two further procedures are used: interobjective comparison and hypothetical substitution or commutation tests (more details on this procedure are presented later). The interobjective comparison procedure helps explain how associations with a particular piece of music may be influenced by the resemblance of particular pieces to other musical pieces, styles, and genres within the same musical culture. It is argued that "the same musical structure . . . in two radically different musical cultures is very unlikely to connote the same thing in both of them" (Tagg & Clarida, 2003, p. 96), which may illustrate an example of the above "limits" of secondary signification. Again, in Rodman's (2010) account of style topics in television music, he advances an analogous argument: "Topics are . . . open signs that rely heavily on interpretation from the culture viewing/hearing these signs" (p. 118).

Middleton (1990) appreciates the process of interobjective comparison as a "richly suggestive technique, easily the most fruitful method at present available for the analysis of secondary signification in popular music" (p. 233ff.), and the process is highly relevant to the study of music in commercials, as I suggested previously. The process aids in identifying the *potentials* of musical signification that a particular piece of music conveys—consistent with the assertion by Cook that music has the potential for specific meanings to emerge—and the sign typology can function as an instrument with which to analyze these potentials in greater detail. However, before initiating a closer examination of how the sign typology may assist exploring secondary audiovisual signification in commercials, it is important to emphasize that this level of analysis is indeed "audiovisual." Thus, the process of musical signification is not "limited" only by, for example, the prior distribution of similar types of music within a given musical culture. In fact, the process is also restricted by the particular cotextualization of the music in the commercial. Tagg does not consider this (audiovisual) level of text analysis in detail, and rather tellingly, the respondents in his study were exposed to only the music but not to the films. Thus, when Tagg's sign typology is used in analyzing a commercial, it is not sufficient to consider how the music in the commercial relates to music outside the commercial (the perspective used in Chapter 2). It is necessary to include an examination of the specific cotextualization of the music in the commercial. Tables B.1 and 5.1 illustrate the particular cotextualization of "There Goes My Love" in the iPad commercial, and this particular cotextualization—for example, "the frequency and placement of synch points . . . help create meaning" (Chion, 2009, p. 268) and "meaning inheres not in similarity, but in the difference that similarity articulates by virtue of the transfer of attributes" (N. Cook, 1998, p. 80ff.)—forms the basis for the following brief illustration of how the sign typology can help inform the analysis of secondary audiovisual signification in the Apple/The Blue Van commercial.

Tagg (2013) presents three types of sign or sign functions: style flags, anaphones, and diataxemes.[6] Style flags use "particular sounds to identify a particular musical style and often, by connotative extension, the cultural genre to which that musical genre belongs" (Tagg, 2013, p. 522). Two subtypes are presented: the style indicator and the genre synecdoche. The genre synecdoche is "a set of musical structures inside a given musical style that refer to another (different, 'foreign,' 'alien') musical style by citing one or two elements typifying that 'other' style when heard in the context of the style into which those 'foreign' elements are imported" (Tagg & Clarida, 2003, p. 101). The genre synecdoche is said to be "doubly metonymic: (1) part of a music style represents the entire musical style; (2) the solely musical-structural (stylistic) aspects of a genre signify the complete set of behavioural traits that constitute the genre" (Tagg & Clarida, 2003, p. 101). Style indicators—referring to a set of musical structures that are "either constant for, or regarded as typical of, the 'home' musical style" (Tagg &

Clarida, 2003, p. 102)—thus complement genre synecdoches; style indica-tors provide the background against which genre synecdoches are perceived as referring to something else. Thus, "none of the musical sign types . . . are mutually exclusive, except for one pair. A genre synecdoche cannot be a style indicator or vice versa" (Tagg & Clarida, 2003, p. 102); however, style indicators can be used by "foreign" musical styles as genre synecdoches. The identification of style indicators makes it possible to characterize music as a specific type and arguably makes it possible to examine the aspects of a genre. In other words, "particular styles of language (lyrics, paralinguistic, metadiscourse, etc.), gesture, location, clothing, personal appearance, social attitudes and values, as well as modes of congregation, interaction, presenta-tion and distribution, are all sets of rules identifying particular genre" (Tagg, 2013, p. 266; see also Tagg & Clarida, 2003, p. 101).[7] This perspective appears to be especially relevant to commercials (see Chapter 4); thus, "one or two notes in a distinctive musical style are sufficient to target a specific social and demographic group and to associate a whole nexus of social and cultural values with a product" (N. Cook, 1998, p. 17).

The style indicators of "There Goes My Love" include a busy, relatively fast-paced rhythm (212 bpm—as Moore, 2001, p. 42, notes, however, there is no simple answer to the issue of tempo in music that is not notated) with a clear backbeat and slightly swung quavers. Moreover, the style is marked by small-scale instrumentation (drums, bass, guitar, and lead vocals); dominant, simple, and repetitive guitar riffs; a melody-and-accompaniment texture; jagged and almost-shouting lead vocals; and a verse–chorus structure with a higher-pitched melody line in the chorus and an abrupt break. There is limited use of chords and chord progressions; the song (and the excerpts) are in C major and utilize a three-chord, eight-bar progression (i.e., I–I–VII–VII–V–V–I–I) that is repeated in the verses and the chorus. Accordingly, the song resembles the turn-of-the-millennium "garage rock revival" by bands such as The Strokes, The White Stripes, Jet, and the Yeah Yeah Yeahs (i.e., examples of interobjective comparisons). This relatively simple, repetitive, rugged, and energetic music has typically been accompanied in videos and concerts by performances from animated young male artists with a non-chalant and nostalgic style reminiscent of the 1960s, including messy or shaggy hair, white belts, skinny ties, simple T-shirts, and leather or denim pants and jackets. For example, the promotional pictures of The Blue Van by Iceberg Records (2010) present examples of "a paramusical field of con-notation" (Tagg & Clarida, 2003, p. 96), and the music video for the song[8] presents a specific example of a piece for interobjective comparison. In the commercial, this particular style is not matched by the clothing or setting of the iPad users, for instance, and the style in the commercial arguably helps portray iPad users as imaginative by meeting their needs and by giving them the ability to handle information rapidly and joyfully. The commercial implies that users have their fingers on the pulse of up-to-the-minute music that is yet unknown to other people. Defining the "charming type," these characteristics are offered for viewers to identify with or to strive for—"this is like me" or "this is what I would like to be." In this view, the musical style used assisted Apple's iPad in presenting itself as a resource that can reinforce ("the iPad fits me") or enhance ("the iPad will bring me there") the identity of the viewer.

Some of the style indicators also function as anaphones, which are musical expressions with a perceived similarity to paramusic, such as sound (sonic), movement (kinetic), and touch (tactile; Tagg, 2013, p. 487ff.). For example, through its concurrent appearance with the tapping hand and finger, the up-tempo drumbeat is simultaneously sonic, kinetic, and tactile. The beat is homologous to repeated, regular, and swift tapping (an example of the "fine-motoric aspect of kinetic anaphones"; Tagg, 2013, p. 499) or knocking (sonic) on something hard and solid (tactile). Thus, the beat helps to characterize both the users' activity and the iPad's materiality. In combination with the dolly in and the fast-forward motion on the iPad screen (see Shot 22 in Table B.1), the drum roll accentuates the intensified accumulation of events (which arguably includes kinetic, tactile, and sonic dimensions) and appears to suggest that the iPad's functions are so numerous and varied that they cannot all be included at a regular pace during the restricted timeframe of a 30-second commercial.

The drum roll and subsequent break also play a role as a type of episode marker and thus as a diataxeme, that is, "an identifiable element of meaning relating to the music's episode order of events" (Tagg, 2013, p. 515). The episode marker is a musical expression that marks the end of an episode while indicating that something new is about to begin. Parallel to the shift from demonstration to announcement, the drum roll acts as a propulsive reiteration (Tagg, 2013, p. 518), signaling that the demonstration of the iPad is coming to an end and that an announcement is commencing. Furthermore, the following break directs the viewer's attention to a change in the order of (musical) events. Indeed, breaks occur between events, and breaks often prepare for a new musical episode in the musical style of "There Goes My Love." As the musical break and the cut to the last shot are synchronized—in fact, this is the only remarkable synch point between the cuts and the musical beat—the written text (i.e., the future launch date) is highlighted. In combination with the visual cut and the text, the break indicates that something new is about to occur outside the setting of the commercial.

The particular cotextualization of the music and moving pictures further characterizes the imaginative users, the brand, and the product. For example, the busy rhythm and steady beats in synch with the users' movements help characterize the iPad as a solid piece of technology that reacts promptly to the user's actions. These readings exemplify how dependent musical secondary signification processes are on the actual cotextualization of the music; a different cotextualization of the same music would result in a perceived similarity to alternative paramusical dimensions. For example, the up-tempo beat might help illustrate the energetic bouncing of a ball, the heartbeat of an aroused human being, the precision of a tool, or the efficiency and dependency of running shoes. These readings are not clearly offered through the particular cotextualization of the music in the Apple/The Blue Van case; although human beings are shown, their relaxed postures at the table do not clearly allow for a reading of an aroused physical state. Thus, the same piece of music—with the same potentials for signification according to the procedure of interobjective comparison—will inevitably contribute to dissimilar processes of secondary signification in different cotextual settings.

Although this example illustrates how processes of musical signification vary according to dissimilar cotextualizations of the same piece of music, dissimilar musical accompaniments to the same pictures will also lead to differences in signification (also, these examples illustrate the procedure of commutation test; see the following section). An empirical example is presented by the marketing researcher Hung (2001). Based on questionnaires and focus group interviews, Hung "examine[d] at the micro-level how music may help form audiovisual images that influence viewer perceptions" (2001, p. 40). Hung illustrated how the evaluation of a shopping mall varies according to what type of music has been deployed in a commercial for that particular shopping mall. The shopping mall is evaluated as "upscale" in a version of the commercial in which a piece of classical music is deployed (i.e., excerpts from the Allegro movement of Antonio Vivaldi's baroque *L'Amoroso*, Violin Concerto in E major), and "Young, 'in,' and Active" in a version of the commercial in which a rock song is deployed (i.e., an instrumental excerpt from the Garbage song "Supervixen"; Hung, 2001, p. 42f). Furthermore, the commercial that includes Garbage's music is evaluated as "quick," "hurried," and "bright" (Hung, 2001, p. 45), whereas no such evaluations are associated with the version that includes Vivaldi's music. Moreover, specific events in the commercial are valued differently, apparently because of the musical cotextualization. For example, in the commercial that includes Garbage's music, a shot featuring a man with his mouth open is synchronized with a heavy guitar riff. Some of the respondents observed that the man is "shouting," although no such observation was made in relation to the version that includes Vivaldi's music (Hung, 2001, p. 46). Additionally, a shot featuring a man trying out a bed is valued differently by respondents; in the Vivaldi version, the man "seemed to be relaxed," whereas in the Garbage version, the man is described as having a "big, muscular chest" (Hung, 2001, p. 47). Hung concluded as follows:

> Thus, the meaning enactment role played by any one part of the music or video may be influenced by the configuration as a whole, so that a feature that may not be salient in one context becomes salient in an alternative context in which the feature corroborates with other ad elements to create an emergent, global perceptual unit.
>
> (2001, p. 47)

Generally, these examples illustrate that musical style is not the only source of considerable influence on the processes of signification. The specific cotextualization of music is also relevant. As N. Cook has observed, "the alignment of the other media with music . . . induces a specific perceptual selection from its available attributes" (1998, p. 83). In a similar vein, "it [music] is a bundle of generic attributes in search of an object" (N. Cook, 1998, p. 23), and "when music is combined with other media, the music readily finds an object" (N. Cohen, 2001, p. 263). "The object" may be understood generally as any non-musical dimension explicated or implied in the commercial. For example, the object could be interpreted specifically as the brand or the product (as discussed in Chapter 3) or as other materials, emotions, attitudes, ideologies, and behaviors. The selection of "available attributes" is dependent on the actual cotextualization of the music, and Tagg's sign typology has been suggested for use as an instrument to examine the significance of those "attributes" regarded as musical structures. The case of Apple/The Blue Van has illustrated that the possible "linguistic attributes" of the music in a commercial must also be considered when analyzing musical signification. At the level of secondary audiovisual signification, pronouns in particular can be considered "in search of an object," and they typically will "readily find an object"—frequently in the form of a noun that designates a user, a place, or a thing—although the relationship between the lyrics and the nonmusical aspects of the commercial is not always presented unambiguously. The Apple/The Blue Van case further illustrates how the cotextualization of a song's lyrics essentially alters the signification of those lyrics. Interestingly, what appears to be a case of intertextuality when only listened to (i.e., the music from the album version compared with the music heard from the commercial) actually presents itself as a case of parody when watched in the commercial; hence, although the musical style of the original is retained, the subject (or perhaps rather the object referred to by the lyrics) is diverted (Lacasse, 2000, p. 41; see Chapter 2).

These examples indicate that although Table 5.1 may function as a framework for the examination of cotextual relationships at the level of primary audiovisual signification, there exists no general model of the relationship between music and moving pictures at the level of secondary signification. Indeed, a number of models have been proposed, and all appear to be relevant to the study of music in commercials at the level of secondary audiovisual signification. For example, Pauli (1976, p. 104ff.) offers three types of musical functions: "paraphrasing," "polarizing" and "counterpointing." In an earlier contribution, Tagg (1979) identifies two main types of relationships between music and visuals: "congruity" and "disparity" (p. 321ff.). N. Cook (1998) has categorized audiovisual relations in terms of a continuum among "conformance," "complementation," and "contestation."[9] Bode (2009) has proposed two "modes of music-image interaction, i.e., "musicalization of the image" and "visualization of the music" (p. 86ff.). Finally, within marketing studies, the concept of "fit" or "congruity" has emerged. For example, in a review article, Oakes (2007) suggests that "'musical congruity' is used to replace alternative but equivalent authorial terms such as 'musical fit,'" and this contribution offers an overview of "the impact of 10 variants of congruity between musical stimulus and advertisement upon purchase intent, brand attitude, recall facilitation, and affective response" (Oakes, 2007, p. 38).

Regarded as general models, the preceding examples of categories tend to reduce the complex forms of "interactions" between music and its cotexts to a simple binary or tripartite construct. The Apple/The Blue Van case illustrates how music and picture can be said to concord on certain dimensions (e.g., the parallel structure—see Table B.1—and the synchronizations of beats and visual movements; see Table 5.1) and to discord on others (e.g., when comparing the clothing style displayed [visuals] and indicated [music] and the quality of pictures and visuals, respectively; see Table 5.1). Although not applicable as general models, these proposals may be helpful in identifying *specific* dimensions of the relationships between music and moving pictures:

> Anyone fabricating such categories [of audiovisual interrelations] and making such assessments would do well to state clearly the basis for his or her evaluations: Are they based on a general sense of concord versus discord that derives from perceptions of mood and cultural/stylistic appropriateness, or do more formal criteria come into play, such as temporal synchronization?
>
> (Richardson & Gorbman, 2013, p. 21).

5.3   COMMUTATION TEST

In this section, I introduce the procedure of commutation test. Essentially, a commutation test provides "a simple control mechanism for testing the validity of a semiotic deduction" (Tagg & Clarida, 2003, p. 98). The commutation test procedure originates from linguistics (e.g., Hjelmslev, 1943) and consists of (1) introducing a change in the plane of expression (signifiers) and (2) observing whether this change generates a correlative modification on the plane of contents (signifieds). Philip Tagg has systematically applied commutation tests to the monomodal (i.e., auditory) musical texts of title tunes (for an example, see Tagg, 1979, p. 121ff). However, neither Tagg nor Middleton offers a systematic demonstration of the possible uses of commutation tests for *audiovisual* texts, apart from introducing an illustrative example:

> The first lesson in my course on Music and the Moving Image has begun with an well-tried commutation trick . . . This old trick consists of playing the same thirty-second sequence three times in succession, first with

no music, to establish the visual sequence of events, then with the music written expressly for the sequence, and finally with music of contrasting character.

(Tagg, 2006, p. 163)

Although it is not entirely clear whether the music deployed for the third version is "contrasting" with the music from the second version and/or the visual sequence (and, if so, on what grounds this contrast occurs), Tagg (2006) observes how the change that is introduced alters the significance of the sequence:

Instantly recognizable to anyone belonging to our culture is the fact that the two different music scores create two completely different narratives from the same visual sequence . . . Narrative one is that of a pastoral idyll . . . Narrative two is that of a horror story.

(p. 165)

The procedure described by Tagg resembles the procedure used for the empirical research by Hung and exemplifies one particular type of commutation test.

I aim to provide a foundation for a systematic examination of audiovisual signification based on commutation test procedures based on the conviction that the commutation test technique "has the potential to tell us quite a lot about the relative distinctiveness and importance of 'elements'" (Middleton, 1990, p. 180). Although the procedure arguably assists in identifying the distinctiveness and importance of particular 'elements,' the significance of a given element cannot be measured using a simple binary construct (i.e., "significance" or "no significance"). As maintained by Middleton, "no musical device is semantically neutral"; hence, "*any* substitution, however small, will probably be agreed by attentive listeners to 'make a difference'; but what kind of difference and how great?" (1990, pp. 236, 182, respectively). Correspondingly, the relative importance of any given element varies according to different musical styles; for example, it appears likely that the sung melody pitch is relatively unimportant in a punk rock style (characterized by hoarse, shouting types of vocals) compared the singing of nineteenth-century Lied. As Middleton observed, "Tagg's approach provides an excellent method of delineating and checking such style codes" (1990, p. 182). Additionally, once a considerably significant element has been identified, the product does not specify precisely *what* that particular element signifies. When the approach is applied to audiovisual texts, this lack of specification becomes clear, because the substitution of an element includes the substitution of a *relationship* between elements, such as musical and visual expressions. As indicated, relationships between elements (e.g., "interactions" and "transfers of attributes") are relevant above all when examining audiovisual signification (see, e.g., Table 5.1).

A commutation test at the level of audiovisual signification thus involves substituting, reordering, adding, and deleting specific auditory (or visual) elements while holding all other elements constant. Consistent with the purpose of this book, the following discussion focuses primarily on music when exemplifying various forms of commutation texts, whereas visual commutations, for example, are illustrated more briefly (see "d." in Table 5.2). Table 5.2 presents an overview of some of the most obvious commutation tests used for analyzing music in commercials. This overview is inspired by previous research that has (more or less) explicitly addressed commutation tests of musical elements in audiovisual texts (e.g., Bjurström & Lilliestam, 1993; Chion, 2009; Gorbman, 1987; Tagg, 1979; Tagg & Clarida, 2003). Table 5.2 includes three columns: in the left column, the commutation text procedures are briefly described; in the middle column, the commutation

Table 5.2   Overview of commutation tests of music in commercials

Commutation test process	Specification of tests	Examples of tests
1. Deleting	a. Music	a. No music[1]
This procedure tests the significance of deleting some of the existing elements	b. Some of the music	b. No music during the "announcement period"
	c. Musical elements	c. Music without the lead singer or the lyrics
	d. Nonmusical elements	d. Commercial without the shots including either the brand logo or the brand logo and product name (Shot 24 in Table B.1)
2. Adding	a. Music	a. A musical logo accompanying the last shot (following the musical break)
This procedure tests the significance of adding elements to the existing elements	b. Some of the music	b. A jingle accompanies the presentation of the brand logo
	c. Musical elements	c. A trumpet accompanying the melody of the lead vocal
	d. Nonmusical elements	d. A voice-over speaking the verbal elements during the announcement period
3. Substituting	a. Music	a. Excerpts from The Blue Van's "Silly Boy"[2]
This procedure tests the significance of replacing existing elements with alternative elements	b. Some of the music	b. Excerpts "of Allegro" from Vivaldi's Violin Concerto in E major, *L'Amoroso*, only for the announcement period
	c. Musical elements	c. A female singer[3]
	d. Nonmusical elements	d. Children featured as the performing users[4]

Commutation test process	Specification of tests	Examples of tests
4. Reordering This procedure tests the significance of restructuring existing elements	a. Music	a. The music begins a half-second later than the moving pictures
	b. Some of the music	b. The music of the announcement is played at a lower decibel level than the music in the demonstration is played
	c. Musical elements	c. The tempo of the music is reduced to 160 bpm (from 212 bpm)
	d. Nonmusical elements	d. The two sections are inverted; i.e., the commercial begins with the announcement and ends with the demonstration

[1] This example appears in the first version deployed in Tagg's commutation technique as described in the text.

[2] A similar procedure is referred to by Gorbman (1987), who maintains that the commutation test "focuses attention on the existing music versus the music that might have been" (p. 18). See also the study by Hung (2001), the second and third versions of Tagg's commutation trick, and Rodman (2010, p. 44).

[3] This type of substitution is exemplified by the above musical branding in commercials for McDonald's, in which the jingle is varied in terms of, for example, tempo, rhythm, melody, tonality, key, instrumentation, accompaniment, and the gender and generation of the possible singer(s).

[4] For a similar example of the substitution of non-musical elements in a commercial, see Thompson (1978), who discusses a commercial for Chanel No. 5 in which Catherine Deneuve is hypothetically replaced by Margaux Hemingway.

test procedures are specified; and in the right column, the procedures are exemplified with reference to the Apple/The Blue Van case.

As indicated, the exemplification of specific tests (see the right-hand column) is based on the Apple/The Blue Van case. Obviously, other examples of music in commercials would encourage the use of other specific tests. For example, when a commercial includes other sounds (e.g., a voice-over and object sounds), the test should include those sounds and their relationship with the music. Additionally, when a commercial includes more than one piece of music (e.g., the Samsung/The Blue Van commercial with excerpts from "Silly Boy" and two original jingles), the tests should involve changing those musical excerpts, for example, by deleting the jingles or "Silly Boy" (see 1.b in Table 5.2). Generally, Table 5.2 can function both as insight to determine which particular elements could be changed and as a framework to evaluate the result of a particular change; for example, commutations 4.a and 4.c would result in different synchronizations between the sequencing of shots and sound structures (see Table 5.1) as well as between the visual content and the auditory structures.

Although the commutation tests listed in Table 5.2 are all principally relevant to the analysis of all commercials that include music, some tests might appear to be especially relevant to specific commercials or analytical interests. This possibility indicates that a commutation test should not necessarily include all the tests in the succession implied by the list in Table 5.2. For example, to evaluate whether a piece of music (e.g., an example of what is assumed to be "original genre music"; see Chapter 2) is in fact insignificant (or indistinct; see Chapter 6) in a commercial in which it appears as an auditory background for a voice-over, the following tests could be performed:

1. Delete (or mute) the music from the commercial, that is, 1.a. in Table 5.2.
2. Rearrange the structural relationship between the music and the voice-over and moving pictures, that is, 4.a in Table 5.2.
3. Substitute the music with a piece of music of a similar type (in terms of style and genre), that is, 3.a in Table 5.2.
4. Substitute the music with a piece of music of a dissimilar type (in terms of style and genre), i.e., another variant of 3.a in Table 5.2.

If the first three tests do not result in significant changes in the analytical observations—for example, (a) the lack of music does not significantly alter the commercial message, (b) no obvious synch points are lost or become salient, and (c) there is no apparent difference between the two types of music—then the music can be regarded as relatively indistinct and as contributing only marginally to processes of signification (for a similar argument, see Bjurström & Lilliestam, 1993). The last test (see the fourth test listed earlier) may aid in demonstrating that no musical expression is semantically neutral (as maintained by Middleton, 1990). For example, the substitution of a given type of music (e.g., a musical vamp; see Chapter 6) in a synth-pop style presenting a circular harmonic expression in a slow tempo) with a piece of music of a remarkably different style (e.g., a speed metal piece presenting distorted guitars and a hoarse, shouting-style vocal) will most likely alter the commercial message significantly although both musical expressions would appear as auditory background.

To provide another example, when evaluating the significance of a piece of preexisting music assumed to present "preexisting unknown opusmusic" (see Chapter 2), the following tests could be performed:

1. Delete the lyrics of the music, that is, 1.c in Table 5.2.
2. Substitute the excerpt from the piece of music in the commercial with another excerpt from the same piece of music, that is, 3.b in Table 5.2.
3. Rearrange the structural relationship between the music and the moving pictures, that is, 4.a in Table 5.2.

4. Substitute the music with another piece of music of a similar type, that is, in Table 5.2.

If these tests result in significant changes in the analytical observations— e.g., (a) the lack of lyrics precludes the manifestation of significant associations based on the relationships between the lyrics and the visual content, (b) the rearranging of the music and its lyrics alters the possible associations based on the relationships between the lyrics and the visual content, (c) obvious synch points are lost and new points emerge, and (d) there is a lack of associations and synch points although new ones might emerge—then the music can be interpreted as relatively distinct and as prominently contributing to processes of signification.

Commutation tests present a procedure to assist the text analysis of musical signification in commercials. The procedure can be performed "as a mind game"—that is, without actually changing the audiovisual expression (also indicated by the term "hypothetical substitution"). However, the actual changing of elements could strengthen the analysis. For example, whereas specific alternative synch points can be difficult to anticipate (e.g., when 3.a or 4.a is deployed), in practice, they would manifest relatively clearly. In addition, the actual changing of elements would allow for reception tests similar to the procedures described by Hung (2001) and Tagg (2006). The procedure could also be constructive during the production process. For example, it is not uncommon for the production process for a commercial to begin with nonmusical elements and end by adding sounds, such as voice-overs, object sounds, and music (see Graakjær & Jantzen, 2009c). For example, the selection of a particular piece of music for a commercial could be based on a series of commutation tests of various pieces of music accompanying the same film (e.g., 2.a and 3.a in Table 5.2), and once a particular piece of music has been selected, commutation tests may be used to determine precisely which excerpts from the music should be included in the commercial (e.g., 4.a, 4.b, and 4.c in Table 5.2).

This chapter has illustrated how processes of musical signification are heavily influenced by the cotextualization of the music. While it is important to examine the music's origin from a transtextual perspective (as demonstrated in the first part of the book), this examination needs to be supplemented by an analysis of the way in which the music is positioned in relation to the visuals and (possible) other sounds. For example, the significance of "There Goes My Love" in the commercial for Apple is highly dependent on the exact excerpt used and the precise cotextual positioning of that excerpt. I have indicated how a number of commutation tests can help pertinently illustrate this insight, and I have emphasized how the cotextual analysis requires an examination of both primary and secondary levels audiovisual signification. The examination of musical signification has laid the foundation for the following examination of how to analyze musical structures and functions in commercials.

NOTES

1. Bruner (1990) appears to illustrate this position: "the following postulates summarize . . . what can be safely concluded: (1) Human beings nonrandomly assign emotional meaning to music; (2) Human beings experience nonrandom affective reactions to music; and (3) Music used in marketing-related contexts is capable of evoking nonrandom affective and behavioral responses in consumers" (p. 99).

2. Middleton (1990) presents a compendium of a wide variety of theories and methods for the analysis of popular music. Comparable but not completely overlapping, the distinctions between two levels of musical signification (i.e., primary and secondary signification) can be found in other contributions, e.g., *congeneric* and *extrageneric meanings* (Coker, 1972, p. 60) and *intra-* or *extramusical meaning* (Martin, 1995). However, for the purpose of this book, I prefer the terminology and perspective presented by Middleton (1990).

3. In addition to the earlier mentioned inspiration from Middleton and Cook, the framework is based on a number of text analytical contributions related to the structural composition of sound and music in audiovisual media—particularly music videos, films, and television series (e.g., Björnberg, 2000; Donnelly, 2014; Goodwin, 1992; Kershaw, 1992; Tagg, 2013; Vernallis, 2004).

4. The particular observations are based on what I have been able to detect by watching the commercial on numerous occasions in brief intervals, as indicated in the introduction to this book. The purpose here is to present an analytical framework that should be applicable to the analysis of music in commercials without needing to rely on, for example, computer technology for the examination of synch points. Computer technology for such purposes has long existed, and it may indeed be used to supplement the present procedure, bearing in mind that attention should not be focused on "coming to terms with the 'nuts and bolts' of synchronization, with less awareness of aesthetic potentials" (Kershaw, 1992, p. 466).

5. This perspective resembles the congruency-association model of music and multimedia (Cohen, 2013). For example, "whereas the discussion of the concept of Congruence focused on the separate structure of the musical and visual information, the concept of Association focuses on the semantic aspect" (Cohen, 2013, p. 25). However, because this model is more psychological than musicological (see Cohen, 2013, p. 24) and because the potentials of musical signification are less detailed than in, for example, Tagg (2013), I do not include further details on this model in this context.

6. Compared with a previous version of this typology (e.g., in Tagg & Clarida, 2003), the structure of the typology has been modified. Most significantly, style indicators and genre synecdoches are grouped together to represent one main sign type (i.e., style flags), the episode marker is nuanced under a new heading (i.e., diataxeme), and new subtypes are added to account for anaphones.

7. Here, style is viewed as a set of "musical-structural rules or norms," and genre is viewed as "a larger set of cultural codes that include also musical rules" (Tagg, 2013, p. 267).

8. See the music video here: www.youtube.com/watch?v=kMonw5hUvWc.

9. Although the analytical perspective is inspired by Cook, I do not include the test procedure presented because I do not find that the resulting "three basic models of multimedia, which I am calling conformance, complementation, and contest" (Cook, 1998, p. 98) capture the complexity of the relationships in the present case. In fact, Cook does not appear to systematically rely on the test procedure during his own text analysis (see, e.g., Cook, 1998, p. 147; for a similar reception, see Moore, 1999). Moreover, in Cook (2001), the test procedure is not mentioned, although conceptual blending theory is introduced.

6　Musical Structures

In this chapter, I aim to provide an overview of the various ways in which music in commercials is structured, and I tentatively identify patterns in the use of music across the six volumes. At the most general level, the distribution of music in the six volumes is presented in Table 6.1.

This table suggests that music has been deployed in an increasing number of commercials, up to a certain point. Beginning with the 2004 volume, the percentage of commercials that use music appears to have stabilized. Arguably, this trend can be understood from the perspective established in Chapter 4: Both converging and diverging strategies are involved in promotion. Because an increasing number of commercials are using music, producers are generally more likely to at least consider using music. However, because the vast majority of commercials use music, the absence of music itself can mark a commercial as distinct, can confound expectations and can thus attract the attention of viewers (see more in Chapter 7 on the functions of "no-music").

With respect to commercials that include music, their musical structures appear to fall into two groups. Some musical structures appear to be prominent and to attract attention, whereas others do not. In the following, the concept of distinctiveness is introduced to differentiate between musical structures.

Distinctiveness is essentially the effect of a particular musical expression that is dissimilar to music in other contemporary commercials. Thus,

Table 6.1　Enumeration of commercials that include music in the six volumes

Year of sample	1992	1996	2000	2004	2008	2012
Commercials in the volume/with music	210/158	197/163	269/243	301/278	258/23	443/409
Percentage of commercials including music	75.2%	82.7%	90.3%	92.4%	92.6%	92.2%

synchronic analysis is necessary for assessing structural distinctiveness: a structure can be identified as distinctive in one period but nondistinctive in another period, which could be said to illustrate a continuing process of (de)familiarization (Shklovsky, 1917/2012) and "rotation of aesthetic norms" (Mukarovsky, 1979, p. 51). A source of inspiration with respect to the analysis of structural distinctiveness is the work of Burns (1987), who offers "a framework of categories to facilitate what might be called hook analysis of pop records," with a hook defined as "a musical or lyrical phrase that stands out and is easily remembered" (Burns, 1987, pp. 17, 1, respectively). Some contributions have compared hooks to music (specifically jingles) in commercials: "The so-called musical 'hook' is just a species of jingle oriented toward the achievement of the same purpose" (Huron, 1989, p. 571; see also Pekkilä, 2009). I shall return to this comparison later and specify how the functions of a jingle can be claimed to differ from the function of a hook. Burns's presentation of various hooks clearly indicates that an absolute and universal definition of the specific musical expression functioning as a hook cannot be given—an insight similar to that explicitly offered here with respect to distinctive commercial music. As is the case with hooks, the distinctive structure of music in commercials is assessable by scrutinizing the various aspects of musical expression, such as melody, rhythm, harmony, and sound. However, with respect to understanding distinctive music in commercials, this type of analysis will not suffice. The actual audiovisual framing and embedding of music (i.e., its cotextualization) is also highly consequential for generating distinctiveness.

In the words of Ritscher (1966, p. 142), "distinct music" is characterized by *Prägnanz* ("conciseness") because the melody, rhythm, harmony, dynamics or instrumentation is pronounced, thus allowing the emergence of a figure or *Gestalt*. Furthermore, distinctiveness can be defined in terms of "markedness" (Hatten, 1987; Monelle, 1992). In its strict sense, a marked musical event "conflicts with stylistic expectations" (Monelle, 1992, p. 271), and therefore, "markedness" is an internal feature of musical structure. In an extended sense, "markedness" can also be understood as "a comparatively significant event in a universe of lesser significance" (Monelle, 1992, p. 269). This significance could then be "related to the context" (Monelle, 1992, p. 270). In the case of commercial music, this significance implies the "universe" of other spots in the same commercial break and the "universe" of other audiovisual elements (i.e., the contexts) in the same commercial. Distinctive music either makes the commercial prominent relative to other commercials or makes the music a pronounced feature of a commercial's overall audiovisual structure.

As indicated, the following specification of musical structures is inspired by previous research (e.g., Bjurström & Lilliestam, 1993; Helms, 1981; Krommes, 1996; Leo, 1999). However, the definitions of structures offered here do not unambiguously match previous contributions. First, the sample for this book includes musical structures that do not fully match previously defined categories. Second, previous studies do not always contain pre-cise definitions, and the lack of consensus on terminology and definitions impedes replication. For example, a significant category in terms of quan-tity, such as "background music," is defined differently by Ritscher (1966), Helms (1981), Bjurström and Lilliestam (1993), and Leo (1999); similarly, a "jingle" has been defined in numerous ways (see more below). Third, studies occasionally use various criteria to classify music (e.g., Leo, 1999). In Leo's account, the following formats (and frequencies) are affirmed: "Background music: 35%, song/jingle: 16%, classical: 10%, classic pop: 6%, film music-like: 2%, jazz: 4%, rock//beat, 5%, ethnic: 4%" (Leo 1999, 38). At least three analytical perspectives appear to be involved: musical formats (song/jingle), musical functions (e.g., background music) and musical genres (e.g., classical). A categorization based on musical genres may provide important insights into the (ab)use of (types of) preexisting music in commercials (see Chapter 2); however, from the perspective of this book, any given genre can function in various ways (e.g., classical music can function either as back-ground or as foreground). In Krommes, to present another example, the typology is less ambiguous because it does not account for musical genres. However, this typology is rather undifferentiated in that it comprises only three formats, one of which is defined by several subformats: "14.4% a sig-nature motif, 20.4% a jingle, a commercial song or a pop song and 53.2% background music" (Krommes, 1996, p. 425).

In the following section, I begin by considering distinct musical struc-tures, and I subsequently introduce indistinctive music and the significance of the possible absence of music in commercials. Thus, distinctiveness is used in a somewhat crude sense in that high and low (i.e., the poles on a continuum) are the focus.

6.1 DISTINCT STRUCTURES

In this section, I examine distinct musical structures in greater detail, and I focus primarily on music in the categories of music–product partnership and productmusic or brandmusic (see Chapter 3). Distinctive music tends to be clustered in specific types or "formats" (i.e., standard characteristics of musi-cal structures that manifest across commercials). Distinctive formats can be differentiated with respect to (a) the musical dimension that presents the musical hook and (b) the duration of the musical expression. Additionally, the various formats tend to serve different functions in commercials (see more in Chapter 7). In general, in the examination of this book's sample, the prevalence of distinctive formats appears to have increased moderately until the 2004 volume: approximately 40% of the commercials from 1992 and 1996 include a distinct format, whereas the proportion is greater than 45% in the 2000 and 2004 volumes. However, in the 2008 and 2012 vol-umes, this increase does not continue, and in fact, a moderate decrease in the commercials with distinct formats can be observed, as only approximately 40% of all commercials in the 2008 and 2012 volumes include a distinct musical format. There is no simple explanation for this apparent decline in the appearance of distinct musical formats. One could, for example, speculate as to whether the financial crisis (beginning in 2007) has resulted in reduced budgets for the production and distribution of (distinct music in) commercials or whether a "maximum ratio of distinctiveness" has been reached—that is, following the delineation of distinctiveness (which includes an intercommercial comparison), not all commercials can include distinct music. However, it is beyond the scope of the sample and the purposes of this book to examine this question in greater detail. In the following, I begin by considering the distinctive short formats (i.e., the jingle and the emblem), and I present the distinctive long formats (i.e., the groove, the tune, and the song).

Short Formats

Emblems and *jingles* are formats of short duration; *emblems* represent a relatively recent development, and *jingles* embody commercial music par excellence. The significance of the jingle format is attested to by the large number of books and articles on how to craft a perfect jingle (e.g., Edel, 1988; Karmen, 1989, 2005; Miller, 1985; Rule, 1997; Teixeira, 1974; Wüsthoff, 1999; see also Rodman, 2010, p. 84ff). The alleged positive effect of utilizing jingles for advertisers has also attracted the attention of experimental researchers. For example, Macklin (1988) studies the effects of a jingle on attitudes toward ads and brands, on the formation of product preferences and on recall effects. Wallace (1991) and Yalch (1991) focus on this last issue in their studies on the efficiency of the jingle as a mnemonic device.

Jingles have a long history. For example, "the first musical advertising jingle was heard in the air in 1929, when a barbershop quartet sang about the breakfast cereal Wheaties on a Minneapolis radio station" (Rodman, 2010, p. 84). The jingle has sometimes denoted commercial music as such (e.g., Miller, 1985). Although the jingle may be understood as the closest representation of a unique musical structure in commercials (i.e., no other audiovisual genre presents quite the same musical format and function), music in commercials includes a much wider variety of musical formats and functions.

From the perspective of this book, whose focus is on music "seen on the screen" rather than merely "heard in the air," a jingle is defined as a short, rounded, melodic motif that (a) consists of at least two musemes (see the following discussion), (b) appears without other concurrent sounds, and (c) is synchronized with the presentation of a logo (and possibly a slogan). The distinctiveness of a jingle is conveyed by an effortlessly remembered and easily recognizable structure and by its synchronization with a logo and slogan. The definition is partly etymologically inspired in that the term originally referred to the shrill clinking sound of small objects of metal (e.g., coins in a pocket or a handful of keys). Thus, a commercial jingle is potentially instrumental. Consequently, contrary to their relevance in differentiating song and tune, lyrics are not considered essential with respect to a jingle's musical function and signification (for more information on songs and melodies, see the following discussion).

With respect to scale and duration, the jingle is here distinguished from either melodically developing (song and tune) or rhythmically intensified (groove) musical expressions of a longer duration (typically lasting throughout most of the commercial). Additionally, a jingle is closely related to the presentation of a logo, whereas songs and melodies are more related to a commercial's overall structure. Compared with the emblem (i.e., the other distinctive short format; see more in the following discussion), the jingle is composed of at least two musemes. The term *museme* is coined by Tagg (inspired by Charles Seeger) to refer to "a minimal unit of musical discourse that is recurrent and meaningful in itself within the framework of any one musical style" (Tagg & Clarida, 2003, p. 808). For the purposes of this book, the minimal unit consists of a musical impulse such as a tone beat or chord (see, e.g., Tagg & Clarida, 2003, p. 563). Consequently, the jingle is composed of at least two such musical impulses, whereas the emblem is composed of only one impulse. Normally, jingles will last longer than emblems, but the definitive difference between the two formats is the musematic composition of jingles. Because it presents more than one museme, the jingle is often more significant in terms of characterizing a brand and product being advertised compared with the emblem, which is more significant in terms of attracting the attention of viewers, although these two functions are not mutually exclusive (see Chapter 7).

Although the preceding sections have compared the jingle to other musical formats in commercials, it may be illustrative to compare the jingle to two musical expressions or functions outside the universe of commercials, namely, leitmotifs and hooks (the latter of which is mentioned above). All three (i.e., jingles, leitmotifs, and hooks) are relatively short musical expressions that aim to attract and (re)direct the attention of listeners. However, these expressions differ in terms of their specific appearance and function.

A leitmotif can be defined as "a musical figure (a chord, a melodic gesture, a phrase), that, through repetition in a narrative text (like an opera, a film, or television program), becomes identified with a character, an idea, or a situation" (Rodman, 2010, p. 110). For a musical figure to function as a leitmotif, it must first be strategically placed so that there is an unequivocal and very clear interplay between the sound and the image—in other words, it must represent a distinctive musical expression in a universe of lesser significance. Second, the figure must be

enforced and anchored in the memory by repeated association, until the linkage is so stable that the musical motif or sound object alone is capable of representing the entire complex of association. Repetition is thus an obligatory component in the creation of a leitmotif.

(Flueckiger, 2009, p. 163)

This function is similar to the function of a jingle as a musical brand; for example, the McDonald's jingle could cause listeners to associate the song with the brand when hearing it in a radio commercial because of the recurrent and consistent exposure to the music–brand relationship in television commercials. Additionally, both leitmotifs and jingles can be structurally varied according to the specific circumstances of their appearance; the McDonald's campaign presents a case in point with respect to jingles. However, whereas the leitmotif in a film is repeated within a narrative and thus "constructing meaning within a work" (Flueckiger, 2009, p. 163), a particular jingle is normally repeated across different commercials for a specific brand. Thus, in view of the definition of leitmotifs presented earlier, a jingle could be defined as a musical figure that, through repetitious exposures in association with a logo across different commercials for the same brand, becomes identified with that particular brand.

Leitmotifs bear a resemblance to hooks in that both function within a text, as implied in the definition of hooks by Burns, but the following definition of a musical "idea" of a hook highlights this particular aspect: "a relatively independent, memorable element within a totality" (Middleton, 1990, p. 51). However, hooks differ from jingles (and, to some extent, differ from leitmotifs) in that a hook attracts and directs the attention of listeners toward "itself" or toward the musical piece of which the hook is an integral part (this function is arguably also part of the function of a leitmotif, e.g., in an opera). A jingle attracts the listener's attention to a nonmusical product, whereas a hook *is* the attraction.

As implied, the definition of jingle does not correspond unambiguously to previous contributions. With respect to the duration of a jingle, the definition inspired by Bjurström and Lilliestam (1993) is inconsistent with previous contributions that do not distinguish between songs and jingles (e.g., Helms, 1981; Leo, 1999; Miller, 1985). Additionally, with respect to the status of lyrics, the definition differs from studies maintaining that lyrics are an essential constituent of jingles, for example, "usually brief, catchy tunes with lyrics that include the name of the product being advertised" (Rodman, 2010, p. 82; for similar definitions, see, e.g., Taylor, 2000; Wüsthoff, 1999). A possible reason for many studies' emphasis on the lyrics of jingles is that jingles in television commercials historically descend from jingles on the radio, which in turn arguably descend from the songs of street merchants, as noted earlier (see Chapter 4). In other words, radio jingles tend to have lyrics because brand and product names cannot be presented visually. Lyrics appear to have historically played a pivotal role in jingles in television commercials, which could explain why some contributions (i.e., those examining historical examples of music in commercials) highlight lyrics. For example, Rodman (2010) explores "the structure of early television commercials and how music was used in them" (p. 80). More recently, the use of jingles with lyrics of the type defined by Rodman appears to have declined: "Jingles, meaning an original happy melody written about a product or service that extols the benefits, qualities, and excitement that come from owing or using that product, are no longer considered honest" (Karmen, 2005, p. 21; for similar arguments, see, e.g., Block, 2003; Bullerjahn, 2006; Klein, 2009; McLaren, 1998; Taylor, 2000, 2012). Arguably, this trend corresponds to the purported increase in the use of both preexisting music and more understated, indirect modes of address (see also Rodman, 2010, p. 205). Incidentally, Karmen's (2005) definition of jingle highlights further differences compared with the definition adopted in this book. Thus, a jingle is not necessarily "happy" (although Karmen does not elaborate on this characteristic)[1] or "original" (i.e., it does not necessarily present a piece of original music; see Chapter 2). Given the perspective and sample used in this book, the jingle, which functions as a musical brand, is most often characterized by original music. Because the sample does not include pre-1992 commercials—unlike researchers such as Rodman (2010), who examines commercials from the 1950s and 1960s—it is not possible to examine whether commercials demonstrate a decline in the use of lyrics in jingles over a longer period.[2] Nevertheless, within the limitations of the brief period included in the present sample, two analytical perspectives can offer an indication.

First, I have previously indicated that the prevalence of jingles with vocals has decreased significantly over time when I compared samples from 1992, 1996, 2000, and 2004 (see Graakjær, 2009a). When examining the April 2008 and 2012 volumes, I noted that this trend appears to continue. Almost all (more than 95%) of the jingles in these volumes lack vocals and, thus, lyrics. Because the jingle is the most typical distinctive format in the 2008 and 2012 volumes—approximately every second distinctive musical format is a jingle, and jingles are present in nearly 20% of all commercials—this format is significant to the evaluation of musical lyrics in commercials in general (see the following discussion for more on the song format).

Second, with respect to the musical change in the jingle during the McDonald's *i'm lovin' it* campaign, the lyrics disappear as the campaign progresses. At the beginning of the campaign, the jingle is not yet "emancipated" from the song in the first commercial. In this first commercial, the subsequent jingle thus functions as part of the chorus or hook of the song. However, the end of the first commercial features a version that will subsequently emerge as the jingle for the campaign. Three motifs are included in this musical expression: (a) "McDonald's," (b) "parapapapa," and (c) "i'm lovin' it."[3] Subsequent versions of the jingle have changed considerably. The jingle has been changed as a result of "repetition" and "variation," following Burns's (1987, p. 2) account of "little" and "moderate" changes, respectively. The jingle has also been "modulated" (with "much change") on various occasions.[4] First, a modulation has occurred regarding the motif "McDonald's": Since August 2004, McDonald's commercials broadcast for the first time on TV 2 have not included this motif (and, thus, the lyrics). Second, a modulation has transpired with respect to the motif "i'm lovin' it": Since December 2005, the lyrics of this motif have disappeared from McDonald's commercials, and the melody has continued to appear in only a small portion of commercials. Finally, a modulation has appeared regarding the "parapapapa" motif. Although the melody has continued to appear in nearly all commercials (although in numerous variants across commercials), since June 2007, the motif has appeared without human voicing. Moreover, in the vast majority of commercials since that time, this motif has become the sole musical expression during the presentation of the logo and the slogan at the end of all commercials.

During this process of change, the jingle has not been transformed; the process does not present a case of mutation or metamorphosis. The instrumental parapapapa motif has presented a relatively consistent musical structure (marked by a tendency toward a particular rhythm and melody line across variations), and the unvarying visual anchoring of the jingle with the presentation of the logo and slogan has helped preserve the jingle as the musical brand for McDonald's. The gradual omission of lyrics and human voices during the campaign arguably illustrates how the use of music in commercials can quite literally activate a brand name and a slogan in the minds of viewers. Because both Justin Timberlake and other human voices "left the jingle" during the modulation process, the "I" of the visualized slogan reveals a type of "identity crisis." "I" presents an "open space" (Iser, 1974) that must be interpreted and "filled in" by listeners. Each commercial for McDonald's will (to some extent) influence the potentials of interpretation, but the "I" is always present for listeners to identify with across all commercials. The parapapapa motif plays an essential role in this respect: Because the motif concludes the auditory expression of the commercial, viewers are left with the visualization of the logo and slogan. Perhaps fortified by previous exposure to the "i'm lovin' it" motif that would previously end the commercials, viewers can finish the jingle by singing—illustrating a simple type of karaoke devoid of musical accompaniment—or merely by psychologically activating the words of the slogan.

The McDonald's jingles further illustrate that jingles are not necessarily "happy." In fact, the changing structures of the jingle have shown a wide variety of musical expressions. With respect to the auditory cotextualization of the jingle, McDonald's commercials demonstrate that jingles can, for example, end a commercial with no other music, end a commercial in a musical style quite different from the previous background music, or end a commercial in a musical style similar to the previous background music. The McDonald's jingle also illustrates the most typical placement of the jingle. Because of their relatively short duration, jingles (and emblems) can be positioned in various places throughout a commercial (for an overview of "five typical placements of jingles," see Wüsthoff, 1999, p. 25). In the examined commercials for McDonald's, the jingle is consistently placed at the end of the commercial in synch with the presentation of the logo and slogan. For example, in the 2012 volume, all 93 of the commercials with a jingle at least include it at the end, and in a few commercials, the jingle also appears in other places. For example, in a commercial for JYSK (a Danish supplier of bedding materials; see Graakjær, 2009b for more on JYSK and its particular jingle), the jingle is placed both at the beginning and at the end; at the beginning, the jingle functions to attract attention and prepare listeners for what is to come (i.e., new bargains from JYSK). When placed at the end of the commercial, the jingle functions as a type of musical signature that draws attention to the sender and validates what has occurred throughout the preceding parts of the commercial. The jingle thus functions both as an exclamation mark rounding off and underlining the preceding message and as a colon presenting and pointing to the concurrent logo and slogan. Moreover, the jingle can help secure product and brand recognition, as the preceding parts of the commercial might not have explicated the brand or the commercial message: as indicated previously, such understated or indirect modes of address are most commonly found in fictional formats (i.e., montages and dramas).

Emblems are also short musical formats, but compared with jingles, emblems lack melody and are often even shorter. Typically, the duration of an emblem is only approximately one second. Moreover, emblems are defined here as presenting only one museme, whereas jingles present at least two musemes as mentioned. An emblem can thus be defined as a single sound or musical impulse that, similar to the jingle, appears without other concurrent sounds and is synchronized with the presentation of a logo.

The emblem attains distinctiveness through its sound and its detailed synchronization with the logo. It is the exact idiom of the sound (e.g., instrumentation, phasing, delay, panning, timbre) that is relevant when analyzing distinctiveness. In the terminology of musical sound envelope, the attack, the sustain, and the decay have relevance: "This initiation of the sound event is termed *attack*. It is followed by the *sustain*. How long is the note hold? How long does it stay at full volume? Finally, the sound fades away. This stage is called *decay*" (Altman, 1992, p. 18). The apparently recent advent of emblems in commercials (the first example is identified in the April 2000 volume) may be an indication of producers' increased awareness of the importance of sound in commercials. Thus, all commercial formats may feature sound as at least one distinctive element of expression (see more on the format of groove in particular).

Emblems have not been discussed much in previous research, perhaps because of the apparently recent advent and rare appearance of this format (in all the volumes studied, only 12 examples were identified) and the fact that the aesthetic dimension of sound has normally been regarded as secondary to musical dimensions, such as melody, rhythm, and harmony (see, e.g., Helms, 1981). However, emblems appear to be included in the contribution by Riethmüller (1973), who focuses on the "Tonsignet" or "tone signet." Although the tone signet also appears to include what I have termed a jingle (e.g., the tone signet is characterized by "a consistent tone sequence" at one point), the reference to the tone signet as a "musical particle" and "musical miniature" (Riethmüller, 1973, p. 76) calls to mind the concept of emblem that has been delineated here. Additionally, the importance of sound is highlighted when characterizing the tone signet: "The timbral effect of the music, its sound, is virtually the most important dimension" (Riethmüller, 1973, p. 73).

Because of its somewhat limited dimensions of expression, the functions of the emblem are typically more confined than the functions of the jingle. The emblem functions primarily to attract attention and to serve as a mnemonic cue, whereas the jingle additionally allows for a significant characterization of the brand and product being advertised. In this respect, the emblem resembles the numerous everyday sound signals (indeed, the tone signet is observed to present the character of a signal; Riethmüller, 1973, p. 71) that inform us that something is here or has occurred (Blattner, Sumikawa, & Greenberg, 1989; Flueckiger, 2009), such as the signals of the loudspeaker system in airports or shopping malls, the doorbell in private houses, and the announcement of incoming mail on personal computers. However, these signals often include a few tone beats and thus more than one museme. The fact that the emblem is composed of only one museme implies that the emblem lacks melody and hence the possibility of being reproduced by listeners. For example, "as the listener hums a tune or sings a jingle, he or she engages in a rehearsal strategy that results in better memory" (Macklin, 1998). Whereas jingles (as well as songs and melodies, see below) may be hummed, sung or silently recalled in the form of an "earworm"—a term inspired by the German *Ohrwurm* to refer to a musical phrase that becomes "stuck in the head" of listeners—no such potential or risk is associated with the emblem. Compared with other distinctive formats (e.g., the jingle, the tune, or the song), the emblem may thus be less prone to "wear-out" effects; for example, "frequent repetition of commercials with a simple or familiar advertising song may guarantee the opportunity to process the ad but may also result in a 'wear-out' effect, thereby diminishing motivation to process the ad" (Bullerjahn, 2006, p. 213; see also Millward Brown, 2008, p. 3). Another implication of the emblem's limited dimensions of expression is that emblems can challenge the definition of music that has been presented for the purposes of this book (see the introduction). For example, rhythmic structure is not clearly allowed, and only the timbre and envelope of the tone or possible harmonic structure (e.g., a musical chord) can indicate a musical dimension of an emblem.

An example of a musical emblem is presented by a commercial (from the April 2000 volume) for Fona (a Danish provider of electronics). A soft attack introduces a musical impulse. The subsequent relatively short sustain is characterized by a synth-chord with a "metallic" sound in a high register. The decay is long lasting, and during the fade-out of the chord, a voice-over introduces the brand name and current slogan: "Enter Fona. We know what you are talking about." In total, the emblem lasts nearly seven seconds, and it illustrates how emblems can occasionally outlast jingles (e.g., many McDonald's jingles last approximately two to three seconds). The "metallic" sound of the emblem contributes to characterizing Fona as a company focused on electronics. Another example of an emblem appears in a commercial (from the April 2012 volume) for Billed Bladet (a Danish weekly magazine focused on celebrity news). The ending logo shot (i.e., a presentation of the front page of the this week's magazine on a black background) is presented in synch with the introduction of a distinct attack—and a subsequent short sustain and decay—of chiming bells in a high register. Through its potential associations with something magical and fairy tale–like in this setting, the sound arguably supports the Billed Bladet brand, a magazine that is particularly focused on the members of the Danish royal family (and their relatives and colleagues across Europe), which is also addressed by the slogan "Billed Bladet. Denmark's royal weekly magazine."

Several additional examples from the April 2012 volume can illustrate that object sounds may function as sound brands in a similar manner as the (musical) emblem and that the distinction between music and object sounds can be ambiguous. In a commercial for HjemIs (a provider of ice cream), chiming bells are also manifest during the presentation of the logo at the end of the commercial. However, compared with the "magical bell" of Billed Bladet, the sound of the HjemIs bell resonates in a lower register, includes numerous attacks, and is visualized in synch with a HjemIs van, which is well known in Denmark for promoting and selling ice cream on streets with private houses. On the van's arrival, the sound of its bells signal that now is the (limited) time to purchase ice cream. The sound is not to be considered music(al); however, it functions as a strong index of—and "(object) sound brand" for—HjemIs. In a commercial for Netto (a supermarket chain), the concluding logo shot is accompanied by the sound of the cash register. This sound is not normally heard in a Netto store and is in fact anachronistic compared with the sound of present-day registers. However, because the sound represents a stylized stereotype of a cash register and thus money transfer, the object sound helps brand Netto as competitive in their prices. Moreover, because the sound signals the conclusion of a transaction, the object sound may suggest that the viewer has "cut a deal" with Netto while watching the commercial and the products promoted—that, the viewer is "rewarded" for having viewed the commercial and is finally "certified" to shop at Netto. The examples illustrate how brands can aspire to "colonize" and "monopolize" (or "connotatively hijack," to use the term offered by Tagg, 2013, p. 184) the signifying potential of object sounds from outside the commercial universe, which in turn influences listeners to potentially associate the brand with the particular object sound when encountered in everyday life.

Long Formats

Long formats include musical structures that continue throughout the majority or entirety of a commercial. Previously, I have briefly introduced the medley, which can be considered a distinctive long format type of music-product (see Chapter 3). A medley is a musical expression structured as a collage of excerpts from more than one piece of music. The distinctiveness of this format originates from its various excerpts, which typically present highlights or hooks from preexisting music. The medley is thus normally deployed when a musicproduct is promoted. For example, in a commercial for *Hits for Kids 27* (Universal 2012) from the April 2012 volume, hooks from seven different songs are arranged during the 30 seconds of the commercial and are introduced by a voice-over: "Now it is here . . ." In general, visual parts are structured on the basis of musical expressions: for example, the artists are dancing and gesticulating in time with the music, not unlike the "visualized music" of many music videos that have functioned as another obvious method of promoting musical products (see, e.g., Goodwin, 1992; Kaplan, 1987; although with the advent of, e.g., YouTube, current "music videos" come in many forms and serve many functions; see Hearsum & Inglis, 2013; Korsgaard, 2013; Vernallis, 2013, p. 207). The music is typically featured without many distracting auditory elements; however, a voiceover will normally ensure that potentially distracted listeners will be informed of the present promotion of a musical product. Such vocal information—for example, "Now it is here . . ." (featured at the beginning of the *Hits for Kids* commercial), "A new great album by . . .," and "Twelve new songs by . . ."—is actually potentially counterproductive because music is an auditory product, but the voice-over will almost necessarily result in masking some of the music. Accordingly, a voiceover of only a few words is normally present. Whereas the medley is prevalent in commercials promoting a musical product, long formats (i.e., the song, the tune, and the groove) manifest in commercials for nonmusical products.

A song is defined here as a sung (with lyrics) melody that lasts for the majority of the commercial and is organized in detailed synch with the visual elements of the commercial. Compared with a jingle, a song allows for musical development, as more than one motif and phrase are presented during the commercial. Moreover, the song, alongside the other distinctive long formats (see the later discussion), typically contributes to the structuring of commercials. A song normally includes episode markers (see Chapter 6) and present harmonic as well as melodic progression. In view of the geometric metaphors for musical structure introduced by Björnberg (2000), the song is linear or elliptical (not circular). Consequently, contrary to the rather "stationary" musical structure of jingles and emblems, the song typically crescendos toward the end of the commercial and therefore ends "on a different note" than it began. As described previously, "There Goes My Love" is an example of a song considered a musical format. Additionally, the first commercial of the McDonald's campaign *i'm lovin' it* presents an example of a song. This case further illustrates that a "song" can include rap and that a jingle can descend from a song used in earlier commercials; as indicated previously, the refrain or hook of the initial song presents the subsequent musical brand for McDonald's (see Chapter 6).

With respect to the function of lyrics, it may be beneficial to reconsider the modes of address previously introduced. From this perspective, a song can manifest as a testimonial, a presenter, or a voice-over(+). Arguably, the visual and auditory appearance of Justin Timberlake illustrates the former, because the product and brand are blatantly praised through the song's lyrics (e.g., "*I'm lovin' it*"). The intradiegetic appearance of "There Goes My Love" may be considered a type of voice- or "musicover+," as indicated previously. Because there is no mention of the product or brand, viewers must determine for themselves what the lyrics mean and how they relate to the visuals, the product, and the brand. These examples indicate three different ways—representing the specific modes of address—in which lyrics can relate to the brand and product being advertised. First, as exemplified by the McDonald's/Timberlake case, the lyrics can explicitly refer to the brand and product name in addition to some straightforward characterization of (the enjoyment of) this particular brand and product. Second, as exemplified by the Orange/(Hey You) The Rock Steady Crew case, the lyrics may explicitly refer to the brand and product name; however, the characterization is marked by some type of metacommunication (e.g., being parodic or ironic). Third, as exemplified by the Apple/The Blue Van case, the lyrics may not explicitly refer to the brand and the product name and may thus leave a semantic gap between the two for viewers to complete. From this perspective, it is most likely the first type mentioned earlier that Karmen and others refer to (Karmen's quote exemplifies that many previous definitions do not distinguish between jingles and songs, as delineated in this book). As already indicated (and mentioned in, e.g., Allen, 2008), studies have not empirically validated whether the use of songs (or jingles) that include product-praising lyrics has declined in favor of the use of preexisting popular music (as suggested in, e.g., Rodman, 2010, p. 205).

In the sample for this book, the song format appears to have gained momentum during the last two volumes. Although a decline in the appearance of songs is registered during the first four volumes, the prevalence of songs appears to have stabilized in that approximately one of four commercials that embody a distinct format presents a song in the two most recent samples. Most typically, a song presents a case of preexisting music; for example, in the 2008 volume, 19 of 27 songs present excerpts from preexisting songs, and for 2012, the number is 26 of 28. Thus, approximately 7 of 10 songs present a case of preexisting music in the two most recent volumes studied here. This finding indicates that although the use of (an excerpt) of a preexisting popular song may not have replaced other types of songs or music in commercials in general, this type of song is much more common than, for example, openly product-praising jingles.

From a transtextual perspective, the songs differ in terms of their distribution and familiarity. Some songs present "known opusmusic." For example, in a commercial from the April 2012 volume for Telenor (a Norwegian multinational telecommunications company), excerpts of Stevie Wonder's "Happy Birthday" appear to highlight the company's 20th anniversary. Other songs appear to present "unknown opusmusic" or "postexisting music." For example, in a commercial for Ecco (a Danish shoe manufacturer and retailer) from the April 2012 volume, excerpts from Treefight for Sunlight's song "Facing the Sun" (released in 2010 on Tambourhinoceros) are used to promote the company's summer collection. A commercial from the April 2012 volume for Mattel's Disney Sparkling Princess illustrates that the openly product-praising jingle has not entirely disappeared. In this commercial, an original song accompanies the illustration of sparkling princesses "in action" while characterizing the dolls and including the product name numerous times.

A tune is defined here as an instrumental (without lyrics) melody that continues for the majority of the commercial and is organized in detailed synch with the visual elements of the commercial. In many ways, the characteristics and functions of tunes are similar to those described for the song format. However, the lack of lyrics makes the tune more likely to interact with a voiceover. An example of a tune has already been mentioned by the appearance of "Champagne Galop" (see Chapter 2), which is a case of known opus music. In this commercial, the structure of the musical excerpts contributes significantly to structuring the commercial and highlighting specific visual dimensions. The musical excerpts are the predominant auditory element of the commercial; in fact, a voice-over is not introduced until the end of the commercial. In the beginning, the introductory musical fanfare (i.e., an ascending melodic gesture presenting a broken triad in the major mode played by trumpets in a fast 2/4 time) is in synch with the visual presentation of a Tivoli guest being prepared for a ride. The fanfare and subsequent music present a variety of anaphones with sonic, kinetic, and tactile qualities. The rhythm offers an approximate stylization of horse hooves hitting the ground powerfully during the fastest running gait of a horse, that is, "diddle dum, diddle dum, diddle dum . . ." Moreover, the fast tempo of the music and the grouping of two quick notes at the beginning of the fanfare motif present a kinetic anaphone that propels energy forward and indicates fast movement (see Tagg, 2013, p. 509, for more on the musical renderings and signifying potentials of the gallop). The fanfare leads to a "popping" sound that resembles the sound of a champagne cork popping from a bottle. The popping sound is visually synchronized with the "release" of the ride, which subsequently occurs and is viewed from the first-person perspective of a Tivoli guest. The music thus parallels the ride and contributes to the characterization of The Demon as fast, forceful, and vibrant. As indicated previously, the added hip-hop-style beat augments this impression. Whereas the commercial for Tivoli's The Demon illustrates a case of preexisting music, a commercial (from the April 2012) for REMA 1000 (a chain of supermarkets) illustrates the use of an original tune. Additionally, the super-market commercial illustrates how a tune can interact with a voiceover, with significant melodic motifs foregrounded in the pauses of the voice-over.

A groove is a musical format that has not been identified in previous studies of music in commercials, perhaps because of the recent advent of this particular format in commercials (see the following discussion). Additionally, the concept does not appear to have been widely used in scholarly research on music until recently. For example, although the concept of groove has long been familiar in producers' and musicians' own usage, only recently has it been theorized by analysts (Middleton, 1999, p. 143). The concept is inspired by the definition offered by Tagg (2013): "one or more rhythm patterns lasting, as single units, no longer than the extended present (usually just a couple of seconds), but those patterns have to be repeated several times before they constitute grooves" (p. 296). Here, a groove is defined as a non-melodic, rhythmically composed repetitive expression that lasts for the majority of the commercial and is organized in detailed synch with the visual elements of the commercial. In view of the geometric metaphors for musical structure, a groove is cyclical (not linear or elliptical; see also Tagg, 2013, p. 296). A groove differs most significantly from songs and tunes by its lack of melody. The distinctiveness of grooves emanates from the sound and "feeling" of a specific, predominantly rhythmic configuration that is prominent on its own accord, unlike the indistinctive structuring of *vamps* (discussed later). Consequently, in commercials, the groove is an "independent" musical expression in the sense that it is does not function as a background accompaniment or preparation for a voiceover or singer, and the groove typically presents the sole auditory expression during the majority of the commercial.

Grooves are pervasive in popular music genres such as jazz, rock, soul, and funk, and the groove "marks an understanding of rhythmic patterning that underlies its role in producing the characteristic rhythmic 'feel' of a piece" (Middleton, 1999, p. 143). Although the lack of melody does not invite listeners to hum or sing, a groove can engage listeners in some form of physical or rhythmic entrainment, such as "tapping" or "semi-dancing" (as described in relation to the music in A&F; see Chapter 4). In commercials, grooves are typically arranged in detailed synchronization with the visual parts of commercials, thus generating interaction at the level of cotext. Moreover, grooves are often effective in increasing intensity toward a peaking roundoff, such as in the presentation of logo and/or slogan. In two commercials from the April 2012 volume for Hennes & Mauritz (a Swedish multinational clothing retailer), a groove presents the only auditory expression. In both commercials, the groove sets the scene for a visual pre-sentation of the clothes worn by women moving in slow motion. In one of the commercials, a relaxed groove—characterized by a slow, laid-back tempo and a simple instrumental arrangement of acoustic drums and slid-ing, echoing guitars—accompanies the slow-motion footage of women in swimsuits. The groove assists in characterizing the possible situation of the clothes (e.g., a relaxed holiday at the beach), and the slow motion of the visual presentation not only allows for careful scrutinizing of how the clothes react to bodily movements but also makes the commercial distinctive from other commercials (this example is the only commercial in the sample that is fully set in slow motion).

Normally, only one distinct musical format will manifest during a commercial, as illustrated by the Apple/The Blue Van case. However, a com-mercial often includes both indistinct and distinct music (e.g., music in the background of a voiceover in the first part of the commercial and a jingle at the end). More than one distinct musical expression in a commercial could conceivably lead to a "crowding" and "blurring" of the music's ability to attract attention and to contribute to musical signification. Nevertheless, notable examples of the use of multiple distinct expressions exist, and the previously mentioned commercial for Samsung/The Blue Van presents a case in point, as three distinct musical structures manifest.

First, excerpts from The Blue Van's song "Silly Boy" are heard during the majority of the first part of the commercial; this musical expression illustrates the distinct format of a song. After approximately 22 seconds, a voice-over is introduced. For the next four seconds, the music is positioned in the background of the following voice-over message: "Amazing phone needs amazing camera. It's Samsung behold. Exclusively from T-Mobile." Subsequent to the T-Mobile announcement, a jingle (i.e., T-Mobile's musical brand) is presented as the song continues to form the auditory background. The visuals have now shifted from a montage that includes diegetic settings to the presentation of the product (i.e., a Samsung mobile phone). At the end of the commercial, the song fades, and a Samsung jingle accompanies the visual presentation of the associated animated logo. Whereas this final jingle presentation conforms to the description of typical jingle positions, the T-Mobile jingle is quite unusual: It does not present the only auditory expression at the time of exposure, and it is not accompanied by a display of the T-Mobile logo.[5] This example illustrates the relative importance of sound over visuals when promoting a brand in a commercial. The visual presentation of the T-Mobile logo is thus omitted to allow for both the placement music to unfold and the final exposition of the Samsung brand. In return, one could say that the auditory exposition of T-Mobile is doubled, first through the verbal specification and second through the musical con-firmation of the jingle. The case also appears to illustrate the criteria of consistency in musical brands (see Chapter 3); whenever a particular brand is exposed, the musical brand element should be activated. This auditorily crowded commercial can be considered the result of the co-promotion of two brands, both of which make use of a musical brand and one of which makes use of placement music. The latter initiative is comparable to the use of music in many Apple commercials; however, as indicated previously, Apple does not deploy a specific musical brand, for instance, in the form of a jingle. With respect to the musical structure of the two jingles, they appear to be symptomatic of a more general trend originating from the Intel jingle. Thus, the two jingles show some of the "symptoms" of what could be termed "Inteluenza" (i.e., a nonvocal single-voiced melody line that includes a few notes in rapid succession). In the sample for this book, this characteristic applies to at least ten different jingles: The McDonald's jingle is illustrative. The Intel jingle appears to have effectively set the tone for a particular norm of jingle structure. As indicated, the Intel jingle has often been highlighted for its exemplarity success and influence in the literature aimed primarily at practitioners (see, e.g., Groves, 2011, p. 109; Jackson & Fulberg, 2003, p. 2).

6.2 INDISTINCT STRUCTURES

Indistinct music refers to musical expressions in commercials that are not prominent and do not attract attention. In other words, elements other than music are foregrounded during the commercial message. Hence, this music can be termed background music in the following sense:

> Background music is music that is subordinated to the background, to accompany either the visual images and the dialogue between characters in a commercial or the voiceover of a narrator. Background music functions much like background music in film and television, where it sets the mood for a story but is not the focus of it.
>
> (Rodman, 2010, p. 82)

Background music is not necessarily insignificant in terms of musical signification and, thus, in the construction of the commercial message. For example, commutation tests indicate, for example, that the music accompanying a dramatic sequence has considerable influence over the process of signification, as indicated by the commutation "trick" by Tagg referred to previously. Additionally, the case analysis by Killmeier and Christiansen (2011) of a 2004 Bush–Cheney campaign commercial illustrates that background music (in the sense of the earlier quote) can significantly "frame" the commercial message, thus establishing interpretive categories and generating expectations for what is to follow.

Perhaps because of operating in and as a background, indistinct music appears in many forms that do not clearly allow for the identification of formats as such (see also Bjurström & Lilliestam 1993, p. 82). However, in the following, I introduce three types of indistinct music: vamps, drama music, and (apparently a recent development) preexisting popular music with lyrics. In this context, drama music refers to primarily those typically instrumental musical expressions that originate from the commercial format of a drama. The function of the music is generally to accompany visual images and dialogues between characters. Another rarer example of this format is the music that accompanies a film or television series that is promoted through commercials.

A vamp is defined here as a non-melodic, repetitious expression that lasts throughout the majority of the commercial in the background (e.g., the background of a voice-over). Vamps are in some respects similar to the musical format of a groove: repeating and non-melodic characteristics that last throughout the majority of a commercial. However, unlike grooves, vamps lack rhythm and sound distinctions. A vamp is characterized by "short chord progressions" that "operate as a loop" (Tagg, 2013, p. 517), have a medium tempo, and feature only instrumental sounds. Moreover, a vamp is not musically "independent." The typical function of vamps in musical genres such as jazz and pop is thus to define the tempo and harmony for a soloist (as implied in the expression "vamp until ready"; see, e.g., Tagg, 2013, p. 517). In commercials, vamps are commonly subdued and have no particular synch-points with other sounds or moving pictures. Thus, for example, a displacement of half a second will not influence the signification of the commercial as a whole. The style of vamps in commercials is often unclear, as the music will appear as an auditory background at low volume with a limited arrangement of style indicators. Operating as a type of "neutral background" (Bjurström & Lilliestam, 1993, p. 79), this music can be quite elusive and thus difficult to describe or analyze. Such music is not entirely lacking signification—as indicated previously, no musical expression is neutral—but its signification is restricted. According to Middleton's analysis of specific pop music styles, the main function of such music is to "fulfill grammatical expectations rather than to stimulate mental associations" (Middleton, 1990, p. 236). The function of vamps is neither to attract the attention of listeners nor to highlight the characteristics of the brand or product. Rather, the music can be argued to contribute to a phatic communicative function of sustaining contact with the viewer (see Chapter 7 for more on communicative functions). This purpose further implies that the music functions "defensively" to avoid irritating and losing viewers, contrary to the typical "offensive" function of formats such as distinctive musical short formats, which aim to attract the attention of as many as possible (inspired by Björnberg, 1987, p. 49). A commercial from the April 2004 volume for the women's weekly magazine *Q* illustrates the vamp. A rock-styled groove appears to function as a background to the foreground voice of a presenter. The music ends abruptly in the middle of the chord progression without an episodic marker function of, for example, finalizing or climaxing the commercial, which is symptomatic of indistinct background music in the form of a vamp.

In what appears to be a recent phenomenon, preexisting popular music that includes lyrics can function as an indistinct background to a voice-over. In previous volumes, the use of preexisting popular music with lyrics would normally have entailed the absence of speech sounds, conceivably because of the possible mutual masking of the two verbal addresses (see, e.g., the discussion in Olsen & Johnson, 2002). However, in the April 2012 volume, there are several examples of the appearance of preexisting music with lyrics in the background of a voiceover. For example, a commercial[6] for Sadolin (an international provider of paints and coatings) includes excerpts from the song "My Days" (released in 2011 on Labrador) by Cecilie Noreng. The song, which presents a case of preexisting unknown opus music/postexisting music (see Chapter 2), is heard in the background of a voiceover, and the two verbal addresses clearly overlap during the commercial. In the commercial, excerpts from the beginning of the song accompany the visual staging of a young woman in the joyful process of painting what appears to be a living room. The female singer and the lyrics of the song—for example, "I paint my days, I use all the colors of a rainbow"—emphasizes the situation, although a focus on the lyrics of the song would most likely imply that the semantics of the voice-over are missed. Although this approach may appear to be a commercially unclear and unfortunate form of address, the viewer can adjust his or her attention during the commercial or focus exclusively on the musical lyrics (or the voiceover) when the commercial is revisited, which may in turn prevent wear-out effects. To provide another example, a commercial for Bilka (a Danish chain of hypermarkets) includes excerpts from Maroon 5's "Moves Like Jagger" (featuring Christina Aguilera and released in 2011 on A&M/Octone). The music, which presents a case of preexisting well-known opus music, is positioned in the background of a voice-over that energetically presents current offers. The music has no obvious relationship with Bilka or with the offers on display, and the music functions more generally as a positive mood enhancer based on the popularity of the music (the music was highly commercially successful in the months leading to its inclusion in the commercial). The use of music in this example resembles the prevalent use of preexisting popular music with lyrics in stores, for example. As indicated in Chapter 4, preexisting popular music with lyrics may, more or less loudly and intrusively, accompany a store visit and thus accompany occasional conversations between consumers and service assistants (e.g., the example of music in the Apple Store). Whereas the manifestations of lyrics were once considered distracting factors in commercial settings—for example, "vocals were thought to demand too much attention from listeners" (Kassabian, 2013a, p. 84)—no such concern currently appears to exist. Listeners are positioned as people who can effortlessly alternate between paying attention to and "engaging with" both the lyrics of a song (see, e.g., the possible use of lyrics in A&F) and the concurrent voiceover or conversation. In other words, listeners can alternate between "foregrounding" and "backgrounding" the music. This tolerance and ability arguably reflect listening practices in everyday life for many people, for whom music essentially functions as a controlled accompaniment to various activities (see, e.g., Bull, 2007; DeNora, 2000; Kassabian, 2013a).

This chapter has provided an overview of the various ways in which music in commercials is structured. As indicated, distinctive music tends to be clustered in specific formats, and Table 6.2 presents an overview of the previously referenced distinctive formats of music in commercials. Additionally, the table indicates the most typical relationship among musical formats, musical origin and promoted products. As indicated at the beginning of this chapter, this particular selection of formats is deduced from the sample for this book and is inspired by the existing literature. As indicated frequently, the typologies offered in previous studies are not perfectly comparable to the typology presented here. For example, the sample examined for this book includes formats that may not have been particularly notable or may not have even existed at the time of previous studies, such as grooves and emblems.

With respect to the relationship between distinctive musical formats and commercial formats, there is no unambiguous correlation. Distinctive music may prevail in all formats, but in general, a wordy voice-over will essentially place all music in the background, as already noted with respect to the medley. However, several tendencies can be identified: Montages are typically accompanied by one of the distinctive long formats, functioning,

Table 6.2 Outline of distinctive musical formats in relation to a typical origin and product

Musical format	Jingle	Emblem	Song	Tune	Groove
Predominant dimension of musical expression	Short, rounded melodic motif	A short-lived (one museme) musical sound	Longer accompanied and sung melody	Longer accompanied instrumental melody	Repetitious turn of phrase. Distinct via rhythm and sound
Cotext	Synchronized with logo and slogan presentation, typically at the end of the commercial		Throughout the commercial. Privileged auditory exposition and significant synch points		
Transtextuality	Original (or preexisting)	Original	Preexisting (or original)		
Relation to product	Brandmusic (or music–product partnership)	Brandmusic	Music-product partnership (music placement) or brandmusic		

for example, to bind together the visual progression. For such tethering purposes, music is privileged compared with a voice-over, which is inevitably characterized by auditory gaps and thus does not present a continuous auditory expression (as exemplified by the Apple/The Blue Van case). The distinctive short formats can be found in every commercial format, but they appear to play a specific role in the format of drama, in which a jingle can ensure, for example, that the sender and brand can be recognized. In the following chapter, I examine how music(al structures) in commercials function.

NOTES

1. See, for example, Tagg (2013, p. 264) for a short introduction to musical indicators of happiness and sadness.
2. Generally, sample-based diachronic studies of (early) commercials—that is, including precise information on the number of commercials examined and criteria for sampling—are rare. However, a few studies show an interest in characterizing earlier commercials. For example, Kilpiö (2001) examines Finnish cinema commercials in the 1950s and observes that "the commercials imitated the ways of Hollywood musical entertainment: using . . . lots of dance and singing." With respect to commercials from the 1960s, "during the first half of the decade, the advertisers continued to believe in singing" (Kilpiö, 2001, p. 72; see also Rodman, 2010, and Taylor, 2012, for historical accounts of commercials broadcast in the United States).
3. These three musical motifs, which will come to constitute the jingle in subsequent commercials, can be heard in synch with the presentation of the logo and slogan at 0:55 in the commercial (see www.youtube.com/watch?v=dI-xHMM8wXE).
4. The following observations are the result of an examination of all newly broadcast commercials for the McDonald's campaign *i'm lovin' it* on the Danish channel TV 2 during the period September 2003 to November 2011. This examination includes 267 unique commercials.
5. See the end of the following commercial for a more typical position of the T-Mobile jingle: www.youtube.com/watch?v=LaN3PnPfzCU. Incidentally, this commercial as a whole also illustrates the sometimes ironic appearances of music in commercials; that is, the somewhat disordered vocals and simple accompaniment can be heard as parodying the stereotype of a "song for a commercial"—an impression fueled by the metareference written on the screen at one point: "maybe next year we'll do a commercial with an overpaid movie star."
6. The commercial can be seen here: www.youtube.com/watch?v=8UbR2bDTBDY.

7 Musical Functions

Whereas previous chapters have specified what music in commercials *is*, how it *relates* to other music, and how it *appears*, this chapter focuses on what music *does* or should do (Rodman, 2010, p. 81). In this context, a function specifically refers to "an active relation between an object [i.e., music] and the goal for which this object is used" (Mukarovsky in Middleton, 1990, p. 256). Furthermore, a function denotes the "reasons for its [music] employment and particularly the broader purpose that it serves" (Marriam, 1964, p. 210). In this chapter, I focus on the functions of music in commercials from a cotextual perspective (i.e., musical functions will be examined with respect to the specific cotextualization of the music in the commercial), although the functions of music in commercials clearly have also contextual implications. For example, from the perspective of musical functions in society, music in commercials is generally associated with "economic functions" that apply "to cultures where, music making and music production are economic activities and, most especially, where a commercial music industry operates" (S. Brown, 2006, p. 12; for musical functions other than "economic," see, e.g., Marriam, 1964; Dissanayake, 2006). Music in commercials is therefore in the business of selling, and the purpose of music in commercials predominantly lies outside the music heard in the commercial. In other words, music is predominantly deployed in a commercial to contribute to the promotion of a product that is available outside the setting of the commercial (e.g., toothpaste, a car, or a full-length version of the music itself). Thus, given the functions of music in commercials, non-aesthetic functions appear to predominate: "For the non-aesthetic functions the goal lies outside the object, but for the aesthetic function it is the object itself"; the aesthetic may be further defined as "that aspect of our 'appropriation' of material reality (of the 'signifier') which, in a reversal of the semiotic norm, throws the weight of attention not on the *self*, its interests, concepts and goals, but on the object, the *other*, in all its materiality" (Middleton, 1990, p. 257). However, aesthetic functions are not entirely absent: "all communicational activities . . . are polyfunctional, so 'aesthetic' and 'practical' functions coexist in them all"; the "balance of functions varies, and the aesthetic function can be dominant, subordinate or even latent" (Middleton, 1990, p. 257). For example,

> One can . . . find cases in which the aesthetic function is only an accompanying function and not a dominant one. These are, e.g., melodic signals . . . and semi-sung outbursts of advertising (in train stations or on the streets) whose main purpose is to call attention to commercial products.
>
> (Mukarovsky, 1979, p. 11)

Thus, whereas music can contribute to an aesthetization of a commercial, the appearance of music in commercials can be generally viewed as a non-aesthetization of that music. This argument is most evident in cases of preexisting music in which the music's prior or "primary" function is "re-" or "metafunctionalized" as a result of the conditions of the new commercial setting (Eggebrecht, 1973, pp. 5, 13; for similar arguments, see, e.g., Björnberg, 1991; Edström, 1989; Leo, 1999; Tagg, 1979).

This introduction may appear to suggest that the functions of music (i.e., what the music does) in commercials is limited (e.g., to call the attention to a product being advertised with the ultimate goal of selling the product). Although this function is indeed essential from a marketing perspective, music can contribute to this purpose in numerous ways and contribute to other supplementary purposes: music is not necessarily deployed with the aim of attracting attention. For example, music can play a role from the perspective of all the communicative functions identified by Jakobson (1960) (for general introductions to this perspective in music theory, see, e.g., Fabbri, 1982; Middleton, 1990; Monelle, 1992).

Previous commentators on music in advertising have highlighted the emotive function: "emotive function dominates advertising jingles" (Fabbri, 1982, p. 12). Music can thus help illustrate and express the current characteristics, attitudes, and intentions of the sender. This function is illustrated by the commercial in which Justin Timberlake's singing endorses McDonald's. However, music in commercials also typically includes aspects of other functions. For example, the quote by Mukarovsky demonstrates that music can play both conative and referential roles, although the latter is sometimes considered unusual for music in general (or as art): "The referential function . . . is probably the least characteristic of the tonal arts" (Monelle, 1992, p. 19). Indeed, music in commercials can refer to something outside the music and the commercial message: the product or service promoted in the commercial; see also "call attention *to commercial products*" discussed earlier (Mukarovsky, 1979, p. 11; italics added; see also the discussion of secondary audiovisual signification in Chapter 5). The conative function is illustrated by the direction to "*call attention* to commercial products" (Mukarovsky, 1979, p. 11; italics added); this function involves addressing and positioning the viewer. In general, music in commercials contributes to the interpellation of viewers as possible consumers (following Althusser, 1971; see also Middleton, 1990, p. 242). Specifically, the possible vocatives and imperatives of the lyrics can more or less explicitly (commonly the latter) position the viewer as someone who is expected to do, feel, and think something in particular. For example, in the course of the McDonald's *i'm lovin' it* campaign, the slogan is arguably increasingly offered for viewers to identify with because of the musical changes. Similarly, the vocatives and imperatives of the lyrics of "There Goes My Love" have also been demonstrated to offer specific readings to viewers. The non-lyrical dimensions of the music may also perform a conative function because that function has been illustrated by the possibility of rhythmic entrainment as a response to a groove, for example. The metalingual function is found in relatively rare cases in which the music presents an ironic rendering of an established, perhaps stereotyped format of musical address in commercials (for example, see the Orange case in Chapter 2). Although the poetic or aesthetic function is generally not the most dominant function of music in commercials, the music may become the focus of interest regardless of its direct relevance to the promotion of a product or the actual situation of the sender. Perhaps the fact that viewers may find interest in and search for a particular piece of music from a commercial testifies to this function. The phatic function (i.e., establishing and continuing confirmation of contact) has already been illustrated by vamps (another example of this function with regard to the commercial use of music is on-hold music on the telephone; see Monelle, 1992, p. 18).

Specific functions of music in commercials have been illustrated throughout this book, including during the presentations of musical structures (Chapter 6) and signification in commercials (see Chapter 5). In the following, I address this issue in greater detail with the aim of presenting an overview of musical functions. I will introduce the most significant previous research on music in commercials (for overviews of musical functions that include other audiovisual texts, see, e.g., Corner, 2002; Goodwin, 1992; Lissa, 1965; Schneider, 1990).

One of the first researchers to address the functions of music in commercials was Motte-Haber (1972): "Music has three tasks to do, to attract attention, to stimulate memory, and to add a specific flair to the product being advertised" (p. 146). In a similar vein, albeit more systematically, Helms (1981) identifies three main functions of music in commercials and typical music forms that serve these functions. First, music may contribute to drawing attention to a product and overall message. This function is typically served by a fanfare, signaling that something interesting is about to occur. Second, music may enhance the learning and remembering of a product and message. Jingles, signature tunes, and composed songs may increase the audience's likelihood of understanding and memorizing a product and message. Third, music helps in constructing an attractive impression for a message or product. Preexisting classical or popular music is presumed to be particularly apt for generating this effect.

The seminal nature of Helms's contribution is demonstrated by its following by the claims of other researchers (e.g., Rösing, 1982, Steiner-Hall, 1987). Rösing (1982) claims that music provides important nonverbal clues for understanding the overall message of commercials. Music provides additional information about a message at three levels. At the illustrative level, music as a "sound image" can represent extra-musical events. The temporality of music can imitate movement, whereas the sound of music can represent the acoustic aspects of objects represented in a commercial. At the second level, association, stereotypical music styles, and genres can activate culturally formed schemes or interpretational frames for identifying the setting or action depicted in a commercial. The third level, emotion, helps the audience interpret whether the visuals of an advertisement should be understood in a positive (e.g., joy or love) or negative (e.g., mourning or loss) vein.

Conversely, Steiner-Hall's (1987) contribution is focused on the functions of music for market communication, studying the effects that music generates in the audience. The three functions identified by Helms (1981) are further specified in 10 functions, each exemplified by a brief case analysis. The following list includes the 10 functions identified by Steiner-Hall:

1. Grabbing attention and enhancing memory
2. Generating a positive mood
3. Increasing arousal/excitement
4. Reducing tension
5. Triggering or enhancing associations
6. Illustrating or showing the product's effects
7. Commenting on or interpreting the plot
8. Solving dramaturgical conflicts
9. Instigating the positive evaluation of the commercial
10. Providing a motive for buying the product

These functions and many of the examples are illustrative, although the logic is perhaps not entirely clear; for example, Functions 3 and 4 can be seen as specifications of Function 1; Functions 2 and 9 appear to overlap, and some of the functions appear to be text-internal, that is, Functions 6 through 8, while others appear to be text-external, Functions 1 through 5, 9, and 10. Also, the focus of Steiner-Hall's (1987) study is to describe *that* commercials may function in specific ways rather than to illustrating textually *how* and *why* this functioning is possible. Therefore, the scope of that study resembles that of the experimentalist perspective (see the introduction), although the methodologies vary considerably. This remark also applies to Leo (1999), who offers the only study that explicitly follows Steiner-Hall's research (more on this study later).

Huron (1989), one of the earliest Anglo-Saxon researchers studying music in commercials (see also Deaville, 2011, p. 16), proposes another categorization in an essay that identifies six functions and classifies them historically. The first and oldest function, derived from *Vaudeville*, is "entertainment," which serves to engage the attention. The second function is claimed to originate from film and functions to create "continuity" between each cut. The jingle is perceived as an example of the third function, which serves to increase a product's "memorability." "Lyrical language" is the fourth function, which comprises emotional, nonrational arguments that are believed to be more efficient when sung rather than spoken. The two last functions, "targeting" and "authority establishment," are presumed to be closely related. The stylistic properties of music lend authority to both commercials and products.

One of the seminal contributions to the field, that of Bjurström and Lilliestam (1993), presents five functions of music in commercials:

1. Creating a mood or background for the advertisement
2. Illustrating or emphasizing the dialogue or the plot
3. Signaling the beginning or end of the commercial spot
4. Emphasizing certain features or associations related to the product
5. Supporting memory of the product or the advertisement

These five functions elaborate those described by Helms (1981), Rösing (1982), and Huron (1989) in a more systematic manner, as illustrated in Table 7.1.

This model illustrates how some of the early classifications can be interpreted as related to Bjurström and Lilliestam (1993). The brackets indicate that an extended definition of a function may also cover another of Bjurström and Lilliestam's functions. Helms (1991) and Rösing (1982) lack at least one of the functions in Bjurström and Lilliestam's list. In each case, at least one of the author's functions covers several functions addressed by Bjurström and Lilliestam. For Huron, it seems straightforward to compare the first three functions with those used by Bjurström and Lilliestam. The fourth function is more difficult to place, indicating that this function's definition may lack precision. The last two functions should perhaps be combined into one function. Bjurström and Lilliestam's classification also presents a more condensed account of many of the functions presented by Steiner-Hall (1987). Although the latter classification lists twice as many functions as Bjurström and Lillienstam do, at least two of these additional functions could be considered merely specifications of Bjurström and Lilliestam, as interpreting the plot (Function 7) and solving a conflict (Function 8) are contained in Bjurström and Lilliestam's second function. The final two functions in Steiner-Hall are not specific to music but are instead related to the overall significance of the advertisement to which music contributes. Only Functions 3 and 4—an increase or decrease

Table 7.1   A comparison of four classifications of the function of music in commercials based on Bjurström & Lilliestam (1993) (adapted from Graakjær & Jantzen 2009a)

Helms (1981)	Rösing (1982)	Huron (1989)	Bjurström & Lilliestam (1993)
	2. The associative level 3. The emotional level	(4. Lyrical language)	1. Creating mood and background
1. Drawing attention to the overall message	1. The illustrative level	2. Continuity	2. Emphasizing plot and dialogue
(1. Drawing attention to the overall message)		1. Entertainment	3. Signaling the beginning and end
3. Creating an attractive image	2. The associative level	5. Targeting 6. Authority Establishment	4. Emphasizing features and associations
2. Enhancing learning and memory	3. The emotional level	3. Memorability (4. Lyrical language)	5. Supporting memory

of tension/arousal—appear to be lacking in Bjurström and Lilliestam's list although they could be seen to be implied under Function 5—supporting memory (see Bullerjahn 2006; Kafitz, 1977; Krommes, 1996, for more on this issue). This function highlights the importance of music in generating neurophysiologic changes in the audience, thereby creating a "present moment" and tuning them to the "right" way to receive a message (see Pfaff, 2006; Stern, 2004).

Bjurström and Lilliestam's (1993) contribution has two additional advantages over most of the other classifications discussed here. First, the authors discuss the relationship between functions and musical forms in considerable detail. Second, their study is based on solid quantitative research on the frequency of different forms of music in commercials. Two studies from the interpretive perspective on market communication that also classify various functions (L. Andersen, 2001; Scott 1990) lack both of these qualities. Scott (1990) identifies eight functions:

1. Creating contrasts by means of dissonance/consonance
2. Representing or emphasizing motion
3. Enhancing learning and memory by means of rhythm and repetition

4. Supporting the plot: music as narrative
5. "Locating": music represents the location depicted
6. Structuring time
7. Forging identifications: music enables identification with the style, genre, or values
8. Making a personal appeal: musical ethos

This categorization appears to add little to those already quoted. Symptomatic of the lack of cross-citation in this field (see the introduction), Scott quotes none of the authors mentioned above. In his contribution, L. Andersen (2001) elaborates on Scott's classification by noting three supplementary functions that he believes may be typical of newer, postmodern advertisements: music as intertextual reference, music as irony, and music as a mediator. As in Scott's (1990) classification, Andersen's account lacks empirical underpinning; thus, it is an open question whether these additional functions are new, widespread, and representative. Interestingly, a humorous and ironic function of music is also (and already) identified in the work of Helms (1981, p. 137).

Following this overview of previous contributions, the functions of music in commercials are numerous and multifaceted. Consequently, a given piece of music typically serves multiple functions with both text-internal and text-external implications. Text-internal implications refer to how music functions in relation to its cotexts. Essentially, text-internal functions relate to the text analytical approach of this book, which addresses text-internal functions throughout the work. For example, the presentation of primary and secondary audiovisual signification can be said to present two meta-functions that provide the foundation for the possible production of more specific text-internal functions, as described by the above contributions— that is, "emphasizing plot and dialogue," "signaling beginning and end," and "emphasizing features and associations" (see the list of Bjurström & Lilliestam 1993). Additionally, in Chapter 3, the presentation of music–product relationships reveals various possible text-internal relationships. Chapter 4 has illustrated how the text-internal functions of music in commercials differ from the functions of music in other commercial settings. For example, Table 4.1 illustrates how the possible text-internal functions of music in commercials differ from those of music on websites, as the latter present a more dynamic text that includes sounds and music as a result of user activity (i.e., in the user mode of navigating and editing). Text-internal functions presuppose an audience and are hence indirectly text-external. For example, the music that emphasizes features and associations presupposes that the viewer can interpret these features and associations. As indicated previously, the distinctive short formats predominantly function to signal the beginning or end of a commercial (the latter being the most typical in the sample used for this book) and to underscore the brand: Jingles and emblems are typically synchronized with the presentation of the logo and the slogan. The distinctive long formats typically serve to structure the commercial and to emphasize features and associations.

Text-external implications refer to the ways in which music can affect viewers. Text-external functions are derived from text-internal functions in the sense that, from the perspective of this book, the text-external function is facilitated by the specific origin, structure, and cotextualization of the music in a commercial. In this book, text-external implications have been hypothesized without actually examining actual effects or viewer responses. Some text-external functions have been examined experimentally, as illustrated by the dependent variables listed in Table 1.1, specifically memorization, recall, attitudes, beliefs, emotional evaluations, images, associations, perception of influence, choice, irritation, and behavioral intent (for a further systematization of what I have termed text-external functions, see, e.g., Bullerjahn, 2006, and Lantos & Craton, 2012). For example, the examination of the *i'm lovin' it* campaign for McDonald's has illustrated how music in commercials may not only attract attention and prompt emotional evaluations. The music in commercials may activate memory of an element that is no longer there; that is, the parapapapa motif could activate an imagined "I'm lovin' it!" Music's text-external functions in commercials differ somewhat from its text-external functions in other commercial settings because commercials do not have a direct musical effect on the physical presence and behavior of viewers in the same way that, for example, stores do. For example, music in stores may influence listeners' perceptions of space and bodily activities throughout the setting. Physical functions of music in commercials are more confined to functions such as an increase or decrease of tension/arousal and the related possible rhythmic entrainment (as mentioned). Generally, the distinctive formats function to attract attention and activate memory, whereas the distinctive long formats primarily function to influence attitudes, emotional evaluations, images, and associations.

In summary, the textual analysis of musical functions in television commercials should consider both text-internal and text-external implications. All instances of music serve multiple specific functions in commercials. The musical vamp illustrates how even a modest musical expression can fulfill both a text-external phatic function and a text-internal background and mood-characterizing function (e.g., co-constructing the emotional tone of the voice-over). When a commercial is accompanied by a vamp, textual elements other than music will normally function to attract attention, stimulate memory and characterize the product and brand, for example. The Apple/ The Blue Van case illustrates how music can serve a much more pronounced variety of functions in a commercial. For example, music has been demonstrated to function text-internally to structure a commercial, to signal its end, to characterize the product and its users, and to function text-externally to foster attitudes, beliefs, evaluations, and increased arousal and rhythmic entrainment.

FUNCTIONS OF "NO MUSIC"

In this section, I briefly address the issue of the significance of "no music" in commercials. As indicated throughout this book, "no music" does not imply "no sound," as object sounds and speech sounds normally appear in commercials that are devoid of music. Actually, no commercial from the sample is completely without sound. I have already briefly addressed the alleged significance of not using music with regard to the specific product category of financial products (see Chapter 3). To provide another example, the following suggestion has been offered: "In the world of advertising, replete as it is with music, there remains one distinct zone in which music is almost absent: . . . the area of the household" (Ala & Ghezzi, 1985, p. 408). However, based on the sample for this book (which clearly differs from the older German and Italian commercials referred to in the earlier contributions), I have suggested that it is not possible to identify an obvious universal correlation between product categories and the use (or nonuse) of music. In the following sections, I examine more closely how the absence of music may contribute significantly to a commercial message by (a) allowing for momentary silence and (b) allowing other sounds to be prominent.

Olsen (1994) focuses on the functions of silence (see also Olsen, 1995, 1997). Primarily based on interviews with advertisers, Olsen finds that "creative directors feel that silence may be used very effectively to generate attention to the ad in general [. . .] as well as to specific pieces of information" (1994, p. 90). Olsen (1994, p. 94) lists the following functions of silence in commercials:

1. To attract general attention
2. To attract specific attention
3. To evoke an emotion
4. To encourage rehearsal of information
5. To demonstrate product attribute

It should be emphasized that the functions of silence are essentially cotextual. Silence can contribute to processes of signification only because silence is produced by (surrounding) sounds. Moreover, the primary function of silence in commercials is to highlight visual elements: Because the audio dimension of an audiovisual expression is lacking, the visual dimension appears to gain prominence. The function of "attracting general attention" illustrates a possible intercommercial distinction: the "use" of silence can make a commercial appear distinctive compared with preceding and succeeding resonant commercials during the television flow. The function of "attracting specific attention" illustrates a possible intracommercial distinction. Within such a commercial, periods of silence may attract and redirect viewers' attention toward specific objects on display. For example, when "silence" is announced as an attractive feature of a promoted product, the absence of music will allow for a demonstration of this feature. As an illustration, in a commercial from the April 1996 volume for an AEG washing machine, a voice-over announces the absence of noise, which is subsequently demonstrated by "silent" moving pictures of the machine in action. Likewise, the non-noisy qualities of a product are promoted in a commercial from the April 2012 volume for a Dyson vacuum cleaner. The commercial begins with the loud suctioning sounds presented as the typical sound of ordinary vacuum cleaners from competitors. As the voice-over identifies the Dyson brand name, the suction sounds become associated with the Dyson vacuum cleaner presented. Shortly after, a decrescendo results in soft and vanishing suction sounds that illustrate the purported lack of (annoying) sound when operating a Dyson vacuum cleaner. On the surface, these examples may appear to conform to the suggestion by Ala and Ghezzi (1985); however, music is not entirely absent from the commercials but is absent only in the parts of the commercials emphasizing the value of silence.

Whereas "silence" may present an attractive feature of a particular product, the sound of a product may also be highlighted. If the sound of a product presents a key dimension of the promotion of that particular product, then the presence of music would risk masking the product's sound, which would in turn be associated with the absence (or pausing) of music in that particular commercial. The challenge presented is the reverse condition compared with the promotion of a musicproduct, in which non-musical sounds are minimized. For example, in a commercial from the April 2012 volume for XL-byg (a Danish provider of tools and building materials), sounds from a construction site (e.g., the sounds of metal and wood being handled) synchronize the sequential "construction" of the logo of XL-Byg without music (or speech), thereby underscoring the companies' claimed expertise related to tools.

The sounds of objects may also play a part in presenting a brand, as previously indicated by the commercials for HjemIs and Netto. For example, in a commercial for SEAT from the April 2012 volume, a whispering presentation of the brand name by the voice-over is accompanied by a low-pitched swaying sound resembling the sound of a heavy sheet that is suddenly shaken. The sound is synchronized with the visual presentation of flames flickering around the logo, and the object sound that appears to arise from the flames adds significantly to the illusion of emotion and passion associated with the presentation of the logo and hence the brand. In addition to accompanying the animation of the logo, object sounds may also help characterize the brand name, the slogan, or the product in various ways. This function is illustrated in a commercial for CBB mobil (a Danish telecommunications company) from the April 2012 volume. In that commercial, the sound of a waterfall accompanies a voice-over presenting the slogan "Tal som et vandfald," which translates to "Run at the mouth" or, literally, "Talk like a waterfall."

In addition to functioning as an expression of underscoring the product and the brand, object sounds can perform a number of more specific functions that indirectly promote a particular product and brand. For example, object sounds can highlight the inclusion and progress of visual graphics, for example, the sudden "arrival," turning, placing, and bouncing of price tags in the form of animated banners widely distributed across commercials. Additionally, to provide an example of a more recent auditory emergence in commercials, the sound of a clicking computer mouse can highlight the cross-media function of television commercials linking to a website (Jessen & Graakjær, 2013). For example, in a commercial for Frisko (the Danish brand name for an international provider of ice cream) from the April 2012 volume, the logo shot ends with a mouse click sound synchronized with a bouncing animation—as if the text is being clicked on—of the e-mail address of the company presented in close proximity to the logo. This animation demonstrates the preceding voice-over's appeal to viewers to visit the company's website, thus illustrating the frequent call-to-action function that is typically performed by a voice-over at the end of a television commercial.

8 Conclusion

With this book, I hope to have provided a platform, that is, a perspective and a vocabulary, from which music in commercials from the perspective of interpretive text analysis need not anymore be considered as a relatively scarce, uneven, and fragmented field of research. In the first part of the book, I focused on contextual aspects of music in commercials. I spent three chapters discussing how music in commercials is textually related to music from outside the universe of commercials, how music in commercials relates to the market of products and brands outside the universe of commercials, and how music in commercials presents a specific type of communication that differs from other music on television and in other types of commercial settings. In the second part of the book, I focused on cotextual perspectives. I discussed the issue of musical signification with a particular focus on how music relates to other text elements, presented the typical structures of music in commercials, and examined the variety of functions that music serves in commercials.

The Apple/The Blue Van case has illustrated these aspects and perspectives. Specifically, the case has demonstrated the necessity to consider not only the prior distribution of the music, that is, its preexistence and familiarity to the viewers, but also the precise excerpt and restructuring of the music in the commercial. The examination has further illustrated that preexisting music should not be considered merely placed but actually, in a sense, produced when deployed in a commercial. This point adds to our understanding of the possible power imbalance between brands and bands in seemingly lucrative music placement partnerships. Additionally, the textual analysis has contributed to our understanding of why—or why not—a band might benefit from music placement. The elements that contribute to this process seem to be the way in which the music is (re)structured and whether it is observed being performed or used by others (e.g., during dancing) although, obviously, more cases must be examined to support this suggestion. As a final point, the case may also point toward a modification of the process of music placement in commercials. So far, it appears as if artists will normally receive a license fee for the corporate use of their music (Klein, 2009, p. 74); however, the observed "Apple awe" indicates that perhaps the time will—or has—come, when labels will pay to have songs placed in commercials (Klein, 2009, p. 75).

I suggest that the presented perspectives—based on evaluations of the existing literature and the book's sample—are indispensable when examining music in commercials from a textanalytical perspective. For example, if an analysis of music in commercials does not include both con- and cotextual perspectives, it runs the risk of becoming unbalanced or biased. However, the analytical procedure need not follow the progression of the books' presentation of perspectives. The book's organization and progression has been inspired by a desire for clarity as well as by the characteristics of the Apple/ The Blue Van case in particular. Other cases might inspire alternative analytical progressions.

It is hoped that the present text-analytical perspective can inspire not only further research from a text-analytical perspective but also research on, for example, the reception of music in commercials as mentioned in the introduction. For example, qualitative interviews and questionnaires may indicate how viewers respond to the music, that is, whether they are familiar with the music's "opus" and genre, how they are positioned in the appeal of the "open spaces" of the lyrics, and how they would characterize the brand and the product. Moreover, observational studies of viewers may indicate the occurrence of rhythmic entrainment, and the deployment of designated instruments could indicate the influence of music in commercial on viewers' levels of arousal. In addition, it is hoped that the book can inspire to nuance the understanding of music as an "independent variable" in the context of experimentation (see the studies listed in Table 1.1). I have suggested that music presents a wide variety of potentials to affect its audiences. It is primarily through music's particular association with its cotexts that these potentials are realized, such that music may be said to contribute to processes of signification, which are in turn offered for particular viewers to interpret. This insight calls for a careful examination of the cotextualization of the music. In fact, it is not "music" that should be considered as the "independent variable" but, rather, the cotextualization of the music that should. I hope the book has provided a useful vocabulary and perspective to approach this insight in the fruitful context of experimentation.

Whether the presented perspectives are sufficient is to my mind a more open question. As far as I have been able to subtract from the existing literature as well as the sample included for this book, I am inclined to suggest, that the presented perspectives are indeed sufficient. However, it shall not be denied that other, for example, future, samples will present alternative propensities in the appearances of music and other sounds. For example, musical formats and functions may vary. So far, the rumors of the commercial's demise have been greatly exaggerated. For example, the following prospect of the future of television commercial can now be evaluated and rejected: "Television commercials will not exist five to ten years from now. It is a very clear tendency" (Jeff Cole in Brundin 2004). This is not to say, however, that commercials' living and environmental conditions referred to in the introduction and further examined in the first part of the book are not dynamic. As the book has focused on commercials from the perspective of (recent, Danish) television programming, this issue has not been thoroughly examined. However, one might speculate whether television commercials present an intermediate or overlapping communicative expression between early cinema commercials and audiovisual commercials in the context of the Internet and new media platforms. For example, "television texts over-flow onto interactive websites, television content is available on myriad platforms, and television networks are part of multi-media conglomerates" (Kackman, Binfield, Payne, Perlman, & Sebok, 2011, 1). Indeed, commercials illustrate how television texts can overflow onto interactive websites. Recently, for example, YouTube, Facebook, and Instagram have allowed for commercials in a textual structure that resembles commercials as encountered during the television flow (see, e.g., Mims, 2013). This also suggests that future research could beneficially include an examination of how music in commercials is possibly versionized for particular media platforms and contributes to cross-media communication. The book has hinted at these issues, by noting the increased explicit announcements of websites in television commercials and by including an examination of music in commercial settings other than television commercials, for example. It is hoped that the book's perspectives can form a platform from which the implications of possible new developments can be analyzed.

Bibliography

Aaker, D., & Bruzzone, D. (1985, Spring). Causes of irritation in advertising. *Journal of Marketing*, *49*, 47–57.

Ala, N., & Ghezzi, E. (1985). Music and advertising on Italian television. In D. Horn (Ed.), *Popular music perspectives II* (pp. 405–416). Exeter, England: A. Wheaton & Co.

Alexomanolaki, M., Kennett, C., & Loveday, C. (2010). Music as first-order and second-order conditioning in TV commercials. *Music and the Moving Image*, *3*(2), 39–50.

Alexomanolaki, M., Loveday, C., & Kennett, C. (2006). Music and memory in advertising: Music as a device of implicit learning and recall. In M. Baroni, A. R. Addessi, R. Caterina, & M. Costa (Eds.), *Proceedings from 9th International Conference on Music Perception and Cognition, August 22–26* (pp. 1190–1198). Bologna: ICMPC-ESCOM.

Allan, D. (2005). An essay on popular music in advertising: The bankruptcy of culture or the marriage of art and commerce? *Advertising & Society Review*, *6*(1), 1–9.

Allan, D. (2007a). Sound advertising: A review of the experimental evidence on the effects of music in commercials on attention, memory, attitudes, and purchase. *Journal of Media Psychology*, *12*(3). Retrieved from www.calstatela.edu/faculty/sfischo/

Allan, D. (2007b). Sound Retailing: A review of experimental evidence on the effects of music on shopping behavior. In T. Lowrey (Ed.), *Brick & mortar shopping in the 21st century* (pp. 33–52). New York, NY: Erlbaum.

Allan, D. (2008). A content analysis of music placement in prime-time television advertising. Journal of Advertising Research, *48*(3), 1–14.

Alperstein, N. M. (1990). The verbal content of TV advertising and its circulation in everyday life. *Journal of Advertising*, *19*(2), 15–22.

Alpert, J. I., & Alpert, M. I. (1991). Contributions from a musical perspective on advertising and consumer behavior. *Advances in Consumer Research*, *18*, 232–238.

Althusser, L. (1971). Ideology and ideological state apparatuses. In L. Althusser (Ed.), *Lenin and philosophy and other essays* (pp. 123–173). London, England: New Left Books.

Altman, R. (1992). *Sound theory. Sound practice.* New York, NY: Routledge.

Anand, S. (2013, August 12). Brands shorten commercials, increase frequency to beat economic slowdown. *The Economic Times.* Retrieved from http://articles.economictimes.indiatimes.com/2013-08-12/news/41332986_1_economic-slowdown-commercials-media-agencies

Andersen, L. P. (2001). Reklamens form og indhold [The form and content of advertising]. In F. Hansen, G. Lauritsen, & L. Grønholdt (Eds.), *Kommunikation, mediaplanlægning og reklamestyring Bind 1—metode og modeller* (pp. 118–152). Copenhagen, Denmark: Samfundslitteratur.

Andersen, T. (2010, March 8). Dansk rockband lægger lyd til ny Apple-reklame [Danish rock band delivers sound for new Apple commercial]. *Politiken*. Retrieved from http://politiken.dk/kultur/musik/ECE918925/dansk-rockband-laegger-lyd-til-ny-apple-reklame/

Anderson, D. R., & Kirkorian, H. L. (2006). Attention and television. In J. Bryant & P. Vorderer (Eds.), *Psychology of entertainment* (pp. 35–54). Mahwah, NJ: Erlbaum.

Anthes, E. (2010, September/October). It's so loud, I can't hear my budget. *Psychology Today*, 40.

Areni, C., & Kim, D. (1993). The influence of background music on shopping behavior: Classical versus top-forty music in a wine store. *Advances in Consumer Research*, *20*, 336–340.

Areni, C. S. (2003a). Examining managers' theories of how atmospheric music affects perception, behaviour and financial performance. *Journal of Retailing and Consumer Services*, *10*, 263–274.

Areni, C. S. (2003b). Exploring managers' implicit theories of atmospheric music: Comparing academic analysis to industry insight. *Journal of Services Marketing*, *17*, 161–184.

Augoyard, J.-F., & Torgue, H. (2006). *Sonic experience. A guide to everyday sounds*. Montreal, Quebec, Canada: McGill-Queen's University Press.

Barnhard, R., & Rutledge, J. (2009, June 5). Music + ads: Advertising is the new radio. *Billboard*. Retrieved from www.adweek.com/news/advertising-branding/music-ads-advertising-new-radio-99496

Barreneche, R. (2006). Hot property. *Interior Design*, *77*(4), 186–191.

Baudrillard, J. (1994). *Simulacra and simulation*. Ann Arbor: University of Michigan Press.

Bay, J., Gudnitz, H., & Jahn, P. (2005). "Musik sælger radio—Sælger radio musik? [Music sells radio—does radio sell music?]. *Radiorapporten 1*. Retrieved from www.pladebranchen.nu/publikationer/RadioRapporten1.pdf

Berland, J. (1993). Radio space and industrial time: The case of music formats. In T. Bennett (Ed.), *Rock and popular music: Politics, policies, institutions* (pp. 104–118). London, England: Routledge.

Björnberg, A. (1987). *En liten sång som alla andra—Melodifestivalen 1959–1983* [A little song like all others—Eurovision Song Contest 1959–1983]. Göteberg, Sweden: Skrifter från Musikvetenskapliga institutionen.

Björnberg, A. (1991). *Analyse af populærmusik: Teorier og Metoder* [Analyzing popular music: Theories and methods]. Aalborg, Denmark: Aalborg: Institut for Musik og Musikterapi.

Björnberg, A. (2000). Structural relationships of music and images in music videos. In R. Middleton (Ed.), *Reading pop—approaches to textual analysis in popular music* (pp. 347–378). Oxford, England: Oxford University Press.

Björnberg, A. (2009). The soundtrack of sales. Supplementary sounds of consumption. In N. J. Graakjær & C. Jantzen (Eds.), *Music in advertising—commercial sounds in media communication and other settings* (pp. 223–236). Aalborg, Denmark: Aalborg University Press.

Bjurström, E., & Lilliestam, L. (1993). *Sälj det i toner—Om musik i TV-reklam* [Sell it in tunes—on music in TV commercials]. Stockholm, Sweden: Konsumentverket.

Blair, E., & Shimp, T. (1992). Consequences of an unpleasant experience with music. A second-order negative conditioning perspective. *Journal of Advertising*, *21*(1), 35–43.

Blake, A. (2007). *Popular music—the age of multimedia*. London, England: Middlesex University Press.

Blattner, M. M., Sumikawa, D. A, & Greenberg, R. M. (1989). Earcons and icons: Their structure and common design principles. *Human-Computer Interaction*, 4, 11–44.

Blau, M. (2011, October 13). 15 songs that defined the sound of Apple marketing. *Mashable*. Retrieved from http://mashable.com/2011/10/12/apple-music-marketing/#

Block, V. (2003, February 3). Death of the advertising jingle. *Advertising Age*. Retrieved from: http://adage.com/article?article_id=36741.

Bode, M. (2004). *Musik in der Werbemittelforschung unter besonderer Berücksichtigung interpretativer Verfahren* [Music in advertising research, especially regardin interpretive approaches] . Frankfurt am Main, Germany: Peter Lang.

Bode, M. (2009). Making sense of music in advertising research. An interpretive model of the interaction between music and image. In N. J. Graakjær & C. Jantzen (Eds.), *Music in advertising—commercial sounds in media communication and other settings* (pp. 121–140). Aalborg, Denmark: Aalborg University Press.

Bollinger, B. K., & Wang, W. (2013, October 18). Sitting through commercials: How commercial break timing and duration affect viewership. *SSRN*. Retrieved from http://ssrn.com/abstract=2342384

Bolter, J. D., & Grusin, R. (1999). *Remediation. Understanding new media*. Cambridge, MA, & London, England: The MIT Press.

Book, A., Cary, N., & Tannenbaum, S. (1984). *The radio and television commercial*. Lincolnwood, IL: NTC Business Books.

Bonde, A. (2009). On the commercialization of Shostakovich's 'Waltz No. 2': A case study of textual, contextual and intertextual meaning of music. In N. J. Graakjær & C. Jantzen (Eds.), *Music in advertising—commercial sounds in media communication and other settings* (pp. 141–167). Aalborg, Denmark: Aalborg University Press.

Bozman, C., & Mueling, D. (1994). The directional influence of music backgrounds in television advertising. *Journal of Applied Business Research*, 10(1), 14–18.

Bridge, F. (1921). *The old cryes of London*. London, England: Novello.

Bronner, K., & Hirt, R. (2009). *Audio branding. Brands, sound and communication*. Baden-Baden, Germany: Nomos.

Brooker, G., & Wheatly, J. (1994). Music and radio advertising. Effects of tempo and placement. *Advances in Consumer Research*, 21, 286–290.

Brophy, P. (Ed.). (1999). *Cinesonic: The world of sound in film*. Sydney, Australia: AFTRS.

Brown, J. (2001). *Ally McBeal*'s postmodern soundtrack. *Journal of the Royal Musical Association*, 126(2), 275–303.

Brown, S. (2006). Introduction. How does music work? Toward a pragmatics of musical communication. In S. Brown & U. Volgsten (Eds.), *Music and manipulation—on the social uses and control of Music* (pp. 1–27). New York, NY: Berghan Books.

Brownrigg, M., & Meech, P. (2002). From fanfare to funfair: The changing sound world of UK television idents. *Popular Music*, 21(3), 345–355.

Brundin, S. (2004, October 22). Internetrevolutionen minskar tevens betydelse [The Internet revolution weakens the importance of television]. *ComputerSweden*. Retrieved from www.idg.se/2.1085/1.26850

Bruner, G. (1990, October). Music, mood and marketing. *Journal of Marketing*, 54(4), 94–104.

Bull, M. (2007). *Sound moves. iPod culture and urban experience*. London, England: Routledge.

Bullerjahn, C. (2006). The effectiveness of music in television commercials. In S. Brown & U. Volgsten (Eds.), *Music and manipulation: On the social uses and social control of music* (pp. 207–235). Oxford, England: Berghahn Books.

Burgess, J., & Green, J. (2009). *YouTube*. Cambridge, England: Polity Press.
Burns, G. (1987). A typology of 'hooks' in popular records. *Popular Music, 6*(1), 1–20.
Burns, G. (1996). Popular music, television, and generational identity. *Journal of Popular Culture, 30*(3), 129–141.
Carah, N. (2010). *Pop Brands. Branding, Popular Music, and Young People.* New York, NY: Peter Lang.
Cheng, F.-F., Wu, C.-S., & Yen, D.C. (2008). The effect of online store atmosphere on consumer's emotional responses. An experimental study of music and colour. *Behaviour & Information Technology, 28*(4), 323–334.
Chion, M. (2009). *Film, a sound art*. New York, NY: Columbia University Press.
Chou, H.Y., & Lien, N.H. (2010). Advertising effects of songs' nostalgia and lyrics' relevance. *Asia Pacific Journal of Marketing and Logistics, 22*(3): 314–329.
Christensen, L.T. (2001). Intertextuality and self-reference in contemporary advertising. In F. Hansen & L.Y. Hansen (Eds.), *Advertising research in the Nordic countries* (pp. 351–356). Frederiksberg, Denmark: Samfundslitteratur.
Christensen, S. (2014). The Blue Van. *Skandinavian*. Retrieved from www.skandinavian.dk/artister/thebluevan/#
Christian, E.B. (2011) *Rock brands. Sellings sounds in a media saturated culture.* Plymouth, UK: Lexington Books.
Clayton, M., Sager, R., & Will, U. (2004). In time with the music: The concept of entrainment and its significance for ethnomusicology. *ESEM Counterpoint, 1*, 1–45.
Clifford, S. (2011, August 17). Abercrombie wants off 'Jersey Shore' (wink-wink). *The New York Times*. Retrieved from www.nytimes.com/2011/08/18/business/abercrombie-offers-jersey-shore-cast-a-paid-non-product-placement.html
Clow, K., & Baack, D. (2004). *Integrated advertising, promotion and marketing communications.* Harlow, England: Prentice Hall.
Cohen, A. (2001). Music as a source of emotion in film. In P. Juslin & J. Sloboda (Eds.), *Music and emotion—theory and research* (pp. 249–272). Oxford, England: Oxford University Press.
Cohen, A. (2013). Congruence-association model of music and multimedia. Origin and evolution. In S. Tan, A. Cohen, S. Lipscomb, & R. Kendall (Eds.), *The psychology of music in multimedia* (pp. 17–47). Oxford, England: Oxford University Press.
Coker, W. (1972). *Music and meaning: A theoretical introduction to musical aesthetics.* New York, NY: Collier-Macmillan.
Collins, K. (2008). *Game sound: An introduction to the history, theory and practice of video game music and sound design.* Cambridge, MA: MIT Press.
Cook, G. (2001). *The discourse of advertising.* London, England: Routledge.
Cook, N. (1994). Music and meaning in the commercials. *Popular Music, 13*(1), 27–40.
Cook, N. (1998). *Analysing musical multimedia.* Oxford, England: Oxford University Press.
Cook, N. (2001). Theorizing musical meaning. *Music Theory Spectrum, 23*(2), 170–195.
Corner, J. (2002). Sounds real: Music and documentary. *Popular Music, 21*(3), 357–366.
Craton, L.G., & Lantos, G.P. (2011). Attitude toward the advertising music: An overlooked potential pitfall in commercials. *Journal of Consumer Marketing, 28*(6), 39–411.
Davies, S. (2001). Philosophical perspectives on music's expressiveness. In P. Juslin & J. Sloboda (Eds.), *Music and emotion—theory and research* (pp. 23–44). Oxford, England: Oxford University Press.

Deaville, J. (2009). TV news music. Television news music in North America. In G. Harper, R. Doughty, & J. Eisentraut (Eds.), *Sound and music in film and visual media. An overview* (pp. 612–616). New York, NY: Continuum.

Deaville, J. (2011). A discipline emerges. Reading writing about listening to television. In J. Deaville (Ed.), *Music in television. Channels of listening* (pp. 7–33). New York, NY: Routledge.

DeNora, T. (2000). *Music in everyday life.* Cambridge, England: Cambridge University Press.

DeNora, T., & Belcher, S. (1999). 'When you're trying something on you picture yourself in a place where they're playing this kind of music'—musically sponsored agency in the British clothing retail sector. *Sociological Review, 48*(11), 80–101.

DiCrescenzo, B. (2011, November 2). How Feist beat being a one-hit wonder. *Time Out Chicago.* Retrieved from http://timeoutchicago.com/music-nightlife/music/15004943/how-feist-beat-being-a-one-hit-wonder

Dissanayake, E. (2006). Ritual and ritualization: Musical means of conveying and shaping emotion in humans and other animals. In S. Brown & U. Volgsten (Eds.), *Music and manipulation—on the social uses and control of music* (pp. 31–56). New York, NY: Berghan Books.

Donnelly, K. (2005). *The spectre of sound: Music in film and television.* London, England: BFI Publishing.

Donnelly, K. (2014). *Occult aesthetics. Synchronization in film.* Oxford, England: Oxford University Press.

Doyle, J. (2011. December 9). The iPod silhouettes: 2000–2011. *PopHistoryDig. com.* Retrieved from www.pophistorydig.com/?tag=tbwachiatday-advertising

Duggan, T. (2006). The Mahler symphonies. A synoptic survey. *Music Web International.* Retrieved from www.musicweb-international.com/Mahler/mahler5.htm

Dyer, G. (1982). *Advertising as communication.* New York, NY: Routledge.

Eckhardt, G. M., & Bradshaw, A. (2014). The erasure of antagonisms between popular music and advertising. *Marketing Theory, 14*(2), 167–183.

Eco, U. (1979). *The role of the reader.* Indianapolis: University of Indiana Press.

Edel, H. (1988). The jingle business. In G. Martin (Ed.), *Making music: The essential guide to writing, performing and recording* (pp. 326–327). London, England: Barrie & Jenkins.

Edström, O. (1989). 'Vi skall gå på restaurang och höra på musik'—Om reception af restaurangsmusik och annan 'mellanmusik' [We are going to the restuarant to listen to music—On the reception of restaurant music and other "in-between music"]. *Svensk Tidskrift för Musikforskning, 71,* 77–112.

Eggebrecht, H. (1973). Funktionale musik [Functional music]. *Archiv für Musikwissenschaft, 30*(1), 1–25.

Elliott, A. M. (2010, July 5). The Apple effect: Ads that have launched music careers. *Mashable.* Retrieved from http://mashable.com/2010/07/05/apple-commercial-songs/

Elliott, S. (2013, September 29). Apple passes Coca-Cola as most valuable brand. *The New York Times.* Retrieved from www.nytimes.com/2013/09/30/business/media/apple-passes-coca-cola-as-most-valuable-brand.html?_r=3&

Ellis, J. (1982). *Visible fictions: Cinema, television, video.* London, England: Routledge.

eMarketer. (2014, April 7). Social usage during TV time still small. *eMarketer,* Retrieved from www.emarketer.com/Article/Social-Usage-During-TV-Time-Still-Small/1010738

Englis, B. (1990). Music television and its influences on consumers, consumer culture, and the transmission of consumption messages. *Advances in Consumer Research, 18*(1), 111–114.

Englis, B., & Pennell, G. (1994). When 'hits' strikeout: Loving the song but hating the product. *Advances in Consumer Research, 21,* 97.

Fabbri, F. (1982). A theory of musical genres: Two applications. In D. Horn & P. Tagg (Eds.), *Popular music perspectives—papers from the first international conference on popular music research* (pp. 52–81). Gothenberg, Sweden, & Exeter, England: Wheaton.

Fehling, R. (1980). Funktionelle Musik—Manipulationsversuch im Gewanden der holden Kunst [Functional music—Attempts at manipulation in the guise of art]. In R. Brinkmann (Ed.), *Musik im Alltag* (pp. 84–95). Mainz, Germany: Schott.

Fill, C. (2002). *Marketing communications. Contexts, strategies and applications.* Harlow, England: Prentice Hall.

Finnemann, N. O. (2001). The Internet—a new communicational infrastructure. *Papers from The Centre for Internet Research, University of Aarhus.* Retrieved from http://cfi.au.dk/fileadmin/www.cfi.au.dk/publikationer/cfis_skriftserie/002_finnemann.pdf

Fiore, S., & Kelly, S. (2007). Surveying the use of sound in online stores: Practices, possibilities and pitfalls for user experience. *International Journal of Retail & Distribution Management, 35*(7), 600–611.

Firat, F., Dholakia, N., & Venkatesh, A. (1995). Marketing in a postmodern world. *European Journal of Marketing, 29*(1), 40–56.

Fiske, J. (1987). *Television culture.* London, England: Routledge.

Flueckiger, B. (2009). Sound effects. In G. Harper (Ed.), *Sound and music in film and visual media.* (pp. 151–179). New York, NY: Continuum.

Flyvbjerg, B. (2006). Five misunderstandings about case-study research. *Qualitative Inquiry, 12*(2), 219–245.

Forsyth, A., & Cloonan, M. (2008). Alco-pop? The use of popular music in Glasgow pubs. *Popular Music, 31*(1), 57–78.

Fouconnier, G., & Turner, M. (2002). *The way we think.* New York, NY: Basic Books.

Fredrix, E. (2010, October 30). TV commercials shrink to match attention spans. *USA Today.* Retrieved from http://usatoday30.usatoday.com/money/advertising/2010-10-30-shorter-v-commercials_N.htm

Friis, H. (2010). The Blue Van—greasing the wheels with advertisement revenue. *Spot Festival.* Retrieved from http://2010.spotfestival.dk/en/news/the-blue-van-greasing-the-wheels-with-advertisement-revenue.html

Frith, S. (1988). *Music for pleaure. Essays in the sociology of pop.* Cambridge, England: Polity Press.

Frith, S. (2002). Look! Hear! The uneasy relationship of music and television. *Popular Music, 21*(3), 277–290.

Galan, J.-P. (2009). Music and responses to advertising: The effects of musical characteristics, likeability and congruency. *Recherche et Applications en Marketing, 24*(4), 3–22.

Galician, M.-L. (Ed.). (2004). *Handbook of product placement in the mass media: New strategies in marketing theory, practice, trends, and aesthetics.* Binghamton, NY: Haworth Press.

Galician, M.-L., & Bourdeau, P.G. (2004). The evolution of product placements in Hollywood cinema: Embedding high-involvement 'heroic' brands images. In M.-L. Galician (Ed.), *Handbook of product placement in the mass media: New strategies in marketing theory, practice, trends, and aesthetics* (pp. 15–36). Binghamton, NY: Haworth Press.

Garlin, F. V., & Owen, K. (2006). Setting the tone with the tune: A meta-analytic review of the effects of background music in retail settings. *Journal of Business Research, 59*(6), 755–764.

Gauntlett, D., & Hill, A. (1999). *TV living*. London, England: Routledge.
Gertich, F., & Motte-Haber, H. (1987). Werbung aus musikpsychologischer Sicht [Advertising from the perspective of music psychology]. *Musikerziehung*, *11*(4), 155–160.
Geertz, C. (1973). *The interpretation of cultures*. London, England: Hutchinson.
Goffman, E. (1983). The interaction order. *American Sociological Review*, *48*, 1–17.
Goodman, S. (2010). *Sonic warfare. Sound, affect, and the ecology of fear*. Cambridge, MA: MIT Press.
Goodwin, A. (1992). *Dancing in the distracting factory—music television and popular culture*. London, England: Routledge.
Gorbman, C. (1987). *Unheard melodies: Narrative film music*. Bloomington: Indiana University Press.
Gorn, G., Goldberg, M., Chattopadhyay, A., & Litvack, D. (1991). Music and information in commercials: Their effects with an elderly sample. *Journal of Advertising Research*, *5*, 23–32.
Graakjær, N. J. (2004). Nyhedernes musik [The music of the News]. *Mediekultur*, *37*, 36–46.
Graakjær, N. J. (2009a). Music in TV commercials—formats, frequencies, and tendencies. In N. J. Graakjær & C. Jantzen (Eds.), *Music in advertising—commercial sounds in media communication and other settings* (pp. 53–74). Aalborg, Denmark: Aalborg University Press.
Graakjær, N. J. (2009b). The JYSK jingle—on the use of pre-existing music as a musical brand. In N. J. Graakjær & C. Jantzen (Eds.), *Music in advertising—commercial sounds in media communication and other settings* (pp. 99–120). Aalborg, Denmark: Aalborg University Press.
Graakjær, N. J. (2010). Beep beats of banking and other money music. *Danish Yearbook of Musicology*, *37*, 57–78.
Graakjær, N. J. (2012). Dance in the store. On the use and production of music in Abercrombie & Fitch. *Critical Discourse Studies*, *9*(4), 393–406.
Graakjær, N. J. (2014). The bonding of a band and a brand: On music placement in television commercials from a text analytical perspective. *Popular Music and Society*. Advanced online publication. doi:10.1080/03007766.2013.861242
Graakjær, N. J., & Jantzen, C. (2009a). Mapping research on music in TV commercials. In N. J. Graakjær & C. Jantzen (Eds.), *Music in advertising—commercial sounds in media communication and other settings* (pp. 13–52). Aalborg, Denmark: Aalborg University Press.
Graakjær, N. J., & Jantzen, C. (2009b). Relevant . . . but for whom? On the commercial (ab)use of music on television. In N. J. Graakjær & C. Jantzen (Eds.), *Music in advertising—commercial sounds in media communication and other settings* (pp. 169–182) Aalborg, Denmark: Aalborg University Press.
Graakjær, N. J., & Jantzen, C. (2009c). Producing corporate sounds. An interview with Karsten Kjems and Søren Holme on sonic branding©. In N. J. Graakjær & C. Jantzen (Eds.), *Music in advertising—commercial sounds in media communication and other settings* (pp. 259–274). Aalborg, Denmark: Aalborg University Press.
Gracyk, T. (2001). *I wanna be me: Rock music and the politics of identity*. Philadelphia, PA: Temple University Press.
Greckel, W. (1987).Die Verwendung klassischer Musik in der amerikanischen Fernsehwerbung [The use of classical music in American TV commercials]. In E. Ostleitner (Ed.), *Massemedien, Musikpolitik und Musikerziehung* (pp. 195–215). Vienna, Austria: VVWGÖ.
Greenspan, C. (2004). Irving Berlin in Hollywood: The art of plugging a song in film. *American Music*, *22*(1), 40–49.

Gregorio, F. de, & Sung, Y. (2009). Giving a shot out to Seagram's gin: Extent of and attitudes towards brands in popular songs. *Brand Management, 17*, 218–235.

Groom, N. (1996). The condition of Muzak. *Popular Music and Society, 20*(3), 1–17.

Groves, J. (2011). *Commusication. From Pavlov's dog to sound branding*. Cork, Ireland: Oak Tree Press.

Hahn, M., & Hwang, I. (1999). Effects of tempo and familiarity of background music on message processing in TV advertising: A resource-matching perspective. *Psychology and Marketing, 16*(8), 659–675.

Hall, E. T. (1967). *The hidden dimension*. New York, NY: Doubleday.

Hampp, A. (2011, August 26). 10 songs Steve Jobs made famous. *AdAge*. Retrieved from http://adage.com/article/news/10-songs-steve-jobs-apple-made-famous/229471/

Hansen, M. (2011, February 21). Derfor medvirkede The Blue Van i iPad-reklame [This is why The Blue Van chose to appear in an iPad commercial]. *MacNation*. Retrieved from http://macnation.newz.dk/derfor-medvirkede-the-blue-van-i-ipad-reklame

Harding, C. (2008, September 9). Synch placement in a TV ad for Apple. *Billboard, 120*(39), 12–13.

Hatten, R. (1987). Style, motivation and markedness. In T. Sebeok & J. Umiker-Sebeok (Eds.), *The semiotic web* (pp. 408–429). Amsterdam, the Netherlands: Mouton de Gruyter.

Haug, W. F. (1986). *Critique of commodity aesthetics: Appearance, sexuality and advertising in capitalist society*. Minneapolis: University of Minnesota Press.

Helms, S. (1981). *Musik in der Werbung* [Music in advertising]. Wiesbaden, Germany: Breitkopf & Härtel.

Hearsum, P., & Inglis, I. (2013). The emancipation of music video. YouTube and the cultural politics of supply and demand. In J. Richardson, C. Gorbman, & C. Vernallis (Eds.), *The Oxford handbook of audiovisual aesthetics* (pp. 483–500). Oxford, England: Oxford University Press.

Henard, D., & Rossetti, C. (2014). All you need is love? Communication insights from pop Music's number-one hits. *Journal of Advertising Research, 53*, 178–191.

Herring, S. C. (2004) Content analysis for new media: Rethinking the paradigm. In *New research for new media: Innovative Research Methodologies Symposium, Working Papers and Readings* (pp. 47–66). Minneapolis: University of Minnesota School of Journalism and Mass Communication. Retrieved from http://ella.slis.indiana.edu/~herring/newmedia.pdf

Hicketier, K., & Bleichert, J. (Eds.). (1997). *Trailer, teaser, appetizer. Zu Ästhetik und Design der Programmbindungen im Fersehen. Beiträge zur Medienästhetik und Mediengeschichte, vol. 3* [Trailer, Teaser, Appetizer. On the aesthetics and design of interludes between programs on TV. Contributions on media aesthetics and history, vol. 3]. Hamburg, Germany: LIT Verlag.

Hirschman, E. C. (1983). Predictors of self-projection, fantasy fulfillment, and escapism. *The Journal of Social Psychology, 120*, 63–76.

Hitchon, J., Duckler, P., & Thorson, E. (1994). Effects of ambiguity and complexity on consumer response to music video commercials. *Journal of Broadcasting & Electronic Media, 38*(3), 289–304.

Hjelmslev, L. (1943). *Omkring sprogteoriens grundlæggelse* [On the foundation of the language theory]. Copenhagen, Denmark: Copenhagens Universitet.

Holbrook, M. (2004). Ambi-diegetic music in films as a product-design and-placement strategy: The sweet smell of success. *Marketing Theory, 4*(3), 171–185.

Horton, D., & Wohl, R. R. (1956). Mass communication and para-social interaction. *Psychiatry, 19*, 215–229.

Hung, K. (1994). *An empirical investigation of the impact of music on brand perception in television commercials* (Unpublished doctoral dissertation). Ann Arbor: University of Michigan.

Hung, K. (2000). Narrative music in congruent and incongruent TV advertising. *Journal of Advertising, 29*(1), 25–34.

Hung, K. (2001). Framing meaning perceptions with music: The case of teaser ads. *Journal of Advertising, 30*(3), 39–49.

Huron, D. (1989). Music in advertising: An analytical paradigm. *Musical Quarterly, 73*, 557–574

Iceberg Records. (2010). The Blue Van. *Deep Dive Music.* Retrieved from www. deepdivemusic.net/files/band134_4.pdf

Inglis, I. (Ed.). (2003) *Popular music and film.* London, England: Wallflower Press.

Iser, W. (1974). *The implied reader. Patterns in prose fiction from Bunyan to Beckett.* Baltimore, MD: John Hopkins University Press.

Jacke, C., Jünger, S., & Zurstiege, G. (2000). Aufdringliche Geschichten—zum Verhältnis von Musik und Werbung [Importunate stories—On the relationship between music and advertising]. In H. Rösing & Th. Phleps (Eds.), *Populäre Musik im Kulturwissenschaftlichen Diskurs* (pp. 25–42). Karben, Germany: CODA Musikservice + Verlag.

Jackson, D., & Fulberg, P. (2003). *Sonic branding.* London, England: Palgrave.

Jakobson, R. (1960). Closing statement: Linguistics and poetics. In T. Sebeok (Ed.), *Style and language* (pp. 350–377). Cambridge, MA: MIT Press.

Janoschka, A. (2004). *Web advertising: New forms of communication on the Internet.* Amsterdam, the Netherlands: John Benjamins.

Jantzen, C., & Stigel, J. (1995). *Reklame i dansk landsdækkende fjernsyn* [Commercials in Danish national television] Copenhagen, Denmark: Statsministeriets Medieudvalg.

Jensen, K.B., & Helles, R. (2007). The silent web. A qualitative study of sound as information and communication in websites. In M. Consalvo & C. Haythornthwaite (Eds.), *Internet research annual 4* (pp. 183–194). New York, NY: Peter Lang.

Jessen, I.B., & Graakjær, N.J. (2010). Sounds of web advertising. In M.S. Eastin, T. Daugherty, & N.M. Burns (Eds.), *Handbook of research on digital media and advertising: User generated content consumption* (535–551). Hershey, PA, & New York, NY: Information Science Reference.

Jessen, I.B., & Graakjær, N.J. (2013). Cross-media communication in advertising: exploring multimodal connections between television commercials and websites. *Visual Communication, 12*(4), 437–458.

Johnson, B., & Cloonan, M. (2009). *Dark side of the tune: Popular music and violence.* Farnham, England: Ashgate.

Jones, C. (2013, August 20). Apple vs. Samsung. Who could win the smartphone war? *Forbes.* Retrieved from www.forbes.com/sites/chuckjones/2013/08/20/apple-and-samsung-who-could-win-the-smartphone-war/

Jones, S., & Schumacher, T. (1992). Muzak: On functional music and power. *Critical Studies in Mass Communication, 9*, 156–169.

Julien, J.-R. (1985). The use of folklore and popular music in radio advertising. In D. Horn (Ed.), *Popular music perspectives II* (pp. 417–427). Exeter, England: A. Wheaton & Co.

Jungheinrich, H.-K. (1969). Hörmassage—Musik in der Werbung [Auditory massage—Music in advertising]. *Musica, 23*(6), 559–561.

Kackman, M., Binfield, M., Payne, M.T., Perlman, A., & Sebok, B. (Eds.) (2011). *Flow TV: Television in the age of media convergence.* New York, NY: Routledge.

Kafitz, W. (1977). *Der Einfluss der musikalischen Stimulierung auf die Werbewirkung eine experimentelle Untersuchung* [The influence of musical stimulation on the effect of advertising: An experimental investigation] (Unpublished doctoral dissertation). Universität Saarbrücken.

Kalinak, K. (1992). *Settling the Score: Music and the classical Hollywood film*. Madison: University of Wisconsin Press.

Kaplan, A. E. (1987). *Rocking around the clock: Music television, postmodernism and consumer culture*. London, England: Routledge.

Karmen, S. (1989). *Through the jingle jungle. The art and business of making music for commercials*. New York, NY: Billboard Books.

Karmen, S. (2005). *Who killed the jingle? How a unique American art form disappeared*. Milwaukee, WI: Hal Leonard, 2005.

Kassabian, A. (2001). *Hearing films—tracking identifications in contemporary Hollywood film music*. New York, NY: Routledge.

Kassabian, A. (2013a). *Ubiquitous listening. Affect, attention, and distributed subjectivity*. Berkeley: University of California Press.

Kassabian, A. (2013b). The end of diegesis as we know it? In J. Richardson, C. Gorbman, & C. Vernallis (Eds.), *The Oxford handbook of audiovisual aesthetics* (pp. 89–106). Oxford, England: Oxford University Press.

Kellaris, J., Cox, A., & Cox, D. (1993, October). The effect of background music on ad processing: A contingency explanation. *Journal of Marketing, 57*, 114–125.

Kershaw, D. (1992). Music and image on film and video: An absolute alternative. In J. Paynter et al. (Eds.), *Companion to contemporary musical thought—vol 1*. (pp. 466–499). London, England: Routledge.

Kilpiö, K. (2001). The use of music in early Finnish cinema and TV advertising. In F. Hansen & L. Y. Hansen (Eds.), *Advertising research in the Nordic countries* (pp. 68–76). Frederiksberg, Denmark: Samfundslitteratur.

Killmeier, M., & Christiansen, P. (2011). Wolves at the door: Musical persuasion in a 2004 Bush-Cheney campaign advertisement. *MedieKultur, 50*, 160–180.

Klein, B. (2009). *As heard on TV: Popular music in advertising*. Farnham, England: Ashgate.

Kloepfer, R. & Landbeck, H. (1991). *Ästhetik der Werbung. Der Fernsehspot in Europa als Symptom neuer Macht* [The aesthetics of advertising. The TV commercial in Europe as a symptom of new power]. Frankfurt, Germany: Fischer.

Knudsen, O., & Jensen, K. (2010, Macrh 8) Brønderslevbandet The Blue Van i Apple-reklame [The Broenderslev band The Blue Van features an Apple commercial]. *Nordjyske*. Retrieved from www.nordjyske.dk/broenderslev/forside.aspx?c trl=10&data=14%2c3515907%2c5%2c3

Korsgaard, M. B. (2013). Music video transformed. In J. Richardson, C. Gorbman, & C. Vernallis (Eds.), *The Oxford handbook of audiovisual aesthetics* (pp. 501–521). Oxford, England: Oxford University Press.

Kotler, P., (1973/1974). Atmospherics as a marketing tool. *Journal of Retailing, 49*(4), 48–65.

Kristeva, J. (1980). *Desire in language: A semiotic approach to literature and art*. New York, NY: Columbia University Press.

Krommes, R. (1996). Musik in der Fernseh-und Rundfunkwerbung [Music in TV and radio commercials]. *Jahrbuch der Absatz-und Verbrauchsforschung, 42*, 406–434.

Kudit, LCC. (2014). Applemusic.info. Retrieved from http://applemusic.info/

Lacasse, S. (2000). Intertextuality and hypertextuality in recorded popular music. In M. Talbot (Ed.), *The musical work: Reality or invention* (pp. 35–58). Liverpool, England: Liverpool University Press.

Lam, S. Y. (2001). The effects of store environment on shopping behaviors: A critical review. *Advances in Consumer Research, 28*(1), 190–197.

Lannin, S., & Caley, M. (Eds.) (2005). *Pop Fiction: The song in cinema*. Palo Alto, CA: ebrary.

Lantos, G. P., & Craton, L. G., (2012). A model of consumer response to advertising music. *Journal of Consumer Marketing, 29*(1), 22–42.

Lanza, J. (2004). *Elevator music: A surreal history of Muzak, easy-listening, and other moodsong* (rev. ed.). Ann Arbor: University of Michigan Press.

Lanza, J. (2013). Foreground flatland. In J. Richardson, C. Gorbman, & C. Vernallis (Eds.), *The Oxford Handbook of Audiovisual Aesthetics* (pp. 622–627). Oxford, England: Oxford University Press.

Lee, J. (2008, October 1). Is Apple the Oprah for indie bands? *The New York Times*. Retrieved from www.nytimes.com/2008/10/01/technology/01iht-01apple.16602972.html?_r=0

Leeuwen, T. van. (1989). Changed times, changes tunes: Music and the ideology of the news. In J. Tulloch & G. Turner (Eds.), *Australian television: Programmes, pleasures, and politics* (pp. 172–186). Sydney, Australia: Allen & Unwin.

Leeuwen, T. van. (1999). *Speech, music, sound*. Hampshire, England: Palgrave Macmillan.

Leeuwen, T. van. (2005). *Introducing social semiotics*. New York, NY: Routledge.

Lehu, J.-M. (2007). *Branded entertainment: Product placement and brand strategy in the entertainment business*. London, England: Kogan Page.

Leo, H. (1999). *Musik im Fernsehwerbespot* [Music in the TV commercial]. Frankfurt, Germany: Peter Lang.

Liebowitz, S. (2004). The elusive symbiosis: The impact of radio on the record industry. Retrieved from http://ssrn.com/abstract=520022

Linz, G. (1985). Musik im Programm—Musik als Programm [Music in program—Music as program]. In W. Hoffmann-Riem & W. Teichert (Eds.), *Musik in den Medien. Programmgestaltung im Spannungsfeld von Dramaturgie, Industrie und Publikum* (pp. 87–98). Baden-Baden, Germany: Nomos.

Lissa, Z. (1965). *Ästhetik der Filmmusik* [The aesthetics of film music]. Berlin, Germany: Henschelverlag.

Lucensky, J. (2011). *Sounds like banding: Use the power of music to turn customers into fans*. London: A & C Black Publishers.

Lull, J. (1992). Popular music and communication—an introduction. In J. Lull (Ed.), *Popular music and communication* (pp. 1–32). London, England: Sage.

MacInnis, D., & Park, C. W. (1991, September). The differential role of characteristics of music on high-and low-involvement consumer's processing of ads. *Journal of Consumer Research, 18*, 161–173.

MacLeod, B. (1979). Facing the Muzak. *Popular Music and Society, 7*(19), 19–31.

Macklin, M. (1988). The relationship between music and advertising and children's response: An experimental investigation In S. Hecker & D. Stewart (Eds.), *Nonverbal communication in advertising* (pp. 225–252). Lexington, MA: Lexington Books.

MacRury, I. (2009). *Advertising*. Oxon, England: Routledge.

Magis, C. (2013). 'Do mess with' Mister In-Between!'. Musicological and socio-ecomomic study of arrangement in advertising covers. *SoundEffects, 3*(1/2), 97–111.

Martin, P. (1995). *Sounds and society. Themes in the sociology of music*. Manchester, England: Manchester University Press.

Marriam, A. P. (1964). *The anthropology of music*. Evanston, IL: Northwestern University Press.

Marx, K., & F. Engels. (1970). *The German ideology. Introduction to a critique of political economy*. London, England: Lawrence & Wishart.

Mattila, A. S., & Wirtz, J. (2001). Congruency of scent and music as a driver of in-store evaluations and behavior. *Journal of Retailing, 77*, 273–289.

McLaren, C. (1998). Licenced to sell: Why the jingle is dead and commercial pop rules. *Stay Free!, 15*. Retrieved from http://ibiblio.org/pub/electronic-publications/stay-free/archives/15/licensed.html

Meier, L. M. (2011). Promotional ubiquitous musics: Recording artists, brands, and 'rendering authenticity.' *Popular Music and Society, 34,* 399–415.

Meissner, R. (1974). Mendelssohns Söhnlein-Musik in der Fernsehwerbung [Mendelssohns Söhnlein-Music in the TV commercial]. *Musik und Bildung, 6,* 305–309.

Mey, J. (1993). *Pragmatics—an introduction.* Oxford, England: Blackwell.

Middlestadt, S., & Fishbein, M. (1994). The effect of music on brand attitudes: Affect-or belief-based change? In E. Clark, T. Brock, & D. Stewart (Eds.), *Attention, attitude, and affect in response to advertising* (pp. 149–167). Hillsdale, NJ: Erlbaum.

Middleton, R. (1990). *Studying popular music.* Milton Keynes, England: Open University Press.

Middleton, R. (1999). Form. In B. Horner & T. Swiss (Eds.), *Key terms in popular music and culture* (pp. 141–155). Malden, MA: Blackwell.

Middleton, R. (2000). Work-in(g)-practice: Configurations of the popular music intertext. In M. Talbot (Ed.), *The musical work: Reality or invention* (pp. 59–87). Liverpool, England: Liverpool University Press.

Miller, F. (1985). *Music in advertising.* New York, NY: Amsco Publications.

Milliman, R. (1982). Using background music to affect the behavior of supermarket shoppers. *Journal of Marketing, 46*(3), 86–91.

Millward Brown. (2008). How to make the best use of music in an ad. Retrieved from www.millwardbrown.com/Libraries/MB_Knowledge_Points_Downloads/MillwardBrown_KnowledgePoint_MusicInAnAd.sflb.ashx

Mims, C. (2013, June 30). It's no accident Facebook made Instagram's new videos exactly as long as a television commercial. *Quartz.* Retrieved from http://qz.com/96475/its-no-accident-facebook-made-instagrams-new-videos-exactly-as-long-as-a-television-commercial/#96475/its-no-accident-facebook-made-instagrams-new-videos-exactly-as-long-as-a-television-commercial/.

Mitchelson, T. (2007). Poseurs paradise! What's it really like to work at the new Abercrombie & Fitch store? *Mail Online.* Retrieved from www.dailymail.co.uk/femail/article-447183/Poseurs-Paradise-Whats-really-like-work-new-Abercrombie—Fitch-store.html#ixzz1dm8m6V5k

Monelle, R. (1992). *Linguistics and semiotics in music.* London, England: Routledge.

Moore, A. F. (1999). Review of "Analysing musical multimedia." *Music and Letters, 80*(2), 328–30.

Moore, A. F. (2001). *Rock: The Primary Text. Developing a Musicology of Rock* (2nd ed.). Aldershot, England: Ashgate.

Moore, A. F. (2010). Review of "As Heard on TV: Popular Music in Advertising." *Popular Musicology Online.* Retrieved from www.popular-musicology-online.com/issues/review%20articles/Moore_Klein.html

Morgan, D. (2012, January 31). Poll: Vote for best classic Super Bowl ad. *CBS News.* Retrieved from www.cbsnews.com/media/poll-vote-for-best-classic-super-bowl-ad/

Morrison, M., Gan, S., Dubelaar, C., & Oppewal, H. (2011). In-store music and aroma influences on shopper behavior and satisfaction. *Journal of Business Research, 64*(6), 558–564.

Motte-Haber, H. (1972a). *Musikpsychologie. Eine Einführung* [Music psychology. An introduction]. Köln, Germany: Musikverlag Hans Gerig.

Motte-Haber, H. (1972b). Das singende und klingende Plakat. Werbung durch Musik [The singing and cinging billboard. Advertising through music]. *Sprache im technischen Zeitalter, 42,* 143–153.

Motte-Haber, H. (1973). 'Erkennen sie die Melodie?' Gedanken zur gewaltsamen Zerstörung von Kunstwerken ['Do you recognize the melody?' Thoughts on the violent destruction of art works]. *Musik und Bild, 5,* 178–181.

MTV Networks. (2010, March 9). The Blue Van Lægger Musik til Apple's iPad [The Blue Van delivers music for Apple's iPad]. *MTV Networks*. Retrieved from www. mtv.dk/nyheder/the-blue-van-l%C3%A6gger-musik-til-apples-ipad-reklame

Mukarovsky, J. (1979). *Aesthetic function, norm and value as social facts.* Ann Arbor: University of Michigan Press.

Mundy, J. (1999). *Popular music on screen—from the Hollywood musical to music video.* Manchester, England: Manchester University Press.

Murray, N., & Murray, S. (1996). Music and lyrics in commercials: A cross-cultural comparison between commercials run in the Dominican Republic and in the United States. *Journal of Advertising, 25*(2), 51–63.

Nattiez, J.-J. (1990). *Music and discourse—toward a semiology of music.* Princeton, NJ: Princeton University Press.

Negus, K. (1999). *Music genres and corporate cultures.* New York, NY: Routledge.

Negus, K., & Street, J. (2002). Introduction to 'Music and Television' special issue. *Popular music, 21*(3), 245–248.

North, A., Hargreaves, D., & Kendrick, J. (1999). The effect of music on in-store wine selections. *Journal of Applied Psychology, 84,* 271–276.

North, A.C., & Hargreaves, D.J. (2006). Music in business environments. In S. Brown & U. Volgsten (Eds.), *Music and manipulation. On the social uses and social control of music* (pp. 103–125). New York, NY: Berghahn Books.

Oakes, S. (2000). The influence of the musicscape within service environments. *Journal of Services Marketing, 14*(6), 539–556.

Oakes, S. (2007). Evaluating empirical research into music in advertising: A congruity perspective. *Journal of Advertising Research, 47*(1), 38–50.

Oakes, S., & North, A. (2013) Dance to the music! How musical genres in advertisements can sway perceptions of image. *Journal of Advertising Research, 53*(4), 411–416.

The Observer. (2002, June 16). Brandenburger with fries? Retrieved from www. theguardian.com/uk/2002/jun/16/theobserver.uknews1

Olsen, G.D. (1994). The sounds of silence: Functions and use of silence in television advertising. *Journal of Advertising Research, 34*(5), 89–95.

Olsen, G.D. (1995). Creating the contrast: The influence of silence and background music on recall and attribute importance. *Journal of Advertising, 24*(4), 29–44.

Olsen, G.D. (1997). The impact of interstimuli interval and background silence on recall. *Journal of Consumer Research, 23*(4), 295–303.

Olsen, G.D., & Johnson, R.D. (2002). The impact of background lyrics on recall of concurrently presented verbal information in an advertising context. *Advances in Consumer Research, 29*(1), 147–148.

Owen, D. (2006, April 10). The soundtrack of our life. Muzak in the realm of retail theatre. *The New Yorker.* Retrieved from www.newyorker.com/ archive/2006/04/10/060410fa_fact?currentPage=all

Paltschik, M., & Lindqvist, L.-J. (1987). *Consumer recall of brand and product class under conditioning of music from television commercials* (Working paper [150]). Helsinki: Swedish School of Economics and Business Administration.

Park, C., & Young, S. (1986). Consumer response to television commercials: The impact of involvement and background music on brand attitude and formation. *Journal of Marketing Research, 23*(1), 11–24.

Pauli, H. (1976). Filmmusik: Ein historisch-kritischer Abriss [Film music. A critical historical report]. In H.C. Schmidt (Ed.), *Musik in den Massemedien Rundfunk und Fernsehen* (pp. 91–119). Mainz, Germany: Schott.

Pekkilä, E. (1998). On musical signification in television commercials. In *Les universaux en musique: Actes du quatrième Congrés international sur la signification musicale. Série esthétique: Nr. 1* (pp. 323–330). Paris, France: Publications de la Sorbonne.

Pekkilä, E. (2009). Music videos and TV commercials—Similarities and differences. In N.J. Graakjær & C. Jantzen (Eds.), *Music in advertising—commercial sounds in media communication and other settings* (pp. 121–140). Aalborg, Denmark: Aalborg University Press.

Percivel, J.M. (2011). Music radio and the record industry: Songs, sounds and power. *Popular Music and Society, 34,* 4, 455–73.

Pfaff, D. (2006). *Brain arousal and information theory. Neural and genetic mechanisms.* Cambridge, MA: Harvard University Press.

Pidd, H. (2009, June 24). Disabled student sues Abercrombie & Fitch for discrimination. *The Guardian.* Retrieved from www.guardian.co.uk/money/2009/jun/24/abercrombie-fitch-tribunal-riam-dean

Phillips-Silver, J., Aktipis, C.A., & Bryant, G. (2010). The ecology of entrainment: Foundations of coordinated rhythmic movement. *Music Perception, 28*(1), 3–14.

Powers, D. (2010). Strange powers. The branded sensorium and the intrigue of musical sound. In M. Aronczyk & D. Powers (Eds.), *Blowing up the brand. Critical perspectives on promotional culture* (pp. 285–306). New York, NY: Peter Lang.

Powrie, P., & and Stilwell, R. (Eds.). (2006). *Changing tunes: The use of pre-existing music in film.* Aldershot, England: Ashgate.

Prendergast, R. (1992). *Film music—a neglected art.* New York, NY: Norton

Radano, R. (1989). Interpreting Muzak: Speculations on musical experience in everyday life. *American Music, 7*(4), 448–460.

Reay, P. (2004). *Music in film: Soundtracks and synergy.* London, England: Wallflower Press.

Redker, C., & Gibson, B. (2009). Music as an unconditioned stimulus: Positive and negative effects of country music on implicit attitudes, explicit attitudes, and brand choice. *Journal of Applied Social Psychology, 39*(11): 2689–2705.

Reinboth, M. (2011, September 12). Music and synchronization: Independents leading the way. *Future Music Forum Barcelona.* Retrieved from http://futuremusicforumbarcelona.wordpress.com/2011/09/12/music-and-synchronization-independents-leading-the-way/

Richardson, J., & Gorbman, C. (2013). Introduction. In J. Richardson, C. Gorbman, & C. Vernallis (Eds.), *The Oxford handbook of audiovisual aesthetics* (pp. 3–35). Oxford, England: Oxford University Press.

Riethmüller, A. (1973). Das Tonsignet. Versuch einer Bestimmung seiner Eigenschaften und Aufgaben [The auditory seal. An attempt to specify characteristics and functions]. *Archiv für Musiwissenschaft, 30*(1), 69–79.

Ritscher, I. (1966). *Akustische Werbung—Ihre Wirkung und Anwendungsmöglichkeiten* [Acoustic advertising—It's effects and potentials]. Berlin, Germany: Duncker & Humblot.

Rodman, R. (1997). 'And now an ideology from our sponsors': Musical style and semiosis in American television commercials. *College Music Symposium, 37,* 21–48.

Rodman, R. (2010). *Tuning in. American narrative television music.* New York, NY: Oxford University Press.

Roehm, M. (2001). Instrumental vs. vocal versions of popular music in advertising. *Journal of Advertising Research, 41*(3), 49–58.

Romney, J., & Wootton, A. (Eds.). (1995). *Celluloid jukebox: Popular music and the movies since the 1950s.* London: British Film Institute.

Rösing, H. (1975). Funktion und Bedeutung von Musik in der Werbung [Functions and meaning of music in commercials]. *Archiv für Musikwissenshaft, 32*(2), 139–155.

Rösing, H. (1982). Music in advertising. In D. Horn & P. Tagg (Eds.), *Popular music perspectives* (pp. 41–51). Gothenberg, Sweden: IASPM.

Rule, G. (1997, March). Jingles all the way. Making music for commercials. *Keyboard*, pp. 69–75.

Rutherford, P. (1994). *The new icons? The art of television commercials*. Toronto, Ontario, Canada: University of Toronto Press.

Sanburn, J. (2012, February 3). Advertising killed the radio star: How pop music and TV ads became inseparable. *Time Magazine*. Retrieved from http://business. time.com/2012/02/03/advertising-killed-the-radio-star-how-pop-music-and-tv-ads-became-inseparable/

Savan, L. (1993). Commercials go rock. In S. Frith, A. Goodwin, & L. Grossberg (Eds.), *Sound and vision—the music video reader* (pp. 85–90). London, England: Routledge.

Schafer, R. M. (1977). *The soundscape. Our sonic environment and the tuning of the world*. Rochester, NY: Destiny Books.

Schank, R., & Abelson, R. (1977). *Scripts, plans, goals, and understanding: An inquiry into human knowledge structure*. Hillsdale, NJ: Erlbaum.

Schmidt, H.-C. (1983).Audiovisuelle Ge- Mis-und Verbrauch von Musik [Audiovisual use, abuse, and consumption of music]. In E. Jost (Ed.), *Komponieren heute—Ästhetische, soziologische und pädagogische Fragen* (pp. 95–107). Mainz, Germany: Schott.

Schmitt, R. (1976). Musik in der Werbung—Ein Beitrag zu ihrer Didaktik [Music in advertising—A didactical contribution]. *Musik und Bildung, 8*, 327–331.

Schneider, N. J. (1990). *Handbuch Filmmusik I—Musikdramaturgie im neuen deutschen film* [Handbook film music I—In recent German films]. Munich, Germany: Verlag Ölschläger.

Schonberger, J. (2011, July). Trend teen retailers make totally hot stocks. *Kiplingers*. Retrieved from www.kiplinger.com/columns/picks/archive/teen-fashion-retailers-totally-hot-stocks.htmlHot stocks?

Schug, S. (2010, May 29). Bands and brands. *The Word*. Retrieved from http:// thewordmagazine.com/dribbles/bandsandbrands/

Scott, L. M. (1990). Understanding jingles and needledrop: A rhetorical approach to music in advertising. *Journal of Consumer Research, 17*(2), 223–236.

Seeking Alpha. (2008, February 13). How Apple's TV ads have a ripple effect on online searches. *Seeking Alpha*. Retrieved from: http://seekingalpha.com/ article/64395-how-apples-tv-ads-have-a-ripple-effect-on-online-searches.

Selberg, T. (1993). Television and ritualization of everyday life. *The Journal of Popular Culture, 26*(4), 3–10.

Sewall, M., & Sarel, D. (1986). Characteristics of radio commercials and their recall effectiveness. *Journal of Marketing, 50*, 52–60.

Segrave, K. (2004). *Product placement in Hollywood films: A history*. Jefferson, NC: McFarland & Co.

Shaer, M. (2010, March 8). Forget "Avatar." How about that Apple iPad ad?' *The Christian Science Monitor*. Retrieved from www.csmonitor.com/Innovation/ Horizons/2010/0308/Forget-Avatar.-How-about-that-Apple-iPad-ad

Shen, Y.-C., & Chen, T.-C. (2006). When East meets West: The effect of cultural tone congruity in ad music and message on consumer ad memory and attitude. *International Journal of Advertising, 25*(1), 51–70.

Shevy, M., & Hung, K. (2013). Music in television advertising and other persuasive media. In S. Tan, A. Cohen, S. Lipscomb, & R. Kendall (Eds.), *The psychology of music in multimedia* (pp. 315–338). Oxford, England: Oxford University Press.

Shklovsky, V. (2012). Art as technique. In L. T. Lemon & M. J. Reis (Eds.), *Russian formalist criticism: Four essays* (2nd ed., pp. 3–24). Lincoln: University of Nebraska Press. (Original work published 1917)

Shuker, R. (2005). *Popular music—the key concepts*. London, England: Routledge.

Smith, J. (1998). *The sounds of commerce—marketing popular film music.* New York, NY: Columbia University Press.

Smith, J. (1999). Selling my heart: Music and cross-promotion in *Titanic.* In K. Sandler & G. Studlar (Eds.), Titanic. *Anatomy of a blockbuster* (pp. 46–63). New Brunswick, NJ: Rutgers University Press.

Smith, P., & Curnow, R. (1966). 'Arousal hypothesis' and the effects of music on purchasing behavior. *Journal of Applied Psychology, 50*(3), 255–256

Spangenberg, E. R., Grohmann, B., & Sprott, D.E. (2005). It's beginning to smell (and sound) a lot like Christmas: The interactive effects of ambient scent and music in a retail setting. *Journal of Business Research, 58*(11), 1583–1589.

Springer, C. (1992). *Society's soundtrack: Musical persuasion in television advertising* (Doctoral dissertation). Ann Arbor: University of Michigan.

Steiner-Hall, D. (1987). *Musik in der Fernsehwerbung* [Music in TV commercials]. Frankfurt, Germany: R.G. Fischer Verlag.

Stern, D. (2004). *The present moment in psychotherapy and everyday life.* New York, NY: Norton.

Sterne, J. (1997). Sounds like the mall of America: Programmed music and the architectonics of commercial space. *Ethnomusicology, 41*(1), 22–50.

Sterne, J. (2005). Urban media and the politics of sound space. OPEN, 9. Retrieved from www.skor.nl/article-2853-en.html

Stevens, C.S. (2011). Touching the audience: Music and television advertising in Japan. *Japanese Studies, 31,* 37–51.

Stewart, D., Farmer, K., & Stannard, C. (1990). Music as a recognition cue in advertising-tracking studies. *Journal of Advertising Research, 30*(4), 39–48.

Stewart, D., & Punj, G. (1998). Effects of using a nonverbal (musical) cue on recall and playback of television advertising: Implications for advertising tracking. *Journal of Business Research, 42*(1), 39–51.

Stigel, J. (2001). The aesthetics of Danish TV-spot-commercials. A study of Danish TV-commercials in the 1990'ies. In F. Hansen & L.Y. Hansen (Eds.), *Advertising Research in the Nordic Countries* (pp. 327–350). Frederiksberg, Denmark: Samfundslitteratur.

Stigel, J. (2004). Tv's egenreklame og kanalstemmen—En kvalitativ undersøgelse [TV's promos and the channel voice—A qualitative study]. *MedieKultur, 37,* 24–35.

Stigel, J. (2006). Continuity og tv-reklame [Continuity and TV commercials] In S. Hjarvad (Ed.), *Dansk tv's historie* (pp. 291–330). Frederiksberg, Denmark: Forlaget Samfundslitteratur.

Stilwell, R.J. (1995). 'In the Air Tonight': Text, intertextuality and the construction of meaning. *Popular Music and Society, 19,* 67–103.

Stilwell, R.J. (2005). Clean reading. The problematics of 'In the Air Tonight' in 'Risky Business'. In S. Lannin & M. Caley (Eds.), *Pop fiction: The song in cinema* (pp. 140–154). Palo Alto, CA: ebrary.

Stockfelt, O. (2006). Music and reuse—theoretical and historical considerations. In S. Brown & U. Volgsten (Eds.), *Music and manipulation—on the social uses and control of music* (pp. 315–335). New York, NY: Berghan Books.

Stout, P., & Leckenby, J. (1988). Let the music play: Music as a nonverbal element in television commercials. In S. Hecker & D. Stewart (Eds.), *Nonverbal communication in advertising* (pp. 207–233). Lexington, MA: Lexington Books.

Stout, P., Leckenby, J., & Hecker, S. (1990). Viewer reactions to music in television commercials. *Journalism Quarterly, 67*(4), 887–898.

Stout, P.A., & Rust, R.T. (1986). The effect of music on emotional response to advertising. In E.F. Larkin (Ed.), *Proceedings of the 1986 conference of the American Academy of Advertising* (pp. R82–R85). Norman: University of Oklahoma Press.

Tagg, P. (1979). Kojak—*50 seconds of television music.* Gothenberg, Sweden: Musikvetenskapliga Institutionen.

Tagg, P. (2006). Music, moving images, semiotics, and the democratic right to know. In S. Brown & U. Volgsten (Eds.), *Music and manipulation—on the social uses and control of music* (pp. 163–186). New York, NY: Berghan Books.

Tagg, P. (2013). *Music's meaning. A modern musicology for non-musos.* New York, NY: MMMSP.

Tagg, P., & Clarida, B. (2003). *Ten little title tunes.* New York, NY: MMMSP.

Talbot, M. (Ed.). (2000). *The musical work: Reality or invention.* Liverpool, England: Liverpool University Press.

Tauchnitz, J. (1990). *Werbung mit Musik* [Education with music]. Heidelberg, Germany: Physica-Verlag.

Taylor, T. (2000). World music in television ads. *American Music, 18*(2), 162–192.

Taylor, T. (2007). The changing shape of the culture industry; or, how did electronica music get into television commercials. *Television and New Media, 8*(3), 235–258.

Taylor, T. (2012). *The sounds of capitalism. Advertising, music, and the conquest of culture.* Chicago, IL: University of Chicago Press.

Teixeira, A. (1974). *Music to sell by. The craft of jingle writing.* Boston, MA: Berklee Press Publications.

Terr. (n.d.). Top 10 Apple commercial songs by emerging bands. *Up Venue.* Retrieved from www.upvenue.com/music-news/blog-headline/1021/top-10-apple-commercial-songs.html/2

Thompson, J. (1978). Acting: Screen acting and the commutation test. *Screen, 19*(2), 55–70.

Tom, G. (1990). Marketing with music. *Journal of Consumer Marketing, 7*(2), 49–53.

Tota, A. L. (2001). 'When Orff meets Guinness': Music in advertising as a form of cultural hybrid. *Poetics, 29,* 109–123.

Traux, B. (2001). *Acoustic communication* (2nd. ed.). Westport, CT: Ablex Publishing.

Treasure, J. (2011). *Sound business—how to use sound to grow profits and brand value* (2nd ed.). Gloucestershire, England: Management books.

Tsang, L. (2007). Sound and music in website design. In J. Sexton (Ed.), *Music, sound and multimedia. From the live to the virtual* (pp. 145–171). Edinburgh, Scotland: Edinburgh University Press.

Turley, L. W., & Milliman, R. (2000). Atmospherics effects on shopping behaviour: A review of the experimental evidence. *Journal of Business Research, 49*(2), 193–211.

Tyler, L. (1992). 'Commerce and poetry hand in hand': Music in American department stores, 1880–1930. *Journal of the American Musicological Society, 45,* 75–120.

Vernallis, C. (2004). *Experiencing music video: Aesthetics and cultural contexts.* New York, NY: Columbia University Press.

Vernallis, C. (2013). *Unruly media. YouTube, music video and the new digital cinema.* Oxford, England: Oxford University Press.

Vihn, A.-L. (1994). *Die Wirkung von Musik in der Fernsehwerbung* [The effect of music in television commercials] (Unpublished doctoral dissertation). Hochschule St. Gallen, St. Gallen.

Wallace, W. (1991). Jingles in advertisements: Can they improve recall? *Advances in Consumer Research, 18,* 239–242.

Wallis, R., & Malm, K. (1988). Push-pull for the video clip: A systems approach to the relationship between the phonogram/videogram industry and music television. *Popular Music, 7*(3), 267–84.

Wells, W. D. (1989). Lectures and dramas. In P. Cafferata & A. M. Tybout (Eds.), *Cognitive and affective responses to advertising* (pp. 13–20). Lexington, MA: Lexington Books.

Williams, R. (1974). *Television: Technology and cultural form*. London, England: Collins.

Wintle, R. (1978). *Emotional impact of music on television commercials* (Unpublished doctoral dissertation). Lincoln, NE: University of Nebraska.

Witt, F.-J. (1989). Musik in der Werbung [Music in advertising]. *Planung und Analyse, 16*(10), 377–380.

Wüsthoff, K. (1999). *Die Rolle der Musik in der Film-, Funk, und Fernsehwerbung* [The role of music in film, radio, and TV commercials] (2nd ed.). Kassel, Germany: Merseburger.

Yalch, R. (1991). Memory in a jingle jungle: Music as a mnemonic device in communicating advertising slogans. *Journal of Applied Psychology, 76*(2), 268–275.

Yeoh, J., & North, A. (2012). The effect of musical fit on consumers' preferences between competing alternate petrols. *Psychology of Music, 40*(6), 709–719.

Yoon, S. G. (1993). *The role of music in television commercials: The effects of familiarity with and feeling toward background music on attention, attitude, and evaluation of the brand* (Unpublished doctoral dissertation). University of Texas, Austin.

Zager, M. (2008). *Writing music for television and radio commercials (and more). A manual for composers and students*. Lanham, MD: The Scarecrow Press.

Zhu, R., & Meyers-Levy, J. (2005). Distinguising between the meanings of music: When background music affects product perceptions. *Journal of Marketing Research, 42*(3), 333–345.

Zigmond, D., & Stipp, H. (2010). Assessing a new advertising effect. Measurement of the impact of television commercials on Internet search queries. *Journal of Advertising Research, 50*(2), 162–168.

Index

For Product Safety Concerns and Information please contact our EU
representative GPSR@taylorandfrancis.com
Taylor & Francis Verlag GmbH, Kaufingerstraße 24, 80331 München, Germany

www.ingramcontent.com/pod-product-compliance
Ingram Content Group UK Ltd.
Pitfield, Milton Keynes, MK11 3LW, UK
UKHW021609240425
457818UK00018B/455